Praise for *Travelling with Ghosts*

'Gloriously rendered, beautifully written, but utterly devastating . . .
an intimate and inspiring experience . . . balm to the soul, as well as
being a necessary witness account of the blackest depths of grief'
Viv Groskop, *Observer*

'A rich and absorbing memoir that shows the reader what it feels
like to lose your future in a matter of seconds in a faraway land . . .
Shannon learns to travel on, to get back in the ocean and to build a
new life' Cathy Rentzenbrink, *The Times*

'Her voice is resonant, calibrated by loss. Fragmented into different
times and places though the memoir is, it pays coherent tribute to
lives cut short' *TLS*

'[A] courageous memoir of love and loss . . . compelling'
Sunday Express S Magazine

'A cross between *H is for Hawk* and *Wild*, this beautifully written tale
follows Fowler's travels through Eastern Europe after her fiancé was
killed by a jellyfish' *Stylist*

'[Fowler] is a writer who is a wonder at conveying pain amid a rush of
emotions. She is a wise writer, too, understanding the nature of danger, confronting it, which can sometimes leave one person unscathed
and another destroyed . . . [Fowler] epitomizes Ernest Hemingway's
classic definition of courage: grace under pressure' *Washington Times*

'Heartbreaking but beautiful . . . As much as this is a tale of grief and
loss, it's one of love, too' *Bustle*

'Movingly and honestly told . . . Her story – rich, unblinking and
adroitly told – is one of strength, of getting past but not getting
over. Few would choose the approach Fowler took to kick-start healing. But hers is a thought-provoking journey that she generously
shares' *USA Today*

'A courageous and finely crafted account soaked in tears of love and
loss' *Kirkus*

'Fowler has turned her **devastating, beautiful, honest,** and personal story into something universal' *Booklist* (starred review)

'Worth waiting for. Our literary editor praises Shannon Leone Fowler's courageous book about the death of her fiancé in 2002'
Harper's Bazaar

'Fowler tells this wrenching story with grace and fortitude ... Just as Fowler's difficult path after Sean's death yields lessons about survival and resilience, her friendship with Anat and Talia, which continues to this day, yields its own lessons of a kindness so extraordinary that it's nearly as affecting as the tragedy at the book's centre'
Christian Science Monitor

'Set against an exotic backdrop of distant lands, Shannon Leone Fowler's memoir, *Travelling with Ghosts*, is a **heartbreaking** story about the randomness of tragedy **told with great courage and tenacity**' Ruth Ozeki, author of *A Tale for the Time Being*

'Shannon Fowler's restlessness in the face of her unimaginable loss makes the reader feel her battered *Lonely Planet* travel guide was aptly named. Like Cheryl Strayed's *Wild*, Fowler makes us feel that a hero's journey is our only hope for surviving grief. *Travelling with Ghosts* is **a brave and necessary record of love, as beautiful as it is heartbreaking**'
Ann Patchett, author of *Bel Canto* and *State of Wonder*

'After witnessing the senseless death of her fiancé, Shannon Fowler sets out on an unforgettable journey of reckoning, paying tribute to her young man's adventurous soul while trying to make sense of the rest of her life without him. **Fowler's voice is powerful and searching,** and the book left me deeply moved, not only by her courage, but by that of all the citizens of the devastated landscapes to which she so beautifully bears witness' Elizabeth McKenzie, author of *The Portable Veblen*

'Shannon Leone Fowler has created **a searing memoir** that recounts the moment her life was shattered by the death of her fiancé, young Australian Sean Reilly, and the months afterward as she stumbles around the war torn and poverty stricken countries of Eastern Europe trying to find a nonexistent balm to ease her grief ... *Travelling* *with Ghosts* celebrates a life cut short, a love never given a chance to grow, and a process of recovery bravely illustrating that while life after tragedy goes on, the chilly fingers of grief touch us in a way that mark us forever'

Elizabeth George, author of the Inspector Lynley series

'Shannon Leone Fowler journeys courageously behind the clichés to explore how nations, cultures, and above all, individuals, grapple with loss; a **vivid, compelling and deeply affecting** memoir'

Manil Suri, author of *The Death of Vishnu*

'Shannon **Fowler's vivid tale of love and loss moved me deeply.** She is a traveller who seeks healing in the most unlikely destinations, and who tells her remarkable story with camera-like precision rather than platitudes. Her book is **a stirring tribute to a beloved fellow traveller, and a reflection of her own abundant courage**'

Nancy Horan, author of *Loving Frank*

'In this **vital and compelling** memoir, Shannon Fowler documents the sudden death of her fiancé and the year of flight that follows. *Travelling with Ghosts* teaches us how to reconcile ourselves with the world once the person we love is no longer in it. This is a book about the kindness of strangers, the consolation of unknown places, and the way that the world can be bright and dark, wide and narrow, all at the same time' Kelly Link, author of *Get in Trouble*

'A **stunningly wise, thoughtful, and thought-provoking** 'survival map' of a memoir ... Drawing from journals of her travels before and after the sudden death of her fiancé, Shannon Leone Fowler shares insights into life, love, and grieving in **prose that is raw and unsentimental, and yet spills over with love**'

Meg Waite Clayton, author of *The Wednesday Sisters*

'This **beautifully written, wonderfully engrossing** book makes real the stubborn process by which we come to accept loss. **Shannon Leone Fowler has made a wonderful gift of her hard won insights,** and comes to a place of compassion that resonates deeply for me'

Dorothy Allison, author of *Bastard out of Carolina*

Shannon Leone Fowler is a marine biologist, writer, and single mother of three young children. Since her doctorate on Australian sea lions, she's taught marine ecology in the Bahamas and Galápagos, led a university course on killer whales in the San Juan Islands, spent seasons as the Marine Mammal Biologist onboard ships in both the Arctic and Antarctic, taught graduate students field techniques while studying Weddell seals on the Ross Ice Shelf, and worked as a science writer at National Public Radio in Washington, DC. Originally from California, she now lives in London. *Travelling with Ghosts* is her first book.

@shannon_leone
shannonleonefowler.com

travelling
with ghosts

SHANNON LEONE FOWLER

WEIDENFELD & NICOLSON

First published in Great Britain in 2017
by Weidenfeld & Nicolson.
This paperback edition published in 2018
by Weidenfeld & Nicolson
an imprint of the Orion Publishing Group,
Carmelite House, 50 Victoria Embankment,
London EC4Y 0DZ

An Hachette UK company

Travelling with Ghosts was first published in the United States in 2017
by Simon & Schuster Inc.

1 3 5 7 9 10 8 6 4 2

Survival Map – The Siege of Sarajevo 1992–1996 – Author: Suada Kapic –
Published by © FAMA, 1995–1996 (www.famacollection.org)

Bubble Toes
Words and music by Jack Johnson
Copyright © 2000 by Bubble Toes Publishing (ASCAP)
All Rights Administered by Universal Music Corp.
All Rights Reserved Used by Permission
Reprinted by permission of Hal Leonard LLC

A CIP catalogue record for this book
is available from the British Library.

ISBN (Mass Market Paperback) 978 1 4746 0598 4
ISBN (eBook) 978 1 4746 0599 1

Book design by Ellen R. Sasahara
Printed and bound in Great Britain by Clays Ltd, St Ives plc

MIX
Paper from
responsible sources
FSC® C104740

www.orionbooks.co.uk

For:

Two teenagers. May 6, 1996. Pulau Langkawi.

British tourist, age 26. October 20, 1999. Ko Samui.

Sean from Australia, age 25. August 9, 2002. Ko Pha Ngan.

Mounya Dena from Switzerland, age 23. August 10, 2002. Ko Pha Ngan.

Moa Bergman from Sweden, age 11. April 3, 2008. Ko Lanta.

Carina Lofgren from Sweden, age 45. February 3, 2010. Langkawi.

Max Moudir from France, age 5. August 23, 2014. Ko Pha Ngan.

Chayanan Surin from Bangkok, age 31. July 31, 2015. Ko Pha Ngan.

Saskia Thies from Germany, age 20. October 6, 2015. Ko Samui.

And for anyone else whose death has not been recognized.

The miracle is not to fly in the air, nor to walk on the water, but to walk on the earth.

—Chinese Proverb

part I

SUNRISE

prologue

T HE OCEAN HAS always had a hold on me, and over the years has
left its mark.

A chipped front tooth from when I was surfing at Tourmaline in San
Diego and the board snapped back on the leash and struck me in the
face. The cold water of the Pacific hit an exposed nerve, and the pain
shot straight through to my skull. It felt as if I'd fractured my jaw, lost
an entire tooth, or even two. But my college roommate, floating on his
board next to me in the swell, just laughed at the size of the chip.

A small white dent in my thumb from shucking raw oysters on Kangaroo Island. Taking a break from studying Australian sea lions and
sitting with a friend, kicking our feet off the wharf at American River
and out over the Southern Ocean. There were bottles of Coopers Red
Sparkling Ale and a bucket of oysters between us. She made me laugh
and the knife jumped from the chalky, rippled shell and straight into my
opposite thumb joint.

A pair of pink mottled splotches, one on each ankle, from when I was
wakeboarding off Saint Kitts in the Caribbean Sea. The inflatable Zodiac
boat had already circled me once, dropping the towrope, but I'd missed it.
The driver, my boss, circled again, faster this time. He thought I had the
rope, when instead it had wrapped around my legs. As he turned hard

on the throttle and sped away, the rope went with him, taking the skin off my ankles before tightening around them and pulling me under. I couldn't come up or scream. It was the kids on board who noticed. They pulled me from the water and we watched the wounds go from white to red as the blood began to pour. In the moist heat of the tropics, I was in and out of the ocean teaching scuba diving all day and it took weeks for the skin to start to heal. Seventeen years later, the scars look like tiny raised maps of forgotten islands.

Those are the scars on the surface, the ones you can see, the ones I can touch. But as it is with the sea, it's really about what lies beneath.

Haad Rin Nok, Ko Pha Ngan, THAILAND

August 9, 2002

T HIS IS WHAT I remember about waiting at the temple—cold, bitter black coffee. Someone had pushed a tiny white plastic cup into my hands. A small dark pool at the bottom. The bitterness I expected, but the cold of the liquid surprised me. I can still taste it, thirteen years later.

It must have been around two a.m., but the temple was full of locals. It didn't occur to me to wonder why. Women were passing out the cups of coffee and snacks, or sitting on mats spread on the rough tile floor. Men stood on the periphery, a small group of them gathered around a red Toyota truck in which the body of my fiancé lay, wrapped in a white sheet.

Two Israeli girls sat next to me on a low wall at the edge of the temple. They had ridden in the front of the truck with me on the drive from the clinic. These girls had been with me through the most intimate and terrible moments of my life. I didn't even know their names.

We were waiting for a key. We had been waiting a long time. At the clinic, they'd explained that Sean had to be kept in a box at the temple. They said it was the only place on the island to keep his body cold. But they hadn't been able to locate the key to the box.

"No problem," someone would say every so often. "They will find the key soon. No problem."

5

As we sipped the cold dark coffee, I watched one of the men reach into the truck and peel back the white sheet Sean was wrapped in. He gestured to the other men, who gathered in closer. They pointed to the red welts encircling Sean's calves. Their conversation grew louder and more animated.

"Oh my God," I whispered. The Israeli girls followed my gaze. One of them, the one with light eyes, jumped up, crossing the short length to the truck in a few strides. She snatched the sheet from their hands and tucked it around Sean's body.

"Show some respect," she said, motioning toward me with a thrust of her chin. "Leave him alone." The men may not have understood English, but they understood. They backed away. Still, she continued to stand, blocking the opened tailgate with her arms crossed in front of her chest.

The other girl, the thinner, darker one, turned to me. "We don't have to wait here. They'll put him in the box as soon as they find the key. We can leave. Do you want to go home?"

"I want to stay with him. I don't want to go back," I said, avoiding the word "home." Back in cabana 214, at the Seaview Haadrin, was the last place I wanted to be. Sean's things spread all over the room, our sea view looking out onto the spot on the beach where he'd collapsed face first into the sand. The sheets on the double bed printed with colorful cartoon clowns, sheets still smelling of him, of our sex earlier that day.

I didn't realize at the time that the Israeli girls were probably tired of waiting and exhausted. But they stayed.

The August nights in Thailand had been uncomfortably hot since Sean and I arrived in the country six days earlier. We'd spent many hours sweating on those clown-printed sheets. But as I waited at the temple, cold began to creep up from my bare feet on the coarse tile floor, seeping through my thin purple sundress as we sat on the abrasive stone wall. Sean had bought the sundress for me in Bangkok. We'd been pushing through throngs of intoxicated backpackers on Khao San Road when he saw it at a makeshift stall. Sean prided himself on his bargaining skills, but this time, he offended the vendor and we walked away empty-handed. Halfway through dinner, Sean decided the vendor's price had been fair and he slunk back to buy the dress at full cost.

I was naked underneath the dress. We'd spent the last two summer months traveling through China, where I'd often declared some days too hot for underwear. I'd tie my long hair up off my neck, and wear a simple sundress and sandals. Sean liked to joke that there was only a thin piece of material protecting my most intimate parts from all of China. But I never felt exposed. Until that night on Ko Pha Ngan.

That night I wasn't naked under the dress because of the heat. Hours earlier I'd been wearing board shorts and a tank top. Hours earlier Sean had been alive.

We'd been holding hands, walking back to cabana 214 along Haad Rin Nok, or Sunrise Beach. The tall palm trees lining the edge of the shore were motionless. The sea was calm. Darkness was starting to fall, though it was still warm and sticky. It was like every other evening on Ko Pha Ngan. We were planning a quick shower, and then drinks and dinner. We knew we were spending too much money on food, but had decided not to worry about our finances in paradise.

Outside our cabana, Sean grinned and flashed his dimple as he set his glasses down on the porch—an invitation to wrestle. I hesitated. He was much bigger and much stronger. I had no hope of not being pinned, much less pinning. But I dropped my sunglasses and kicked off my flip-flops.

I lost badly. Soft white sand stuck to my coconut-scented skin, still oily from a cheap massage on the beach that afternoon. I was not a good loser, and threw sand at him as he disappeared into our cabana.

I headed straight for the ocean to rinse off, the water so warm I didn't hesitate. I could hear boys drinking and laughing on the cliff high above me. Sean reappeared and made his way to the shore. Without his glasses, he couldn't see where I was. I took off my wet tank and threw it at him. He grabbed it and waded over to me, laughing. "I had no idea where you were until you threw your top." I hugged him and circled my legs around his narrow waist.

"You didn't have to throw sand, Miss."

I made excuses. "I was just playing . . . and I was losing."

"Yes, you were losing."

He knew me too well. He paused and I felt guilty for being so immature. "It's only because it got in my eyes and I couldn't see," he said. I rubbed my nipples against the small dark patch of hair on his chest and apologized.

In my head, I was revising our plan for the evening to include sex before showering, and then drinks and dinner. He held me in the warm, waist-deep water as I wrapped my legs tighter around him. We kissed and I could taste the seawater salt on his tongue. I felt something large and soft brush against the outside of my thigh. I flinched and gave a short yelp. Sean had always been afraid of sea creatures and quickly asked what it was. He'd been particularly nervous about sharks and since our arrival on the island had kept asking me, "Don't most attacks happen in shallow water?"

I was studying to be a marine biologist and knew how unlikely a shark attack was, especially in Thailand. I kept assuring him that he was more likely to be struck by lightning.

"I just felt something," I began, but hadn't finished the sentence when Sean flinched and dropped me. I was thinking that he was going to hear about this later, dropping me into whatever had frightened him in the water. But he was already making his way as fast as he could to the beach, running and pulling through the darkening turquoise sea with his hands. His movements were urgent and awkward, his elbows held high, his fingers splayed. I followed him to the water's edge. He sat down on the wet sand.

"Miss, it's all over my legs." I bent down in the fading light and could barely make out a faint red welt rising on his ankle.

"It's probably a stingray."

Whatever bumped me in the water had felt substantial and solid. Other than the small welt, I couldn't see any marks on his legs. After the ray brushed my thigh, Sean must have inadvertently stepped on it. I'd been with people stung by stingrays before and seen how excruciating it could be. So I wasn't surprised when Sean said, "Miss, my head feels heavy. I'm having trouble breathing. Go get help." He was quiet, calm, and coherent.

"Come with me." I'd never heard of venomous marine life in Thailand. And he wasn't sensitive to bees, so an allergic reaction seemed unlikely. I thought he was being squeamish. When we'd gone fishing the year before at Wilsons Prom on the southern tip of Australia, I had to be the one to bait the hooks with sandworms and then pull off the wriggling silver bream we caught. He'd even been scared of the tiny blue soldier crabs there.

"Come with me," I said again as I looked down at him sitting at the water's edge. His dark hair wet, his narrow chest leaned back, and his long white legs now covered with sand.

"I can't."

t w o

San Diego to Haad Rin

1982–2002

I DECIDED I WANTED to be a marine biologist when I was eight years old. It was July of 1982, and the first time I'd traveled alone to San Diego to stay with my grandparents for the summer. Coming from my small, inland, Northern California hometown, I'd felt reckless and daring on the plane by myself. My little brother would never have been brave enough. We banked high above the clouds, the ocean a green expanse broken only by tiny whitecaps. I pressed my nose up against the window, the reflection of my own green eyes lost in all that water, and abandoned my previous aspiration of becoming a tightrope walker for something that felt much larger.

Grandpa Bob was a physical oceanographer at the Scripps Research Institute, and he taught me about spring tides and how to recognize rip currents. My grandma Joy swam laps beyond the breakers, before bodysurfing the waves back to shore. Each summer, we'd spend the weeks together exploring tide pools, shuffling our feet along the sand to avoid stingrays, and watching migrating gray whales through Grandpa Bob's telescope.

During World War II, my grandpa had drawn waterproof maps of ocean currents in the hope that pilots shot down over the Pacific could use these currents to reach Allied territories. I remember pushing myself up onto my knees in a chair in order to reach my grandpa's table. My finger was my plane, suspended in the air above the map, before plummeting from the sky in a fiery crash . . . *here*. And then I would trace my path along the swirling blue lines in the ocean to see where I would end up. *Would I be blown into a spiraling eddy in the middle of the sea, or would I be swept onto the beach of a friendly nation?* It was hard for me to guess which countries had been on our side. The landmasses were just featureless orange blobs. The critical details were all in the ocean.

For ten summers, I made the trip to San Diego on my own. Once I finished high school, I returned again to study biology at the University of California. Every Sunday, my grandparents met me for pecan-banana waffles at Harry's Coffee Shop in La Jolla. I learned to surf and to scuba dive, and volunteered at the aquarium at Scripps, guiding elementary school students' chubby fingers as they handled leathery sea stars and spiny purple urchins.

I took my junior year abroad, studying marine sciences in Sydney, and spent a blissful two weeks diving and counting clown fish in the coral reefs off Heron Island. As a senior, I conducted research on learning behavior in the giant Pacific octopus, and on courtship and mating in fiddler crabs. I spent hours watching the thumb-sized male crabs wave their whitish overgrown claw, hoping to entice females down into their sandy burrow. But the tiny females were picky, traveling great distances (up to fifty feet!) before finally selecting a mate.

After graduation, I wanted to continue to explore the far-off oceans and landmasses I'd first seen on my grandpa's maps. While my friends settled down in California, I taught scuba in Panama and Ireland, and marine ecology to teenagers in the Bahamas and Ecuador. I worked on board ships as a naturalist in the Galápagos and the Caribbean. In between contracts, I'd use my earnings to travel on a shoestring: learning Spanish in Costa Rica, walking the Inca Trail to Machu Picchu in Peru, eating lemon ants in the Amazon, hiking among proboscis monkeys in Borneo, snowboarding in Chamonix. But I never stayed far from the coast for long. The sea kept pulling me back. I had no way of knowing what it would one day take from me.

. . .

"He's hilarious. And super fun. And good-looking. When I first met him I thought to myself, 'Marty's got cute friends.'"

It was my first night at the basic Albergue Palau hostel in Barcelona, and it was beginning to feel as if I was being set up. I'd heard Luisa on the phone earlier telling someone, "There's a bit of talent at my hostel." But I'd had no idea what that could mean.

Luisa was a nurse from Melbourne who was also backpacking through Europe. She'd invited me out for drinks with some guy named Sean—he was staying at another hostel and was a friend of her ex-boyfriend Marty. But I was exhausted from the overnight train from Nice. My contacts were sticky. I told her maybe.

Then Sean bounded up the stairs. His tall, lanky body didn't seem solid enough to contain his energy and enthusiasm. Wire glasses slipped down his angular, crooked nose. But he was definitely good-looking, as promised.

We started barhopping along La Rambla. Sean and I flirted over bottles of Estrella Damm. He also flirted with a couple of blond Swiss girls he'd brought along from his own hostel, and a Kiwi chick with blue eye shadow. Yet he got annoyed when I started to flirt with an Irish bartender. Sean kept pulling the hood of my jacket down over my head. And we got into the usual Sydney vs. Melbourne debate. I'd only visited Melbourne a couple of times and was unimpressed, but I'd loved living in Sydney during my junior year abroad.

Sean was unwavering and bold. "I'll make you love Melbourne more than Sydney once I get the chance to show you around." Which made me laugh.

The next morning Luisa and I moved into Sean's hostel near Plaça de Catalunya. Angie, the owner, was wiry with a manic energy. Her place was cleaner and cheaper, with no midnight curfew or daytime lockout policy. Angie and Sean danced and bounced around the hostel together, Sean wearing purple-striped thermal leggings and a Futbol Club Barcelona scarf he'd just bought.

That night, Sean was up for another one on the town, but Luisa wanted to catch up on her journal and postcards.

"You'll come with me for drinks, won't you?" he asked.

We made our way through crowded streets to the coast and to the bars along the water. I braced against the cold, winter ocean wind and pulled a tube of ChapStick from my jacket pocket.

"Can I have some of that lip stuff?" Sean asked.

It was such a bad line, I never saw it coming. Without looking up, I started to pass him the tube. Instead, he leaned in and he kissed me.

After that first kiss, I fell for Sean fast and I fell for him hard. It was the end of January in 1999. I was twenty-four and he was twenty-two. He had a broad working-class Australian accent, honest blue eyes that wrinkled at the edges when he smiled, and his entire body bent double when he laughed. Together with Luisa and Sascha, a law student from Sydney, we traveled first to Granada and then took the ferry farther south to Morocco. But Sascha left us in Essaouria to return to his studies, and Luisa had decided three was a crowd by the time we made it back up to Lagos.

Sean and I continued on our own for months, zigzagging across Europe and making up the itinerary as we went along. From Portugal to Austria, and then on to Slovenia. In Ljubljana, I wanted to take the short hop to Italy, but Sean had already been and was more interested in the Netherlands, sixteen hours away. On a rainy afternoon at the Slovenske železnice station, our backpacks had been packed but we still hadn't agreed on our next destination.

"Dutch apple pancakes, coffeeshops, late-night chips and mayo." Sean wasn't giving up.

"Pasta and pizza. *La dolce vita*. Right there." I pointed in what I was pretty sure was the direction of Italy. "I can practically taste it."

"We can get pasta and pizza anywhere. C'mon, I'll buy you a Heineken."

"How 'bout we leave it to chance and let the schedule decide. Let Ljubljana pick for us?"

"Deal." Sean grinned and grabbed my hand, rubbing his thumb against the inside of my wrist. Together, we walked onto the platform and looked up while the black and white departures spun, clicking slowly into place letter by letter by letter. Third letter *S*, fifth letter *E*, second letter *M*, first letter *A*, last letter *M*. The next train was leaving for Amsterdam in an hour.

In June, I had to return to a job teaching diving in the Caribbean, and then a PhD program I was starting in the fall in Santa Cruz, California. Sean had a working visa for Ireland. We caught a train out of Prague that would split in Nuremberg for our different destinations, but for the first part of the trip we could ride together. During the night, Sean got up to use the bathroom. I drifted back asleep, without realizing that the train cars had locked and Sean was shut out. I woke up alone in Nuremberg at 3:30 a.m.

My pulse pounded as I rushed to the door. I leaned out into the darkness, searching for Sean. I looked to the right, to the left, and back behind me at our seats. I was tempted to jump, my foot hovering in space outside the carriage even when I could feel the train shifting and creaking as it prepared to depart.

Sean found me there just as my train was pulling away. He'd run up and down the platforms looking. Panting, he forced open the closing doors for an urgent kiss. "I love you!" A conductor's whistle blew, and the doors slammed shut again. We yelled our goodbyes and held our hands to the steamed-up glass as Sean jogged alongside, like a scene out of a tacky romantic film.

I rang Sean from rusting payphones on the islands of Sint Eustatius and Saba, and we wrote letters and postcards. We talked about getting married, until the time and distance apart overtook us, and at the end of August, after seven months together, we broke up.

But we got back together less than two years later, as soon as we managed to make our long distance a little shorter. Sean had come home to Melbourne, and for my thesis, I chose to study the development of diving in the threatened Australian sea lion. I felt lucky to be undertaking such an interesting research project, lucky to have just barely scraped together the funding, and lucky to be seeing Sean. In June 2001, I moved from Santa Cruz to Kangaroo Island, where I could spend every few weekends in Melbourne, and the rest of my time at an isolated sea lion colony on the rugged south coast.

I flew into Melbourne with a ridiculous amount of gear: thick black canvas bags to catch the pups, boxes and boxes of L'Oréal blond hair dye to mark them, hanging scales and tape measures, pencils and yellow Rite in the Rain field notebooks. I was juggling the heavy bags and struggling with jetlag when I turned a corner in the airport and saw him there, waiting for me, in a suit and smiling. "G'day, Miss." He took me out to dinner that night at Blue Train, under the stars and overlooking the city and the Yarra River. We ate and drank and laughed and talked about our adventures in Europe. When we got back to his flat, Sean had planned on maybe taking the couch. I told him he didn't need to.

"When you move like a jellyfish, rhythm don't mean nothing, you go with the flow, you don't stop."

Jack Johnson's *Brushfire Fairytales* scratched out of the car stereo. A stereo so old that even in 2001 it only had a radio and tape deck, so I'd had to record a bunch of CDs onto cassettes. I was on a tight research budget, and Sean helped me find the used '87 Mitsubishi Magna from a friend of his oldest brother in Melbourne. I'd left Sean's flat on my own the day before with all my gear and bags loaded into the back, spending the night in Bordertown as soon as I hit South Australia. Then I'd continued on to Cape Jervis, before taking a SeaLink ferry across the wet and windy Backstairs Passage to Kangaroo Island.

With no streetlights on the island and no nearby houses or cars, winter darkness pressed in around me. Dense copses of eucalyptus trees arched up and over Hog Bay Road, the long thin trunks silvery-blue in the beams of my headlights.

I'd never been to Kangaroo Island, and had no idea what to expect. But I loved discovering new parts of the world, enjoyed my own company, and was comfortable being out of place. When I was fourteen, my parents took us to the UK for a summer holiday; it was the first time

I'd left California. After that, I went to Canada and Mexico on family vacations. But my dad and two of my uncles had all studied abroad, so they'd encouraged me to spend my junior year in Sydney. That was when wanderlust really struck. I'd been traveling as much as I could manage ever since.

I was midreverie—daydreaming about travel and Sean and sea lions—while trying to figure out exactly where I was on the island when a huge shadow bounded out in front of the car. I felt the thump as much as heard it. A sound and sensation soft and hard and more sickening than I could have imagined. And then a bump as the wheels ran over the body.

"Oh my God." I slammed on the brakes and pulled over to the left, looking at the dark, motionless lump in my rearview mirror. "Oh my God." Without thinking, I grabbed my new cellphone and called Sean.

"Miss me already?" He answered on the first ring.

"Oh, fuck. I just hit a kangaroo."

"Shit. Are you okay?"

"Yeah, yeah, I'm fine. But it's not."

"Are you sure you're all right? How's the car? Is the windshield okay? Those grays can do some serious damage, Miss. You're definitely okay?"

"Yeah, I'm fine. I think the car's fine. But it's dead." I started to cry. My hands were shaking. "Fuck. Here I am this conservation biologist, here to save one of Australia's endangered species, and I've gone and killed the national icon in my first twenty minutes on the island."

In an instant, I'd gone from savoring my solitude to desperately wishing he were beside me. It's easy to be alone when times are good, but it's a lot harder when something bad happens, especially far from home. We'd only just gotten back together, and already I couldn't imagine not having Sean.

We talked about our two relationships as Chapter One and Chapter Two. Both were easy and comfortable, but Chapter Two felt more settled and secure. We had grown up a little, and were both working, renting, and paying bills. The future, and our future together, felt more solid and less imagined. Sean was so full of ideas, had so many plans. Before, when he used to talk about a holiday we'd take someday years in the distance, I could only laugh. Now all those quests and ventures together seemed right around the corner.

On Kangaroo Island, my fieldwork was initially intimidating. I'd never seen an Australian sea lion before, much less caught one, and my advisor at UC Santa Cruz was on the other side of the world. It didn't help that I was the only unmarried woman living in Vivonne Bay, a town with forty-two people (mostly sheep-shearing single men in their forties), a general store, and a petrol pump. I lived alone in a tiny, one-room corrugated tin cabin, where I usually spent the evenings writing the next round of grant applications and begging any organization I could think of for money. And although I socialized with the rangers at Seal Bay Conservation Park, I missed Sean—the comfort of his laughter, his confidence in me, and the way his hands could make me forget about everything else. The frustrations of cellphone reception on a small island in 2001 didn't make it any easier. But the days were my own and I fell into a comfortable routine. Each morning I'd drive from Vivonne to Seal Bay to check in with the rangers, before wandering alone up and down the beaches searching for the chocolaty-brown newborn pups (and avoiding their sleek two-hundred-pound mothers), scrambling over cliffs, poking through scrub, breathing in the salt of the Southern Ocean, and taking naps among the sea lions.

Unfortunately, Sean hated his marketing job at Cadbury Schweppes, what he referred to as "selling bubbles." Anxious for a change, he accepted a short-term teaching job for the Communist Party in China.

It was only for five months. It was now 2002, and China was too fascinating a country to turn down. A place torn between communism and capitalism, still faithful to doctrine but seduced by the Western world, and practically undeveloped for international visitors. Besides, we were young and nauseatingly in love. He teased me for saying once that the only things that "filled me up" in life were him and the ocean. "Would you like a bit of bread to go with that cheese, Miss?" But he also told me how excited he'd get in Chángshā when he was expecting my call.

Without a landline on Kangaroo Island, I could only call if I was back on the mainland. Then Sean would run back to his flat from the Institute of Finance and Management and wait by the phone. When I got through, the static of the connection would crackle, and I'd ask how he was. He would always let out a long exhale and say, "Better now."

Before his contract was up in July, I flew to Chángshā to meet him. I saw where he worked, met his bosses and his students, and attended their graduation. Then we traveled. First around China, where we got engaged, and on to Thailand. I was now twenty-eight and he was twenty-five. In October, we were going to move in together in Melbourne. I'd continue to take short trips to Kangaroo Island to finish my fieldwork, but had managed to convince my advisor that I could complete all the labwork with the help of an associate at Melbourne University.

Sean and I discussed our plans on the long summer train rides through China, and while we were sitting on our porch overlooking Haad Rin Nok beach in Thailand. We talked about finding jobs and buying a house, getting married and what we would name our children: Jack, after his grandfather, but we found it harder to agree on a name for a girl (*Jessica? Sally? Lara?*). We even talked about our eventual retirement—how we'd keep traveling, driving a caravan around Australia, and how we'd spoil our grandkids.

Yet it was the day-to-day little things we kept coming back to, like which bars and restaurants we would go to in Melbourne—the Cherry, the Commercial, and Blue Train—and what dishes Sean would cook for me. I was already an enthusiastic fan of most of his staples: chicken satay, spaghetti carbonara, hokkien pork noodles, and a gooey-rich lasagna layered with béchamel, Bolognese, ham, mozzarella, and ricotta. But he couldn't wait for me to try one of his favorites, something that he hadn't had the chance to make for me yet—his chicken and sundried tomatoes with bowtie pasta.

Unlike Sean, I wasn't entirely convinced Melbourne was where I wanted to settle permanently. At twenty-eight, I'd lived in seven different countries on four different continents, and still hadn't quite figured out where my home was in the world. But it was easy for me to see our life together. Sean felt like home.

three

Chángshā, Húnán, CHINA

July 2002

W E'RE WITH SEAN'S students in a dingy private room at the local karaoke bar in Chángshā. Posters of boy bands and David Beckham plaster the walls and the closed windows rattle with the roar of traffic. We've brought our own snacks and the smell of instant noodles hangs thick in the hot, trapped air.

Sean chooses the Red Hot Chili Peppers, a band we have tickets to see in December back in Melbourne. He bounces his knees and twists his narrow hips as he sings first "Scar Tissue" and then "Breaking the Girl."

China hasn't been easy for Sean. Shortly after his arrival, he phoned me in exasperation saying he didn't know what he'd been thinking. He hated crowds, was impatient in lines, and couldn't use chopsticks. But now he can't stop grinning as he talks, and I love the way his dimple pops. He describes a previous night out with his students, a packed nightclub, how he'd ripped off his shirt, leaped onto the stage, and danced in front of a screaming crowd.

Later that night, we discuss our plans to finally move in together when we return to Melbourne—which neighborhoods we'll look at and what kind of flat we want for our first home. I ask him what he'll miss most about China.

He looks off into the distance, and he smiles. "Being a superstar."

four

Haad Rin Nok, Ko Pha Ngan, THAILAND

August 9, 2002

"I CAN'T."

Sean started to sink down onto his elbows in the wet sand. "The key is in your shoe." It was the last thing he said as I turned to go.

There was a bar several hundred feet down Haad Rin Nok beach. But I was topless. I didn't realize he was dying. I thought it was a stingray. I thought he was being squeamish. We were right in front of our cabana, so when I got to it, I peeled off my wet board shorts and threw on the thin purple sundress. By the time I ran back out, he'd collapsed face first into the sand.

I sprinted to him. "Sean! Sean!" There was no response. It was difficult to turn him over. As his head and shoulders touched the sand, there was a brief rush of air. At the time, I thought it was an inhale. I was grateful. I thought he hadn't been able to breathe with his face in the sand. I thought he was unconscious.

I rushed to the bar. It was crowded with August tourists. "My boyfriend's been stung. He's having trouble breathing." I was having trouble breathing myself.

As I ran back to him, I saw a girl walking along the water's edge. She was tall, fair, and thin, with a string bikini top and denim cutoffs. She stopped where Sean was collapsed on the wet sand and she looked down. She continued on for a few steps, then turned around and looked down again, without ever getting too close to him. She walked away before I got near enough to see her face.

A number of people followed me from the bar. When we reached Sean, he had no pulse. A young female backpacker began compressing his chest, her slender white hands folded on top of each other. A thin Israeli with a goatee instructed her in English, criticizing her counting.

I waited for a reaction, a Hollywood-esque splutter and cough as Sean came to and gasped for air. We would exhale in relief and I would tell him how much he'd scared me.

I still thought someone could save him. Save us.

We'd only been doing CPR a few minutes when I realized how totally alone I was. I was the only one on the beach this was happening to. Everyone else was just watching.

"Oh my God. Oh my God. He's dead. He's dead." I was sobbing and screaming and choking. But I was still trying to breathe for him.

"No, he's not. It'll be okay." I felt hands on my shoulders. Felt short, warm summer waves lap at my ankles and soak the edges of my dress.

"We need an ambulance. Can someone get an ambulance?"

"He must have drowned. He has water in his lungs. Turn him upside down," a local man said.

"He didn't drown. He collapsed on the beach. Can someone please get an ambulance?"

"Maybe he's thrown up and he's choking," someone else suggested. "Turning him upside down could empty his airways."

"Maybe his face was in the water. He has water in his lungs. Turn him upside down," another local agreed.

No one was listening to me. They were insistent. I knew they were wrong, but I let them turn him upside down. I was desperate. It eventually took three men to turn him, the heaviness of his liquid weight spilling over their dark bare arms. Upside down, Sean's limbs bent at loose, rubbery angles. His face was slack, his features sliding toward the sand at their feet.

"Can we please get an ambulance?" It didn't occur to me that Ko Pha Ngan wouldn't have one.

Finally, a truck was reversed down to the beach and Sean was moved into the back. With his head in my lap, I continued mouth-to-mouth. The Israeli who'd criticized the chest compression counts and one of the locals who'd insisted he drowned rode with us. No one said a word as we jolted along a dirt road toward the clinic. As I bent my mouth to Sean's and forced my breath into his lungs, the Israeli looked away.

The truck pulled up directly in front of the Clinic Bandon International at Haad Rin. The two men in the back jumped out and carried Sean through a tiny waiting room and straight to a bed against the far wall. The men moved quickly. But we were postponing the inevitable.

"Has he taken any drugs?" a round-faced Chinese doctor asked from behind thick glasses. "Has he been drinking? We will work on him for twenty minutes."

"No problem," the receptionist said, beaming at me.

A British girl was filling a prescription, exchanging crumpled baht notes for a small amber bottle. She was speaking to the receptionist in a combination of clipped English and Thai. She turned to watch Sean's body being carried in and then took a seat on one of the three chairs in the waiting room, her pills clutched in her hand.

We watched through open white curtains as the doctor leaned into Sean's chest. A nurse squeezed a plastic bag placed over Sean's mouth, before pushing tubes down his throat and up his nose.

I paced. I shook. I couldn't figure out what to do with my hands.

They were working on Sean a few feet away from us. The curtains were pulled back on thin metal bars that sectioned off two exam areas from the three chairs placed in front of reception. I watched as twice, a thick dripping needle was plunged into his chest. There was hardly any medical equipment. There was no defibrillator. Not even a bottle of vinegar, a common treatment for jellyfish stings. And certainly no antivenom. There was nothing there that could save Sean.

"No problem," the receptionist said again, smiling.

"Do you want some water? Do you want to sit down?" The British girl gestured to the seat next to her. She was about my age with short, platinum curls. "Why don't you sit down." It wasn't a question. My pacing seemed to make her uneasy.

She told me she lived on the island. "You live here? Is there another hospital? Anywhere else I can take him?" I asked.

"This is the best place. The doctor here is very good. They're doing everything they can."

The receptionist nodded. "No problem."

A group of men waited on the other side of the glass front door. The driver and the two men who'd ridden in the back of the truck with us had been joined by other locals on the narrow dusty street. But two young girls pushed their way past the gathering crowd outside, through the door, and into the clinic.

The twenty minutes passed in an instant, and my heart seized as the doctor walked away from Sean's bed and over to me.

"I'm sorry," the doctor said. I collapsed onto the floor, sobbing into the British girl's lap as she sat in the chair beside me. "There was nothing I could do. He was already dead when he got here."

The British girl gently grabbed my wrists. She disentangled herself from me as she stood. She smoothed down her skirt, running her hands over the damp spot where my face had been. I looked up at her from the floor. "They will take care of you," she said, nodding to the two who'd just come into the clinic. Then she pushed the glass door open and walked out.

I turned to look up at the people who were supposed to take care of me. Two girls with long dark hair looked down. Two complete strangers.

"How are you going to pay?" The three of us left in the waiting room turned to the receptionist.

"She needs to be allowed some time alone with him." The girls pushed me toward the bed at the back and pulled the curtains shut behind me. Their loud, harsh Israeli accents filtered through as they spoke to the receptionist, but I couldn't concentrate on the words. Sean lay staring at the ceiling.

"I'm sorry." I stood next to him, one hand on the side of his face and the other hand on the small dark patch of hair on his chest. "I am so sorry. I didn't know you were dying." I laid my head on his chest, my face in the crook of his neck as I had done so many times before. "Please don't be dead. I love you."

I swept my hand down over his dark eyelashes, but his eyelids kept popping open. His blue eyes stared at the ceiling. His pinched lips and gaping mouth were completely unfamiliar, his face already settling and distorting into features I didn't recognize. I kissed him anyway.

"I am so sorry. I love you." He was wearing loose boxers. His only piece of jewelry was a wide silver ring engraved with pictures and figures. I slid the ring off his finger and felt the cold weight of it in my palm. He had often told me to remind him to put his ring on again after showering. If he washed with it, the little men filled with white soap. But he'd always been afraid of leaving it behind.

The images stamped into the dull metal told the story of the history of Ireland. A shepherd with a crook. A round tower to hold grain. A Viking. A castle. The Union Jack. A tall ship representing emigration after the famine. The separation of Northern Ireland. And a question mark for the future.

The ring was loose on my own finger. I had to shut my fist to keep it from falling.

f i v e

Prague, CZECH REPUBLIC

April 1999

I   T'S OUR LAST night together. After traveling for months, our time has
run out. Sean needs to head to Ireland for his working visa, while
I have to make my way to the Caribbean to teach scuba. But we
have one more springtime night in Prague. Tucked into a dark corner
at a smoke-filled pub, we've been drinking huge heavy pints of the local
Budweiser Budvar and planning how I'll come visit him soon.

Soggy, sloppy, and sentimental, I slide a plain silver band off my thumb
and onto Sean's finger. It's a snug fit, but I can just push it down over the
knuckle. Sean smiles, before pulling his hand back and testing the ring.

"Miss, it won't budge." He looks at me with big, round eyes.

But I'm lost in my drunken moment, and feeling mushy. "It's a token,
something to remember me by while we're apart." I keep trying to gaze
into his eyes, only Sean's looking down at his finger.

"Seriously, Miss, I can't get it off."

I take his hand and dip it into his beer. But the band is stuck. He
keeps working at it, and soon his finger starts to purple and swell. I'm
not worried—we're young and in love, *what's the worst that could happen?* I think we just need a bit of soap. Once I've finished my pint. But
all Sean can focus on is the ring. So I slip the cuff of my sleeve down
over the top of my half-full glass, and we walk a few doors down to the
apartment we've rented for the week.

I finish my beer in our bathroom as we try to soap the ring off. We then move to the kitchen and try butter. The ring won't even wiggle.

"I can't feel my finger anymore," Sean says in a thin voice.

"We could wait until the morning, so that the swelling has a chance to go down." I'm almost sure it will be fine if he just leaves it alone for a while. "Or we could try to find a hospital or something . . ."

I try to make waiting sound like the sensible option. It's late; I, at least, am definitely drunk; and we have no idea where a doctor might be. But Sean isn't convinced, and I'm feeling guilty since it's entirely my fault, so we leave to go find one.

It must be two or three in the morning, and the streets outside are cold and quiet. We manage to hail a cab, but the driver doesn't speak English. I pantomime a doctor with a stethoscope, tapping a heartbeat rhythm against my chest. *"Baa bom, baa bom, baa bom."* The driver looks at me blankly. I whirl a hand above my head, doing my best ambulance-siren impression. *"Woooooh oooh wooooooh oooh."* I point again and again to Sean's swollen finger.

At last, the driver understands. He coasts slowly forward, never pulling away from the curb. He's only gone a hundred feet or so when he stops, and points to the hospital on our right. Then he points to the taximeter.

The hospital is shut for the night. We're standing outside the locked gate, when four young Spanish girls arrive. One girl's heart is racing, and they're all scared for her. I whisper to Sean that I'm guessing drugs of some kind were involved. There's an intercom at the side of the gate, and the girls and I all try to talk to someone on the other end who doesn't speak English or Spanish. We take turns trying to express our need for medical attention. We reason, we beg, we plead, we implore. The girls have the Latin flair for drama, and one of them seems to be speaking in a language that might even be Czech. Eventually the gates swing open.

Sean and I follow the girls through darkened silent corridors, until we see lights on in an empty waiting room. The girls are seen first and I fall asleep, curling up on the plastic-cushioned seats.

"Can I help you?" A good-looking man with dark eyes and a long nose is standing over me. He's wearing a white coat and has a stethoscope wrapped behind his neck.

"You speak English!" I couldn't be more delighted and relieved. I point to Sean, slumped in the chair beside me. "My boyfriend has a ring stuck on his finger. We can't get it off."

The doctor looks at me hard. "You are in internal medicine. I'm a cardiologist."

"Please" is all Sean says.

The doctor looks at Sean, back to me, and then finally at Sean's finger. He motions for Sean to follow. But when I start to get up, he turns and raises his hands. "You"—he points to the waiting room seat—"stay here." They leave me alone, and within minutes, I'm curled up and asleep again.

The next time, it's Sean who wakes me. I'm now a lot less drunk and a lot more embarrassed.

"Did they get it off?" I ask, pushing myself up. I feel my cheeks flame, and check the corner of my mouth for drool.

Sean draws his lips into a tight line. "It was excruciating, Miss." He tosses the silver band back to me.

"I am so sorry. I love you." I take his hand. His finger is red and puffy. The doctor shoved a pair of scissors under the metal to pry open a space, and then threaded a wire around and around, before twisting the ring off by force. A nurse had to hold Sean's wrist, and the wire cut deep grooves into the silver band.

We both stifle a gasp when we're charged over two thousand koruny, about sixty US dollars and a relative fortune in the Czech Republic in 1999. But we catch ourselves, smile and thank them, and pull out the cash.

Dawn is breaking as we leave the hospital, the hazy light over the Vitava River beginning to pale from blue to gold. Our last day in Prague. But we seem to have escaped lightly, and we both know I'll visit Sean in Ireland soon. I feel the pleasure that comes from beginning a day at sunrise. Everything seems full of possibility, and our entire spring day together is stretched out before us. I slip the ring comfortably back onto my own thumb, and run my fingernail along the scars left from the wire.

Haad Rin Nok, Ko Pha Ngan, THAILAND

August 9, 2002

"I AM SO SORRY. I love you."

I kissed Sean once more, his ring heavy in my fist, before walking numbly through the white curtains and out into the clinic. But the Chinese doctor immediately ushered me back in and sat me down at a desk crowded into the corner. Across the small space of the room, I could almost reach out and touch Sean's curled fingers. His blue eyes continued to stare at the ceiling. The doctor handed me a pen and placed a piece of paper in front of me on the desk.

"Please sign the death certificate." The doctor pointed to a line near the bottom of the document. The words were all in Thai. It hardly seemed to matter. I couldn't focus on the print. My gaze pulled to Sean's half-naked body—I wanted to climb up onto the bed and curl myself around him—and my hand moved to the end of the page.

One of the Israeli girls walked into the room and placed her hand over mine. "This needs to be translated." The other girl followed closely behind.

"It will be very difficult to find a translator at this time," the doctor replied. "She needs to sign it tonight."

"She's not signing until it's translated."

I listened to their conversation as if it didn't involve me, detached and staring at Sean. Wishing his eyes would stay shut. Wishing he were dressed. Wishing they would leave us alone.

"She can have it translated tomorrow. After she signs."

"She's not signing something in Thai."

The doctor sighed and pulled up a chair next to me. He translated the death certificate himself, pointing to the rows of dots and curly characters.

"This is the time you brought him into the clinic. This is the time we stopped CPR. This is the official time of death. This is the official cause of death."

"What's the cause of death?" The two girls were looking over his shoulder at the certificate.

"Drunk drowning."

I turned from Sean. The doctor's round face was calm, his jaw set. I finally spoke.

"But I told you he wasn't drunk. I told you he didn't drown. He was stung." My voice sounded high-pitched and strange.

The girls agreed. They had been on the beach. He had not drowned. That was when I finally recognized them. They'd stood behind me as I'd knelt next to his body on the wet sand. The taller one had put her hands on my shoulders when I'd started screaming.

The girls pointed now to Sean's exposed legs. Thin reddish purple lines wrapped around his calves over and over. A delicate tangle of inflamed knots twisted from his ankles to his thighs. The welts seemed to be swelling and darkening before our eyes.

I couldn't pull my eyes away from the rising welts. It hadn't been a stingray. Sean had been holding me in the water, my legs wrapped safely around his waist, as tentacles wrapped around his legs below me.

The girls continued to focus on the doctor. "She will not sign something that says drunk drowning. She will not sign until it's been corrected."

The doctor sighed again and adjusted his glasses. "He must have had an allergic reaction to jellyfish then. Was he allergic to bees?" The doctor looked directly at me, avoiding the other two girls.

"No . . . So, if I had been stung, I would have been fine?"

"You probably were and didn't even know." But none of this made sense. I would have felt a sting, even without an anaphylactic reaction.

And right before he'd left for China, Sean had stepped barefoot on a bee in his parents' driveway with no side effects of any kind. How was it possible he happened to be violently allergic to some benign jellyfish in Thailand?

"He was just unlucky." The doctor crossed out a short jumble of characters with a single thin line. Then he scribbled a long string of swirls, curves, and scratches next to it. The only words I understood on the entire page were my name, misspelled: *Ms. Shannan Fouler*. I wanted *her* to have to sign this piece of paper. I wanted it to be *her* dead fiancé lying on the bed, his body as white as the sheets and his eyes staring blankly at the ceiling.

The doctor pushed the page at me again and pointed a chubby finger to the line near the bottom. I moved the pen, but my signature came out all wrong. The letters oddly squashed together and tilted to the left, before falling apart at the end.

After I signed, we followed the doctor out through the curtains. The receptionist looked up from her desk. "How are you going to pay? Cash?"

"He has insurance . . ." I didn't know how any of this was supposed to work.

There was a brief discussion between the receptionist, the two Israeli girls, and the men waiting outside the clinic on the other side of the glass door. I didn't listen until one of the girls asked if Sean's insurance card and passport were back at the Seaview Haadrin.

We climbed into the truck that had taken Sean's body from the beach. This time I rode in front, with the girls. They said they would wait outside our cabana.

His glasses were on the nightstand. The shirt and shorts he'd been wearing when we wrestled lay in a sandy heap beside the bed, my crumpled, wet board shorts near the door.

Sean kept his passport and insurance card in a concealed pocket of his pack. As I undid the zipper, a rolled-up plastic bag of dusty brown marijuana fell out. I'd been nervous about buying and smoking pot in Thailand, although Sean insisted there was nothing to worry about. But the risk on my own scared me. I had no idea what would happen next; they might insist on searching the cabana. I went to the bathroom and climbed onto the toilet to look out the window. A man walked by, whistling and with his hands deep in his pockets. I had to wait for him to pass before tossing out the bag.

I couldn't stop shaking. Back outside, I told the girls I'd thrown up. I needed an excuse for spending so long in the bathroom. And it seemed like throwing up was the right thing to do, an appropriate way to act following the sudden death of my fiancé. Irregular waves broke in the darkness just off the porch, rolling onto the wet sand and the exact spot where he died. My head was swimming and my heart was crashing.

Being alone in our cabana had been a small relief, a brief respite from the stares of strangers.

We drove back to the clinic. Back to Sean's pallid body lying on a thin bed and staring at the ceiling. Back to the round-faced Chinese doctor peering at me through thick glasses. Back to the crowd gathered on the dirt road outside the glass door.

The girls said I should ring his family and my own. The receptionist looked up from Sean's insurance papers and rested her hand on the phone. "How you pay for the calls? Cash?"

I had no idea what time it was in California. The machine picked up at my parents' house. I left a disjointed message.

"I'm okay. But Sean is dead . . . He was stung by a jellyfish . . . We think he had an allergic reaction . . . I'm at a clinic. I don't know how long I'll be here . . ." Neither Sean nor I was traveling with a cellphone, so I left the number for the clinic.

Then the only number I had for Sean was his parents' in Melbourne, written on the information page of his passport. I would have preferred to call his oldest brother first, or one of his friends. Again, one of the girls placed her hand on top of mine. They wanted me to think about what I would say before dialing. But if I thought of his parents—Keith and Audrey, at home in the same modest single-story house Keith had grown up in, both probably asleep and certainly oblivious—I could never have gone through with the phone call.

"There is nothing I can say that will make this less painful. Sean is their favorite. The baby."

His mother answered. It was horrible, anguished, and brief. "I told him to be careful." She was wailing.

"I know. I am so sorry."

"I'm all alone. I have to go." And she hung up on me.

The clinic began to swirl around me, a dizzying eddy of directions and instructions coming from the different people surrounding reception. We had to move Sean, quickly, take him to the temple, to keep him cold, it was the only place on the island, it had to be done now, it was getting late, we couldn't wait for my parents to call, no, we had to leave now.

And once again, his body was loaded into the truck. Once again, I rode in front with the girls. This time, no one was breathing for Sean in the back.

The girls and I drank cold dark coffee at the temple. We waited a long time for the key. And finally, we slid Sean's pale, stiff, half-naked body from the starched white sheet and into an ornate brightly colored glass coffin. A thick black cord ran from its base. Someone plugged in the cord and a tiny fan came to life and began to blow cold air onto Sean.

Two teenagers.
May 6, 1996. Pulau Langkawi.

In May 1996, two teenagers died after jellyfish envenomation near Pantai Cenang in Pulau Langkawi, off the southwest coast of Malaysia bordering Thailand. Their rapid demise and characteristic skin markings implied a chirodropid, with Chiropsoides buitendijki *blamed.*[1]

seven

Zhāngjiājiè, Húnán, CHINA

July 2002

S EAN TAKES ME to Zhāngjiājiè, in the Húnán province. His students
had suggested it, presenting him with a small guidebook on the
area:

> *The park possesses more than three thousand grotesque peaks and rare
> stones. They appear to be at once human figures and animals, tangible
> or intangible. They display a strong tinge of either uninhibition, or
> delicacy, or uniqueness, or surreptitious.*

We really have no idea what to expect. One of his students says we
might even see a unicorn there.

Zhāngjiājiè turns out to be a highlight—3,100 narrow towering quartz
and sandstone pillars, many almost three thousand feet tall, cloaked in
white mist and covered in delicate patches of dark green forest. I enjoy
Sean's easy company as we hike upward through the July heat and damp
fog, taking turns carrying our sweat-soaked daypack.

Porters pass us, balancing wealthy Korean tourists on slender bamboo-
framed sedan chairs called *jiaozi*. The tourists sip cool drinks from sweating bottles and wave to us languidly as they're carried by.

It's no surprise to find the view at the summit completely obscured.
As we descend the jagged peaks, we catch moments alone in the clouds

where Sean grabs me and kisses me. We're still trying to make up for lost time, and after teaching his last class in Chángshā, Sean is relaxed and happy. He reads fantastical names from our guidebook that fit the surreal landscape: Xiānrén Qiáo (Bridge of the Immortals), Mihuntai (Platform of the Lost Mind), Tiānmén Dōng (Gate to Heaven). And tells me that Chinese water deer, giant salamanders, and clouded leopards hide in the dense, lush woods around us. It's my first real taste of traveling in China, and it's totally unforgettable.

But whenever we try to say Zhāngjiājiè to a native speaker, our pronunciation provokes hilarious laughter. We try over and over again to get the singsong syllables right. We become so tripped up and self-conscious, we begin to stumble over the sounds in our own personal conversations as well. Finally, frustrated and discouraged, we start referring to Zhāngjiājiè as "Your Asshole" and our private nickname sticks.

"Do you remember how that hotel owner kept thinking I was your little sister in 'Your Asshole'?" "I hope this bus ride won't be as chockers as the one from 'Your Asshole,' and we can actually sit together." And, "Miss, was it in 'Your Asshole' where we had that weird black soup with chicken feet?"

eight

Melbourne, Victoria, AUSTRALIA

August 2002

OR TWO MONTHS, it had just been the two of us. It hadn't been easy backpacking around China. But our shared experiences and frustrations became private jokes that only we understood. Secret nicknames and words whispered into the heat of his neck.

Even after Sean's death, it was still just the two of us. Me and his body. At the temple on the island of Ko Pha Ngan, and then up to Bangkok, before finally flying his coffin home to Melbourne.

The Australian immigration officer took my passport. I flinched as she brought her stamp down on the very first page—ARRIVED 16 AUG 2002. Exactly one week since that night on the beach. The officer waved me through, her neat auburn ponytail already turning to take the next person in line. I looked from the wet black ink to my passport's expiration date: AUG 2, 2010. From now on, every single time I opened my passport, that stamp would be there. I knew it was something I would carry for a long time.

The doors from customs parted with a gasp, as if I'd stepped through a vacuum, and my chest tightened when I saw the faces of Sean's parents. Any words I could think of dried in my throat. I stepped toward them on unsteady legs, and hugged first his father and then his mother. It was the first time I'd hugged either of them. His mother and I couldn't stop shaking.

At first, I was relieved to be able to share the burden. I'd all but stopped eating and sleeping, and was close to collapse. I was grateful his father had organized the funeral.

But it wasn't long at all before I missed his weight. Of course I missed Sean, but I found I even missed his dead body, the heavy pull of responsibility. His body had been mine, and mine completely. Once his parents took over, I physically ached to have that ownership of his body again.

I'd only been in Melbourne a few hours when I unpacked Sean's things in his parents' living room, surrounded by his family and friends. His father had already taken our rolls of film to be developed, and in a daze, I explained where the photos had been taken. I shuffled the snapshots of Haad Rin Nok beach to the bottom of the pile, and instead showed them Sean's flat and groups of his students in Chángshā, the two of us smiling among the clouds in Zhāngjiājiè.

The late afternoon sun darkened through the window behind us as I opened Sean's pack. I found the two pairs of small, bright silk pajamas. "These are for the girls." I handed the plastic-wrapped pink and red packages to his oldest brother. "And this is for you." I passed a knockoff Gucci bag to his wife. No one else spoke as I handed out the pirated DVDs to his mates, gave the wooden Buddhist mask to his mother. I pulled out trinkets and ticket stubs and T-shirts, until Sean's empty pack lay in a crumpled heap on the floor.

Then different people claimed the different parts of him that were left. His father tucked Sean's blue passport into his chest pocket, his brother took our *Lonely Planet* guides for China and Thailand, his mates divided up his CDs and clothes. I'd kept a few pieces for myself: his silver ring and his wire glasses, his travel journal, and the Futbol Club Barcelona scarf he'd bought when we first met and had packed for the winter in China. We all wanted to hold on to what we could.

I'd been to Sean's parents' house at 99 Deakin Street many times before. The last time, I'd also been on my own. Sean had already moved to China, but he'd wanted me to visit. He said he liked thinking of all the people who meant the most to him being together on the other side of the world. So on my next trip through Melbourne, I'd gone alone to dinner.

His father, Keith, and I shared an interest in seafood, especially raw oysters, and enjoyed introducing each other to obscure wines. I always brought a bottle or three from Kangaroo Island because although the vintners kept planning to export, each season the locals drank the supply dry. That night, we'd compared the Admiral's Reserve to the Porky Flat Shiraz, before moving on to Dudley's Shearing Shed Red.

That had been in the Australian fall. When I returned to Deakin Street, again on my own, winter had long since arrived, but it wasn't yet spring.

There was a trapped stillness in the house while we waited for the funeral. As if time had gotten stuck somewhere between Thailand and Melbourne. His father hadn't been able to schedule the service because we hadn't known when Sean's body would be released. When I finally arrived with his coffin, early in the morning on the seventh day after he died, the funeral was booked for the tenth day. I stayed with his family as we counted down the hours until he would be buried.

I helped Keith choose the music for the service: the Beatles, Ben Harper, David Gray, and Crowded House. Sean's friends brought over bottles of whiskey and Kahlúa, and we drank Jack and Cokes and White Russians in the middle of the day.

I sat with his older brothers, Michael and Kevin, in the backyard by the swimming pool. Their eyes were the same shade as the flat blue water, the same shade as Sean's. In the thin winter sunlight, we folded and stacked the memorial cards his father had printed. *In loving memory of **Sean Patrick Brian Reilly**, Born 26th October 1976 who died on the 9th August 2002. Aged 25 years. R.I.P.*

Card after card, I folded the photo at the front against the poem on the back—*Do not stand by my grave and weep, I am not there, I do not sleep. I am a thousand winds that flow. I am a diamond's glint on snow*—and pictured Sean rolling his eyes, groaning, and laughing at the elegy. *Would you like a bit of bread to go with that cheese, Miss?*

Of course Sean would have never said this to his parents. He'd been born shortly after two-year-old Kevin was diagnosed with leukemia. There were hardly any baby photos, as he'd spent the first few years of his life in hospitals for his brother's chemo. These years had shaped Sean's personality. He was sunny and cheerful, accommodating and cooperative, helpful and happy-go-lucky. He never wanted to cause any additional concerns or worries.

I slept in Sean's old twin bed in the tiny bedroom he'd grown up in, right next to the side entrance that everyone used instead of the front door. As the last of three sons, the baby, Sean had ended up with the smallest bedroom in the house. He'd once told me that when he was little he slept facedown to try to keep his nose from growing any bigger, something Michael had encouraged. I lay awake at night in his bed, trying to sleep facedown and imagining Sean doing the same. It felt as if I were suffocating.

My parents flew in from California for the funeral and they hovered at the edges, trying not to intrude on the heartbreak. They arrived two days after I did and left five days before, staying with an aunt and uncle of Sean's. Although I appreciated that my parents had come, in those days following Sean's death, I preferred the company of the people who'd been closest to him. But I didn't really belong with his family and friends either.

I wasn't from Essendon, or anywhere else in Melbourne. I wasn't even Australian. I hadn't grown up with him, or known him for as long as they had. We hadn't had the chance to get married. And I wasn't pregnant anymore.

Months before, Sean and I had taken an early morning bus from Xī'ān to Huá Shān. It was a few minutes before eight a.m., but already muggy and hot, and the bus smelled of exhaust and sweat. Sean and I had hopped on thinking how lucky we'd been to catch the bus right as it was leaving. Then the driver had circled the station for hours hoping to collect enough passengers to fill the vacant aisle down the middle. I was shifting in my seat, trying to avoid a broken strut and find a position that put less pressure on my bladder when I realized . . . I'd forgotten to take my birth control pill. But it was only the one missed pill, and I took it as soon we finally reached Huá Shān.

By the time Sean died, I was three weeks late and he was three weeks nervous. Sean adored his two nieces, Eden and Sophie, and was looking forward to being a father. But not just yet. We were too young. There were too many things he still wanted to do.

After his death, I was overwhelmed. The nausea, insomnia, emotions, dizziness, and stomachaches only started then, and seemed more likely to be caused by shock and grief. I was so focused on getting Sean's body released, I kept forgetting I was pregnant. And then I wasn't anymore. Four days after losing Sean, I miscarried alone in a Bangkok hotel room.

The pregnancy had been accidental. It was in the early weeks. I was terrified and on my own. But I desperately wanted that baby. Losing it meant losing that last piece of Sean.

His friends and I spent one of my first evenings in Melbourne out drinking at the Cherry, a loud dark bar on ACDC Lane that was one of Sean's favorites. Shots of Jägermeister were lined up in front of us as Stevie D told me that his heart went out to me. He said it must be so hard with all our intimate moments, and the way Sean painted such a clear picture of our future.

Which was what I couldn't get out of my head: Sean and I should have still been exploring Thailand, maybe visiting Krabi on the west coast or up in the northern mountains of Chiang Mai, before returning to China, and eventually back to Melbourne to move in together. All that was left for me now were the ghosts of the life we would have had. At the end of the night, Stevie and I sat next to each other on his couch and he held me for hours as I cried—ragged, gasping sobs that left a dark wet blotch on his T-shirt.

Still, Australia had never felt so alien and I'd never felt like such an outsider among Sean's friends. The next night, at another bar, Marty told me about an upcoming trip he was taking to Kuala Lumpur. He said he couldn't wait to get there and "just party." He also told me about the night he'd heard about Sean. He and another mate, Dan, had gone to a costume bash in London. They were sulking in a corner until some girl came up to them.

"All right," this girl had said as she pulled them up from their chairs and off to dance. "Enough. We're going to forget about this and have some fun!"

Marty took a long sip from his pint of Victoria Bitter and then wrapped his hands behind his neck. He looked at me and he smiled. "It was just what I needed. You know?"

Even Sean's father, Keith, seemed to respond with a sense of purpose and resilience that I wasn't able to find. He told me he cried only once, in the shower. He took only two days off before returning to work. I knew how much he was grieving. He must have found the demands and distractions easier to bear than the emptiness at home. "Chin up," Keith kept saying. "Enough with all these glum faces. Would Sean want to see us so depressed?"

I knew he was right. Sean wouldn't want to see us so depressed. But I'd still find myself thinking, *He's only been dead for eight days. Sean's just going to have to understand.*

After the intensity of the summer heat in China and Thailand, I was constantly cold in Melbourne. The day before the funeral, a wet gray winter day, a small group of family and friends met to view Sean's body. My parents were there, and Keith, Michael, Kevin, and Stevie. We walked into the Tobin Brothers funeral parlor, and the temperature dropped a few degrees further. I shivered as we waited, and tried to ignore the stale chemical smell hanging in the air. Since I'd already spent so much time with Sean's body, I went last. When it was finally my turn, I entered the room off the lobby, and walked through the rows of empty chairs to his open wood coffin. The first thing I noticed was his hair. It had probably been meticulously arranged to cover the postmortem incisions, but it looked strangely thin and red. Sean had always battled with his thick dark waves, keeping his hair short and simple, smoothing it down with caramel-scented Fudge Putty. The swept, airy, blow-dried bouffant they'd chosen for his last viewing looked absolutely ridiculous. I actually laughed to myself thinking how much he would have hated it.

He'd been dead nine days. His body had spent a week in tropical heat, been dissected in a developing country, been flown halfway across the world, and was now too bloated to fit into his own clothes. His chest was so swollen even his oldest brother's suit was stretched tight.

I was relieved that he at least looked more presentable than he had when I last saw him, pale and naked on a metal autopsy cart in Bangkok. Audrey, Sean's mother, didn't think she could endure seeing his body, so she had stayed at home. But this was how his father had seen him. I couldn't decide if it was better or worse that the body lying there looked nothing like Sean.

When I leaned down to kiss him, he smelled of talcum powder. His lips had long pulled away from his teeth, and his skin was waxy, rigid, and cool. Then I couldn't bear to leave, to turn my back on him. I retreated slowly, sinking first into a chair near his casket, and gradually working my way backward to the chairs closer to the door. It was the last time I would see his body, and I focused on his face as the sides of the coffin began to rise and block my view. I'd only made it about halfway through the rows when my mum finally came in to collect me.

As we were leaving, the funeral director approached. He was tall and thin, and dressed in an appropriate dark suit. He bent low at the waist to take my hand and then kissed my cheek.

"I hear you two had gotten engaged. Congratulations."

I had no idea what to say in response. *Thank you?* Or, *Congratulations?* . . . *Are you kidding me?* It was the first of many instances when some well-meaning person said something that knocked me senseless, that made me want to laugh and cry and curse and scream, all at the same time.

Later that same afternoon, Keith, Stevie D, and I were testing the sound system at the redbrick St. Therese's Parish, where the funeral would be held. "In My Life," "Shall Not Walk Alone," "Don't Dream It's Over," "Say Hello Wave Goodbye," and "Mull of Kintyre." I stood by myself at the back of the dark hollow church, listening to the music and crying. A young priest walked past, his hands tucked into the long sleeves of his robe.

"Thinking of getting married here, love?"

I shook my head, and wiped at my eyes with both hands. I could barely get the words out. "It's for a funeral."

"Well," he said, and he winked. "One day."

The following afternoon, I stood at the front of St. Therese's Parish, wearing the black trousers, tank, and cardigan my mum had brought from California. As I'd walked with his family to the first pew, Audrey had quietly sobbed that everyone was staring at her. But now they were staring at me. I looked out at the sea of well-known and unfamiliar faces and thought there would never be so many people at my own funeral. All of Essendon seemed to be there.

My hands shook as I pulled the microphone down to my chin. I didn't have any notes to hold on to, but I knew what I wanted to say. I drew a long unsteady breath, and could see Michael and Stevie out of the corner of my eye, ready to lead me away. They'd both spoken first, and already, I had no memory of their words. I think one of them might have joked about Sean's snoring. I exhaled and tried to begin, but choked on a sob. Michael stepped forward to take the mike, and I held on to it tighter.

When I'd first said I wanted to give a eulogy, Keith had told me that Michael and Stevie D already were and he didn't think the priest would allow three. But I'd insisted. And there was no way I wasn't going to speak after fighting for my place up there. The packed rows of the church were quiet and still as everyone watched and waited. I blew all the air out of my lungs and tried again.

"When my friends and family back in the US would ask me what I love about Sean, I would tell them that he's spontaneous, affectionate, funny, loyal, honest, considerate, charming, and silly. And that he has the most generous heart I've ever known. Whether it's giving up his seat on a crowded bus, or carrying a stranger's heavy suitcase up a flight of stairs, buying round after round of drinks for his mates, or shopping for gifts for his family. Everywhere we went, he was always thinking of other people.

"As we traveled together through China and Thailand, he'd hand out money and presents to the little kids we met. He'd tickle the girls, wrestle with the boys, and flirt with their mothers. More than once, the women he flirted with at the hotels where we were staying would tell me how lucky I was. And although it's just about impossible to feel lucky right now, when I've lost the person I thought I would spend the rest of my life with, have children with, and grow old with . . . I know that I was lucky to have loved him, and so lucky to have been loved by him."

After the funeral and Sean's burial at Fawkner Cemetery, a wake was held at O'Sullivan's Sibeen, a local Irish pub. I clutched at my pint of Guinness as I wandered among his friends and was introduced to his acquaintances.

Girls who'd gone to elementary school with Sean told me how cute they'd thought he'd been in grade four.

Elderly women I'd never met before squeezed my elbow and told me that I was young and beautiful and that lots of men would be attracted to me. That I'd find someone else. Soon.

Someone's brother asked me if it was true that I'd been in the water with him, true that I'd actually felt the jellyfish first. Was it was true that I'd tried to do CPR, but Sean had died on the beach anyway?

I began to want to be somewhere where I didn't speak the language. It felt as if I was already in a place where no one could understand me, but the fact that we shared a common vocabulary seemed to be getting in the way.

Still clutching my glass of Guinness, I left the wake early with Sammy, who was arguably Sean's best mate. I carried the pint across a couple of busy streets and over the railroad tracks to Sammy's flat on Rose Street.

I'd known Sammy for well over a year. He'd recently survived cancer, and now he was struggling with Sean's death as much as I was. Earlier that day, Keith had pulled me aside and told me to take care of Sammy, and later I found out he'd also pulled Sammy aside and told him to take care of me.

That night was awful. Sammy and I slept fitfully, clinging to each other. We broke out into night sweats that soaked through the sheets. We were so congested from crying that our breathing was labored, and we woke each other up with high-pitched inhalations and exhalations that whistled through our noses. But the day after would be harder.

Since Sean had died, there had been jobs for me to do: dealing with the Thai police and Sean's insurance company and the Australian consulate, getting his body off Ko Pha Ngan and up to Bangkok and over to Melbourne, helping his parents with the funeral and deciding what to say for my eulogy.

The day after was when I had to start figuring out what to do next.

I had assumed I'd have a life with the Reillys. I had an easygoing relationship with Keith, bonding over shellfish and Shiraz. And Sean had said that his mother, Audrey, liked me, and that she'd only decided she liked his previous girlfriends after he had broken up with them. I was a lot more open with my parents about my love life, but Sean said Audrey would understand how serious we were when we moved in together in October.

I rode with the Reillys to Sean's funeral, we sat together in the front pew, and I stepped forward to take the roses from Sean's casket before he was lowered into the ground. After I left Melbourne—after I'd hugged and kissed his parents goodbye, and Keith had driven me to the airport—but before the grass had begun to take root on Sean's grave, his parents stopped returning my phone calls, emails, and letters. During my last visit to Deakin Street, over a year and a half after the funeral, Audrey didn't come out of her room.

Maybe I was too terrible a reminder. Maybe they thought I could have saved him, maybe they blamed me in some other way. Maybe they couldn't help but wish it had been me instead. Maybe even though I thought of them as family, all they could see when they looked at me was their dead young son. In the end, I lost Sean, and the only other people on earth who felt the same way about him.

The photo at the front of Sean's memorial card had been taken at his parents' house on Christmas day the year before, in 2001. I'd spent the afternoon jiggling Sean's younger niece, Sophie, on my knee while I spoke to my own parents on the phone, before reading to his older niece, Eden, on the couch in the living room. Eden had wanted her parents to drive home for her red sunglasses, so that her glasses would match mine.

In the photo, Sean smiles easily into the camera—his dark hair short and spiky, his dimple caught in his cheek, his eyes crinkled near the edges of his square-shaped glasses. In the original picture, I was sitting next to him, my thigh pressed against his and his arm thrown around my waist. But on the memorial card, the image has been cut tight against Sean's body. I've been carefully cropped out of the frame. I imagine, though, that I was smiling. I imagine I was thinking about spending many more Christmases just like that one.

nine

Zagora, Souss-Massa-Drâa, MOROCCO

February 1999

I T TAKES US two days by camel to reach the Berber camp in the Zagora Desert. When we start out, children run alongside with their hands outstretched and hopeful smiles plastered on their small smudged faces. Sean and I hand them the ballpoint pens our guide had suggested we bring.

"No, dollars! Dollars!" The pens are dropped in the dirt, and the kids continue to run with hands that are still outstretched, but faces that are no longer smiling.

I spend the ride photographing the rusted-gold-colored dunes, the enormous sky stretched thin and pale to the horizon. Our guide's footsteps sink into the sand behind us, and the shadows of the camels grow long until their knobby legs look impossibly tall and spindly. Sean is uncharacteristically quiet. When I turn to grin at him, he grimaces in return.

"Camel humps were definitely not designed with the male anatomy in mind."

I suggest sidesaddle, but he's too precariously balanced and too macho.

I'm pleased with female anatomy until we reach the camp and find there aren't any toilets. There's no choice but to walk across the flat, featureless sand to what seems like a respectful distance. I'm grateful Sean is there to stand and try to block the view of the men unpacking the camels.

After the sun sets, we gather around a communal earthenware pot

47

under a large striped tent. Sean and I sit close together, a scratchy carpet spread over our laps. We scoop up lamb and apricot tagine with our right hands, our fingertips stained yellow with turmeric. We sip ridiculously sweet mint tea from tiny glasses. The men sing complicated, arrhythmic Berber songs that rise and fall in the cold desert night. Then they ask us to sing. They want to hear a traditional song from our culture.

"'Barbie World!' 'Barbie World!' You sing that for us, please," the men chorus. They clap their hands together and their dark eyes shine in the low light of the tent.

They're disappointed to have to settle for their second pick, "Hotel California." But Sean doesn't know the words. Though I'm far from confident in my ability to carry the tune on my own, I have no choice but to sing it alone.

t e n

Santa Cruz, California, UNITED STATES

September 2002

ALIFORNIA SHOULD HAVE felt like home. It was where I'd been born, where I'd grown up, where I'd spent most of my life. During the years that I'd lived abroad, I'd always identified myself as being from Northern California. But the desperate desire to escape that had started in Melbourne only got stronger.

Sean had been dead seventeen days, his funeral only a week earlier. When I'd booked my flight from Australia to San Francisco to leave on August 26th, ten days had seemed long enough to be staying first in Sean's old bedroom at his parents' place, and then crashing at Sammy and Jacks's apartment over Scullys handbag shop on Rose Street. I'd also picked August 26th because I was supposed to be the maid of honor at a wedding in Santa Cruz on August 25th.

Dorian had been one of my best friends since we were eleven. During the hot lazy days on Haad Rin Nok beach with Sean, I'd been mulling over what I would say for the champagne toast at her wedding. But after Thailand, I had trouble anticipating what would be expected of me. I couldn't begin to guess what might constitute normal behavior in the wake of my fiancé's sudden death. So I booked my flights for August 26th because I didn't want anyone to feel that if I was in California, I should have been at her wedding.

Of course, Dorian understood. Even if I'd flown to San Francisco a week earlier, she wouldn't have expected me to be there. She probably wouldn't have even wanted me there. It was difficult enough for her to concentrate on a day she had been planning for so long. In her wedding program, she added a note:

> Shannon Fowler, Maid of Honor. "Shannon, words cannot express how much you mean to me and how important you are in my life. It is so hard for me to imagine this day without you here." Unfortunately, Shannon could not be in attendance due to the very recent death of her fiancé while they were traveling together in Thailand.

Later, Dorian told me that a guest I'd never met had told the story of Sean's very recent death as she had her nails painted at a salon before the wedding. Another client, a young girl, overheard. This girl said she'd been there that night on the beach in Thailand. She said she'd watched Sean die.

I have no idea who this girl was. No one from California ever spoke to me during the week that I spent on Ko Pha Ngan. But in my mind, she became the tall, fair, thin girl I'd seen walking along the water's edge. The same girl who'd stopped twice to look down at his body, before turning and walking away.

"I'm worried about how awful the holidays this year will be for us." My mum started to merge her old black Honda Accord into the right lane of traffic, but swerved left again as a truck barreled past. We missed the 41st Avenue exit for Capitola, a seaside village in Santa Cruz, for the second time in a row.

"I don't think it'll get any better for us for a long, long time," she continued, sniffing and wiping at her eyes with the back of her hand. "But I wonder when it will start to get just a little easier for us."

Throughout my life, my mum had been another one of my best friends. I'd grown up asking her questions about politics and puberty, sex, love, and drugs. When I finally lost my virginity to my boyfriend my freshman year of university, the first thing I did was phone her.

But in the car, I felt trapped. I looked back over my shoulder at our exit behind us, and then leaned my forehead against the cold glass of the passenger window. In the confined space, I'd never felt such a distance between us.

Sean had only come to visit my family once in California. Our relationship had taken place in Europe, North Africa, Australia, and Asia. My mum's grief surprised me.

It also angered me. I was pissed off at the world. More than that, I'd become possessive of my grief. When my mum implied that his death was a tragedy we shared, it felt as if she were trying to take another part of him from me.

I kept thinking of my rebroken broken nose. Nine years earlier, my mum had driven eight hours, from Davis to San Diego, to be with me that day. The doctor had made it sound like a simple enough procedure, and said there was an 85 percent success rate. He never suggested that it might be better for my mother to stay outside in the waiting room.

I was given a shot of anesthetic between the eyes, and the doctor placed cotton balls soaked in liquid cocaine up my crooked broken nose. Then he slid a large cold metal rod into one nostril. The nurse held on to my head, and the doctor planted his feet, leaned in, and yanked hard against the rod. There was a crunching pop, and the doctor stood back, shook his head, and leaned in again. A second sickening snap, before he stepped back, and shook his head a second time.

It felt as if a sharp pain were being drilled directly into my brain. I swallowed the metallic taste of blood dripping down the back of my throat. A cool sweat broke out all over my body, and I thought I might throw up or faint.

I heard moaning, which my mum remembers coming from me. But I was sure the sounds were coming from the corner of the room, where she was huddled on a chair, her hands clasped over her mouth, her eyes white and wide. Seeing her reaction was terrifying. Just as a small child after a fall might look to their mother's response before deciding their own. Watching my agony through the expression on my mum's ashen face made the pain brighter and hotter, more certain and more shocking.

Late one night, I came across the bottle of School House Pinot Noir I'd stored in the kitchen cupboard at the small condo my parents owned in Capitola. I'd bought the bottle for Keith earlier that year, when my friends and I had gone wine tasting in Napa Valley for Dorian's bachelorette. There didn't seem to be any point in saving it now.

By the end of the bottle, I was in hysterics. I called my younger brother, Ryan, in LA, crying so hard I couldn't speak, and gulping for air. Ryan waited for me to stop choking. He listened and he cried. At the end of the phone call, he stopped me before I hung up.

"Hannon." Ryan was the only person who called me this. When he was little, he hadn't been able to pronounce the beginning of my name, but "Hannon" had also proved easier to yell. He was still using it at twenty-six. "Hannon, I need to hear that you're going to be okay."

I knew Ryan just wanted the old me back. I knew he thought that eventually, I should date someone I'd known in high school or college, someone who knew the person I'd been before Sean. He also just wanted me home, and he figured if I could finally manage to fall for a Californian, I might settle down and stay put. Ryan himself had gotten married the year before, to a beautiful, bubbly girl who was always able to look on the bright side. She was a good match for him. Ryan wanted to fix things when people were upset, and she wanted things fixed.

"Hannon, just say you'll be all right."

But I couldn't tell my brother what he needed to hear.

. . .

52

"I've got a work conference in Boston," my dad kept telling me. "You could come with me. We could see the Red Sox play at Fenway. We could go whale watching."

I'd never been to Boston, and normally would have jumped at the chance to check out a new city, explore the sights, and eat seafood. But I wasn't ready to share a small hotel room when most of the time I just wanted to be alone. And I definitely wasn't ready for whale watching.

"I've recorded that *Seinfeld* for you where George pretends to be a marine biologist. Let me know when you want to watch it." My dad kept trying.

I'd never been a *Seinfeld* fan, and had never seen the marine biologist episode. But I'd heard about it so many times I knew exactly what happened: George tries to impress a girl by pretending to be a marine biologist, Kramer tries to hit golf balls into the ocean, and George has to save a beached whale in front of the girl—by pulling Kramer's golf ball out of its blowhole. Reciting parts of that episode was the most common response I got when I told people I was a marine biologist.

"You haven't seen it? You gotta see it. So George is walking with this girl along the beach, and then there's this crowd of people on the sand watching a beached whale," yet another person would say, shaking their head and laughing and wiping at the corners of their eyes.

"And then someone in the crowd says, 'Is anybody here a marine biologist?'"

It was weeks before I felt ready to face anyone other than family in California. I finally went for sushi with three of my oldest friends. Dorian was now a newlywed, Mary's wedding was at the end of the month, and Kristen had recently found out she was pregnant. They didn't know what to say, so they talked about everything else: mortgages and IKEA furniture, city trees and unions, book clubs and haircuts. I picked at my miso soup and a spicy tuna roll, and they spent most of that early September evening talking as if I weren't there.

After dinner, they dropped me off at my parents' condo in Capitola. As soon as we walked through the door, I started crying. The three of them stood silent and still under the faint buzz of the fluorescent lights in the kitchen. Their eyes were on the floor and their hands at their sides. I asked them to leave. And then asked them a second time.

I hated them that night for not once mentioning Sean. Saying nothing at all hurt so much more than saying something wrong. After that, I saw them individually. They didn't pretend that Sean hadn't lived, and they didn't pretend that he hadn't died. Our friendships survived, and to this day they continue to be three of the most important people in my life.

After Thailand, the idea of being back inside a medical clinic left me cold. But eventually I went to the student health center in Santa Cruz to see a doctor about the miscarriage I'd had more than three weeks earlier.

I sat on the exam table, naked and wrapped in a stiff paper gown. Tears spilled into my lap as I told the doctor about Sean and what had happened in the hotel room in Bangkok. To my surprise, she suggested that I take a pregnancy test, just to be sure. She drew my blood, and promised to call the same day with the results.

But I didn't hear from her at all that day, or the next morning. I rang three times throughout the following afternoon and left three messages. The doctor's receptionist eventually took pity on me and agreed to give me the results herself. I could hear her shuffling through paperwork on the other end of the phone.

"Good news," she said. My heart leaped and my mind raced. *The baby would be due in April. I'd name him Jack, Sean for his middle name, but should his last name be Reilly or Fowler? I was terrified at the thought of being a single mother. But my life would have meaning. I'd have something to look forward to and a part of him forever. I'd have a place with the Reillys . . .* "You're not pregnant."

Which, I had to admit, I'd already known.

. . .

The time that I spent in Santa Cruz was hazy. Weeks could dissolve in an instant, but minutes and hours dragged achingly slow. The entire month of September felt like one endless Indian summer day. As if that year, California itself couldn't let go of the August sun.

Things that always seemed quirkily cute in an only–in–Santa Cruz type of way took on a nightmarish quality: the homeless guy downtown who asked for a small donation to debate any political or historical topic of your choice, the freshmen of Porter College running naked through campus in the first autumn rain, the clown with his pink parasol and melting makeup who walked one slow step at a time up and down sunny Pacific Avenue. They all seemed to be reminders that my grasp on sanity was tenuous.

I wasn't sure which direction to take, or how to find a way forward. My advisor, Dan, was on a research ship in Antarctica and wouldn't return until later that month. My first time back at the lab, I was relieved when Terrie, a professor on my thesis committee, and Susan, the departmental secretary, were surprised to see me. I'd been feeling that after five weeks, I should be working. But they'd both assumed I'd be taking time off. Terrie even said she was impressed I was mobile. I could at least wait until Dan returned to start thinking about my degree.

Though mostly I figured that I wouldn't go back. I thought about taking off and thru-hiking the Appalachian Trail from Georgia to Maine with the family dog. But the logistics were too overwhelming. I considered volunteering, maybe somewhere in Africa. But the commitment was too frightening. I had no idea what to do with the rest of each day, much less the week, the month, the year, or my life. All I really wanted to do was run away.

Instead I just ran. I spent hours running hard and alone. Whereas I used to jog along the coast, over the bluffs and onto the sand at New Brighton State Beach, now I avoided going anywhere near the water.

Deep in the Santa Cruz Mountains, my feet pounded miles of dirt trails that wound through ancient redwood forests, past black-tailed deer, coyotes, and banana slugs. Or I'd run the dry, dusty tracks up St. Joseph's Hill in Los Gatos, pushing myself to the top for a view inland to the cities and towns of Silicon Valley.

Some days I went to the Pacific Edge Climbing Gym with my friend Steven. There was something reassuring about having to focus completely on the next brightly colored handhold just out of reach above my head, the smell of chalk, and knowing that Steven's belay would catch me when I finally lost my grip and fell.

It felt constantly as if I couldn't catch my breath, or pull enough air down into the depths of my lungs. I could never run far enough or climb long enough to sleep at night. Images of Sean's face while he was dying, or how his features contorted and settled immediately after, would flash into my head as I was drifting off and I'd bolt upright in bed.

Sometimes I'd ring Sammy or Stevie in Melbourne. Since they were seventeen hours ahead, their evening would just be beginning. One night I made the mistake of watching *The Abyss*. I'd always liked the film, and felt I needed to try to get back in the water. I don't know how I could have forgotten about the CPR scene. The crew of the *Deep Core* have pulled Lindsey's body from the pool. They've stopped the compressions, the defibrillations, and the rescue breaths. Lindsey's eyes are vacant, her lips blue, her skin white and waxy. Everyone has given up except Bud. "C'mon, breathe, baby. Goddammit, breathe. Goddammit, you bitch, you never backed away from anything in your whole life! Now fight!" He slaps her hard across the face, twice. "Fight! Fight! Do it! Fight, goddammit!" And she does. She fights and she breathes and she lives and everyone cries and laughs and hugs and exhales in relief and she's fine.

I spent the warm sleepless nights in Santa Cruz creating memorials. I listened to a CD of the songs played at Sean's funeral, changed all my passwords to variations of his name, and finally started putting our photos from Western Europe into a handcrafted album.

I tried to replace the images of his death by surrounding myself with pictures of what we'd had. A framed photo of Sean dipping me tango-style in front of a striped Berber tent in the Zagora Desert—my arms thrown around his shoulders and my head tossed back, his face bent down into the white arch of my neck. Sean with a bottle of red outside our rooftop room at the Hôtel Smara in Essaouira, a pink sun sinking into the ocean in the background. The two of us giving the local quokkas a drink from our water bottles on Rottnest Island. Sean taking a shower fully clothed—*doing his laundry*—in Bled.

When I did manage to fall asleep, the nightmares were worse than the insomnia. In my dreams, Sean was cheating and breaking up with me, or we were fighting and he was dying, or I was the only survivor of a terrible car accident.

In one dream, I was trying to get away from a giant orange jellyfish. There was a man I didn't recognize, tangled up in fishing line in the water beside me. He was struggling, and I had nothing to cut the line.

In another dream, I woke up on the morning of August 9th in cabana 214 at Haad Rin Nok beach. But I couldn't tell Sean what I knew was about to happen. So I had to try to make something up to keep him from going in the water, and to get him to leave Ko Pha Ngan.

One night, when I was half-asleep, there was a soft knocking on my bedroom door. Moments later, Sean and I were in bed together. He was crying, which he almost never did, and I was comforting him. He said he didn't like it where he was.

"I'm new there, and I don't get it, Miss," he told me. "I'm just no good at heaven." Then my bedroom door shut quietly, I was awake, and he was gone.

My grandpa Bob used to warn me not to touch the purple-striped jelly-fish that washed up onto the beaches in San Diego. Without a heart, brain, or central nervous system, jellyfish only require contact for their stinging cells, or nematocysts, to fire, and this could still happen long after they'd died. Even pieces of a jellyfish broken up by the waves could sting. We'd use a stick or stalk of giant kelp to turn over the slippery purple and white blobs. If we were lucky, we might find a young white Cancer crab—hoping to hitch a ride and feed on the jelly's parasites—still hidden inside the bell.

Over the years, I'd taught my students about jellyfish life stages (from larva to attached polyp, then budding into free-swimming ephyra before developing into adult medusa), and how to identify the different species. I'd always been partial to animals with a backbone, but there were a few marine invertebrates I had counted among my favorites: Christmas tree worms and flamingo tongue snails, nudibranchs (a type of sea slug), octopus, and jellyfish.

Now, back in Santa Cruz after Sean's death, jellyfish were suddenly everywhere. Vivid blown-glass sculptures sitting in shop windows in downtown Capitola, huge glossy posters advertising *The Jellies Experience* at Monterey Bay Aquarium, colorful images on screensavers and calendars, within the pages of the latest Bridget Jones novel, during an old episode of *Friends*.

My friend Mary tried to help figure out what kind of jellyfish it had been in Thailand. We'd been friends since the sixth grade. Mary had always been rational, objective, and inquisitive, and was now completing her doctorate in public health. As a fellow biologist, she wanted answers and she wanted to be able to do something. So she searched environmental and medical journals, read scientific notes and articles. She emailed the Israeli girls, who'd been on Haad Rin Nok after I left when the locals dragged nets through the water, and asked them for a description of the jellyfish pulled up onto the beach. The girls emailed her back: *brown color, small head, long arms.*

Mary got in touch with various jellyfish experts and told them what happened, discussed their research. And one bright afternoon, I found myself driving to a Bay Area café to be interviewed by a PhD student from UC Berkeley.

We sat outside at a wobbly table and the sun bounced off the lenses of her glasses. In between gulps from an extra-large latte and doing lots of gesticulating with her hands, Carys asked about the location, the beach, the conditions of the weather and the water. And she asked about Sean's reactions, the signs, symptoms, and scars.

"Holy moly. I'm afraid it sounds like the classic MO for a box. And of all the nasty boxes, my bet would be *Chironex fleckeri*, the biggest and the nastiest by a long shot."

From everything I'd read, my guess had been a box jellyfish. But having expert confirmation, and even a species name, didn't seem to mean as much as I'd thought it would. It didn't really change anything.

"And besides, we actually know so little about the jellyfish in Thailand. It could even be an entirely new species of box."

"So I thought, 'Fuck it.' And I packed up the kids and the balloons and his birthday cake and we drove to the cemetery and we had the damn party there."

Susan brushed her bright red hair out of her eyes and blew her nose into a tissue. "Punch, pin the tail on the donkey, and a freaking piñata all at his grave. You should have seen the looks we got. But the kids loved it."

It was the second Tuesday evening I'd spent with the young widows' group, sitting in the circle of folding chairs in the corner room at the Santa Cruz Hospice community center. The first week, we'd been warned not to take the other women's stories home with us.

Susan's story about waking up next to her husband's body after his heart attack sometime in the night.

Kathy's story of watching her husband's heart attack during a week-end bike ride with their young girls. A passing stranger had caught their daughter, strapped into a seat on the back, but her husband had fallen to the ground.

Lisa had lost her husband after a messy and drawn-out battle with brain cancer. Jill's ex accidentally overdosed in Mexico. And Sara's police officer husband had been killed during a high-speed car chase.

Telling my own story helped some. As did seeing Gary, a patient and kind grief counselor at UC Santa Cruz. Even though I sometimes got the feeling that Gary wasn't quite sure what to do with me, and I was the youngest in the support group by at least twenty years. The other widows had all had the chance to get married, and they'd all had the chance to have children, some of whom had grown up and moved out. They'd built their lives and their families together.

Yet they never once questioned my official status as a widow. And even if the conversations often revolved around school runs, mortgage payments, and life insurance policies, they understood some things my closest friends did not.

"Everything happens for a reason, right?" Susan slid her husband's gold wedding band along the chain she wore around her neck.

"God has a plan," Kathy said.

"God never gives us more than we can handle," said Lisa.

"What doesn't kill you makes you stronger," said Sara.

Then the whole circle of us was laughing and crying and talking at once. "Better to have loved and lost than never to have loved at all." "You have your whole life ahead of you." "Time heals all wounds." "It was just his time." "I know exactly how you feel."

As I drove back to the condo that night, I thought how, more than any of the other well-intended clichés, I hated being told I was strong. "You're so strong, if I lost Rob, I wouldn't survive." "You're being so strong, I would never be able to get through something like this." "You're so strong, I think I would just curl up and die."

I certainly didn't feel strong. I was frantic and scared and barely getting out of bed in the morning. And although I knew it would never have been a conscious decision, it felt as if my friends were choosing not to see how damaged I was.

It also seemed to imply that *something like this* could never happen to them. Because they wouldn't survive, they wouldn't be able to get through it, they would just curl up and die. That it had happened to me because I was strong. It made it feel like a choice. Or my fault.

It wasn't only my friends who tried to reassure themselves. Tourists and scuba divers about to head to Thailand for vacation discussed Sean's death online. People who'd never met him claimed he was hypersensitive or highly allergic. Others blamed us for being in the water during jellyfish season. They didn't seem to notice or care that box jellyfish had never been reported in Thailand, or that even 4,500 miles away in Australia, it was three months early for the box jellyfish season.

One user named Jack said that he hoped the news didn't put off those who'd planned to visit Ko Pha Ngan, especially first timers. He posted that you just needed to be cautious when dealing with Mother Nature: *Love HER, SHE will love you too* ☺.

One of my labmates refused to make eye contact, a neighbor went out of his way to avoid me, an old college buddy stood me up again and again, as if mortality could be contagious. The comments from my childhood friends, the awkward silences from colleagues, the Internet messages from Americans I didn't even know, made the United States feel like a place where death was neither likely nor inevitable. We must have done something wrong to be so unlucky.

My mum bought me a copy of Linda Feinberg's *I'm Grieving as Fast as I Can: How Young Widows and Widowers Can Cope and Heal*. Curled up on the old couch at the condo, I read through it in a single afternoon. I couldn't understand how guilt wasn't included in the five stages of grief she outlined. I recognized the other stages, although I hadn't moved on to acceptance, and denial didn't come easily after watching him die on the beach and then spending ten days with his body before he was lowered into the ground.

I swung back and forth between the other three stages. There were flashes of anger. *A fucking jellyfish. Who the fuck dies from a jellyfish? Why couldn't it have been a car accident, a plane crash, cancer . . . something that actually happens to people?*

There were hours feeling depressed and sorry for myself. I felt picked on by the world, pointless, and empty. My insides scraped clean like a hide, and dried out like a husk.

There were entire days spent bargaining. *Why couldn't it have been the British chick whose boyfriend always ate fried egg sandwiches, or the French guy on the bus, or one of the topless Swiss girls on the beach with the puppy? Or me, why couldn't it have been me?* I tried to trade his death for countless other tragedies: an affair that would break my heart, a crippling accident that would leave one or both of us wounded and scarred. The scientist in me knew it was irrational, yet it also seemed no more unlikely than his death. So I wished on everything I could think of, and made promises to whatever God there might be out there to raise any future children Catholic, Jewish, Muslim, whatever . . . if I could only have that day back.

But the anger, depression, and bargaining were all laced with guilt.

If I had gotten help faster. If I had stayed with him and screamed for help instead of running for it. If I had started CPR the moment he collapsed onto the sand. If we had gotten to the clinic quicker, if they had tried the adrenaline sooner, if they had been equipped with a defibrillator or antivenom. If I had been stung, then maybe he would have done the right thing and been able to save me.

I felt I would never be able to forgive myself for not realizing he was dying. For not even saying goodbye.

And how could his mother ever forgive me for being the one to tell her that her youngest son was dead? For calling her in the middle of the night, without knowing that Keith was out of town and she was all alone?

It was all too easy to think that everything had happened because I deserved it. I knew that Sean loved me, but maybe it was only because he didn't truly know me. I could be self-centered, envious, and painfully stubborn.

It was equally hard not to think that the jellyfish had actually been meant for me. I knew this was called survivor's guilt. But putting a name on it, and knowing other people who survived similarly traumatic events felt the same, didn't make me feel it any less.

It would have been an ironic death for a marine biologist. The days that we'd spent at Haad Rin Nok beach, I'd usually been the one holding Sean in the water, enjoying the buoyancy of the sea and the novelty of lifting someone nearly twice my size. But on August 9th, Sean was holding me.

The jellyfish must have grazed my thigh first, and then wrapped itself around Sean's legs below me. The only reason I wasn't stung was that my own legs were circled high around Sean's waist.

More than likely, it wasn't even an unfortunate case of us accidentally bumping into it. Although most jellyfish are passive drifters, I'd since learned that box jellyfish are active predators—strong swimmers with surprisingly good vision. I couldn't shake the feeling that I was the one who had been hunted, but Sean was the one who was killed.

Three years earlier, when I'd first started my PhD in marine biology at Santa Cruz, Mary had bought me a fish tank as a housewarming present. It seemed like such an appropriate gift. I spent months filling the tank with bubble-cheeked goldfish, blue-striped neon tetras, deep-bellied silver hatchetfish, and golden apple snails.

I even added a couple of fiddler crabs to the tank. Their frantic claw-waving antics reminded me of my undergraduate research days spent on the muddy tidal flats in San Diego. When I first met Sean, I'd tried to explain this research, telling him that I'd studied courtship and mating behaviors by looking at male-biased sex ratios and patterns of female mate searching. After that, whenever I started speaking in overly technical scientific terms, Sean would tease me. "Miss, keep it simple. You watch crabs fuck."

When I moved to Kangaroo Island to study Australian sea lions for my thesis, the fish tank stayed behind in the condo in Capitola. My parents had rented it out to fellow graduate students, who also agreed to take care of the tank. I'd checked in on it during my three visits back, to present at a conference, for my thesis proposal defense, and to teach a lab.

But while I was in Asia with Sean, every single one of the creatures died. I returned to an abandoned and empty box—silt settling in on the rocks and bright yellow shells scattered along the bottom, algae climbing the glass walls, and my scuba diver figurine knocked over onto her side.

For twenty years, I'd wanted to be a marine biologist. Just that year, I'd dragged Sean to three different aquariums in the space of a few weeks: to see the sevengill sharks in Melbourne, the leafy sea dragons in Perth, and even the spotted jellies at Monterey Bay. *Love Mother Nature and she will love you too* ☺? I don't know how I could have loved her more.

And now I felt a lover's betrayal. I hated the ocean. I resented it for everything it had taken from me.

I didn't see how I could continue my degree. I was only halfway through, with three years down and probably three more to go. Yet even if I did decide to abandon my childhood dream, I didn't have a clue what I might do instead. Every other possible career choice I could come up with sounded ludicrous: studying veterinary medicine or viticulture, training to be a pilot or a wildlife photographer or a sushi chef. I felt tormented and conflicted; I could continue or quit. Face the physical, financial, and mental demands of an upcoming field season, or walk away from my studies and the sea lions and into something else entirely unknown.

I couldn't forget that I'd made a promise to each organization that had donated money toward my research, to my advisor, the university, and to myself. But mostly I'd made a promise to the Australian sea lions at Seal Bay Conservation Park. I'd hoped my research would lead to policy protections for these endangered animals. The young sea lions learning to dive were thought to be particularly vulnerable.

There were fifty-five pups at Seal Bay I'd been following since birth. There was Jolie, the pretty blond female. And TV, the lazy male who always lounged on his back as he stared out to sea, one brown flipper tossed over his pink rounded belly. There were Edward and Elvira, Leelou and Fidel, Shady and Wiley. I'd watched a number of them being born, weighed and measured them when they were only a week old, tagged them when they were two months, and begun studying their diving at just six months.

Soon they'd be turning a year old, and my next field season was supposed to be in a month or two. Since I was studying development in the young sea lions, I couldn't put it off. But I didn't see how I could return to that long stretch of sandy beach and the crashing surf of the Southern Ocean.

During my last season, on St. Patrick's Day only six months earlier, my team and I had lost pup number thirty-seven on a sandy spit known as Danger Point. It was a hot afternoon and a difficult capture. We finally caught the pup in a hoop net near the dunes at the edge of the beach, before using a gas mask to anesthetize him. But the pup had a bad reaction to the gas anesthesia. Kneeling around his body in the damp sand, we saw his gums pale from pink to ashen as his heart stopped. We'd tried to do CPR, but he had died on the beach anyway.

I still couldn't even bear to think about his mother, returning from the sea at Danger Point and searching for her pup. She would have hunted up and down all the different beaches at Seal Bay, calling out to him again and again, and trying to listen for his bleating bark in return. How long was it before she gave up and accepted he was gone?

One sunny afternoon, I took a look through my bank accounts. I'd managed to save quite a bit of money from teaching scuba diving in the years before grad school. I'd been planning on putting these life savings toward a down payment on a house. But the future wasn't something I could depend on anymore. On the one-month anniversary of Sean's death, September 9th of 2002, I wrote in my journal: *Seems stupid to have money & not be traveling. Sean would.*

Two weeks later, I went into my lab at the university's Long Marine Center to discuss my degree. I could smell the salt and hear the rush of the waves at Natural Bridges Beach as I made my way into the building.

My advisor, Dan, had returned from Antarctica, where he'd been studying crabeater seals. "I don't want to see you quit," he said as we sat together in his office on the second floor.

"I know." I nodded. "But I just don't see how I can do the next field season."

"I can handle this field season for you. I'm sure most of your labmates will jump at the chance to help out on Kangaroo Island. You should take the time that you need."

Through his office window, I heard the guttural barking of a California sea lion from across the water. The muscles in my back relaxed, the knot in my throat unwound just a little, and I started to cry. I hadn't thought that taking time out would be an option. I was well aware that most people who'd lost a loved one would never have had the choice of taking a break from life's demands and responsibilities. I felt a twinge of guilt, but mostly I felt grateful.

So I did what Sean would have done. That night on the beach at Ko Pha Ngan, in a matter of minutes, I'd lost everything that had kept me grounded. The path I had chosen—a family with Sean, a career in marine biology—had been pulled out from under me. I wasn't ready to forgive the ocean. But I could still travel. Travel was something Sean and I had shared. And it was all I had now.

I would spend the winter traveling alone. I ticked off continent by continent to see what was left of my world. Sean had died in Asia and I wasn't ready to return there. We'd traveled extensively together through Western Europe and Australia, and going back without him felt unbearable. Africa seemed too intense on my own, and the last time I'd been in Latin America, I had been mugged. It was Eastern Europe by default. Although Sean and I had been to the Czech Republic and Slovenia, there were still a number of places to go where I'd find myself in uncharted territory.

It helped that Eastern Europe was cold, English wasn't widely spoken, and I didn't speak any of the languages. I wanted to be left alone. It was also cheap, and even more importantly, inland.

Taking the money I'd saved from teaching scuba diving, and the thousands of airline miles I'd earned flying back and forth between California and South Australia, I booked a ticket to Budapest.

Before I left, I made a list and told everyone on it that I loved them: my mum, dad, and Ryan; Dorian, Mary, and Kristen; Janna, Anne, and Steven. I hadn't told anyone I'd loved them since Sean had died.

My parents must have been terrified to let me out of their sight. They wouldn't know how, or even where, I was. My Australian cellphone, packed away in a box in Melbourne, didn't work abroad. It had hardly worked on Kangaroo Island. Skype wouldn't be introduced for another year, so it would only be payphones and email. And none of us knew how hard it might be to find either of those in Transylvania in 2002.

But my parents didn't try to stop me, or talk me out of it. They knew if they pushed, I'd only push back harder. And they understood it was something I needed to do, even if they didn't understand why.

At the time, even I didn't understand why.

I didn't bring a camera; I'd stopped taking photos. I didn't have a map, or a single reservation, no itinerary or real plan. Just a blank journal, a *Lonely Planet* guide for Eastern Europe, my old green Eagle Creek backpack, and a return ticket several months later out of Barcelona. I chose to end my trip there because it was where, almost four years earlier, I'd met Sean. It was where we'd had our first kiss, and although I didn't tell him until weeks later in Salamanca, it was in Barcelona where I first began to fall in love with him.

eleven

San Diego, California, UNITED STATES

June 1983

"LOOK, THEY CAN'T sting. They can't bite. And they won't pinch. I promise. They cannot hurt you." My grandpa Bob scoops his hands through the water, cupping one of the bright red crabs in his palms. "See, they're tiny."

I'm nine years old, and it's my second summer on my own with my grandparents in San Diego—a typical June Gloom foggy day, except the beach at La Jolla Shores is carpeted in red. We've stepped over hundreds of dead crabs to make our way to the ocean, their shells crunching under our feet and giving off a rotten, fishy stink. Fat gulls wander along the shore, bits of red hanging from their beaks. I'm standing with my grandpa waist-deep and the water around us is thick with them—their hard little bodies bumping into me, their sharp scratchy legs scuttling against my bare skin.

I look down at the thumb-sized crab my grandpa has in his hands, all long spindly legs and two round black eyes. It reminds me of the crawdads we'd raced in the first grade for the school science fair. Mine hadn't been particularly fast, but he'd outlived almost all of them after the fair. I'd named him Armor, made him a rocky home in a glass fish tank, fed him salad and frozen peas, and scrubbed his shell with an old toothbrush. And just like Armor, the crab in my grandpa's palms does have pincers, even if they are small.

"They're pelagic red crabs, or tuna crabs," my grandpa continues. "Brought up from Mexico with the warm water. Totally harmless. And they'll be gone soon." My grandpa is calm and logical. But he can't persuade my little brother when he comes to visit later with my parents. Ryan takes one look at the sea of red bodies, turns around, and heads straight for the chlorinated swimming pool. He refuses to set foot in the ocean that entire summer and the next, and remains suspicious of it for years.

I'm not going to give up on the ocean. I stand with my grandpa in the water; the sensation of hundreds of tiny legs skittering across my skin, sometimes poking my stomach through my swimsuit, is incredibly unsettling, even scary. But I want to be brave. I try to be brave. I am going to be brave.

British tourist, age 26.
October 20, 1999. Ko Samui.

On October 20, 1999, a 26-year-old male British tourist swimming in early evening calm seas off Chaweng Beach, Koh Samui, suddenly exited the water, walking unsteadily and calling for water to drink. Within minutes he collapsed, stopped breathing, and became pulseless. At a nearby hospital, dilated, nonreactive pupils were noted on arrival shortly afterwards. Extensive typical chirodropid welts were present across his neck, chest, and back. Resuscitation was unsuccessful.[2]

twelve

Budapest, Közép-Magyarország, HUNGARY

October 2002

S EAN HAD PROMISED me in Thailand that I'd never holiday alone
again, that I was stuck with him. I hadn't really known how I felt
about the promise when he made it. I'd always liked traveling on
my own. Most of the trips I'd taken had been alone. But traveling with
Sean felt more relaxed, easier, safer—it was just more fun. Flying by myself
to Budapest, I regretted feeling ambiguous about his offer. *If only I could
have that now, take it back.* I wasn't sure I could do this alone, wasn't sure
I could do this at all. Or even wanted to try. Maybe I was too old. I was
definitely too sad.

It had been two months and eight days. The next day, October 18th,
it would be ten weeks. Ten weeks since that promise had died with him
on the beach at Ko Pha Ngan.

As I watched black suitcase after black suitcase spin past me on the
baggage carousel, my stomach twisted and my face went hot. My knees
buckled and I sank down onto the cold metal of the luggage cart, closed
my eyes, and willed myself not to throw up in Budapest's Ferihegy airport.

I'd spent the night before in Earls Court in London, sobbing and
drinking with Sean's friends who lived there, Marty and Dan. I'd fallen
asleep on their fraying sunken couch, my head in Dan's lap. When I
woke up, I was still drunk. I'd managed to make my flight to Hungary,
but had already lost one of the small memorial cards Sean's father had

handed out at his funeral. *Do not stand by my grave and cry, I am not there, I did not die.*

I'd planned to carry the card in my back pocket through Eastern Europe—to have something of him that was immediate, physical, and constant. The loss of that card would have felt like an irrecoverable crisis if I didn't already have a second one with me in my wallet, or hadn't saved a whole stack back in California.

The bus from the airport into what I hoped was Central Pest wound its way past squares and parks, the stone footpaths buried under loose piles of fading yellow and orange leaves. I climbed the stairs to the cheerfully painted Museum Guest House worried about not having a reservation; I was in no shape to be searching the city on foot with my pack. But there was plenty of space, and I spent the rest of my first day in Eastern Europe collapsed at the coed dorm, in the bed I chose in the corner.

In and out of sleep and from under the covers, I heard giggles and young voices in various languages. The few in English were discussing plans for a pub-crawl tour. I forced down the taste of something sour rising into my throat, and curled toward the wall.

I stumbled through Budapest in a daze. I wrote incessantly in my journal about missing Sean, and sobbed during phone calls to my parents. If I'd still been pregnant, I wouldn't have been traveling, and I'd have traded my freedom and that trip for the baby in an instant. I wondered constantly if I'd made the wrong decision to come. Before I'd left, I kept saying that I could always change my ticket and come back. Even as I said it, I hadn't believed it.

But what the fuck was I doing in Budapest? I hardly knew anything about Eastern Europe. None of my friends had ever been and there didn't seem to be many other people visiting in 2002, especially in October. Twelve years after the fall of communism, EU membership was still a long way off and the winter tourists were few and far between.

I wasn't interested in sightseeing. I couldn't make myself care about the city's most important medieval monuments on Várhegy (Castle Hill), or the world's largest supply of electricity-consumption meters at the Elektrotechnikai Múzeum.

I did, at least, have time alone with my thoughts and with Sean. I began signing his name in every guest book I came across, kept notes in my *Lonely Planet* anytime I remembered anything about him. How he hated mushrooms and cantaloupe, but loved meat pies and olives. The scrunched-up way he held a pen. Or that night we were walking back from playing pool and drinking White Russians at the Edinburgh Castle. I was in the middle of telling some story, and he spun me around on the sidewalk and kissed me. Each time I thought of something new, it felt like a small gift, and I rushed to write it down before I lost it forever.

My fourth day in Hungary, I spent a warm afternoon walking for hours on the curved banks of the silver Danube and talking to Sean. The fall colors were turning to winter. Red leaves becoming brown, before curling in at the edges, and dropping into papery heaps along the paths. I passed skinny-legged women in miniskirts and knee-high stiletto boots, walking contented-looking dachshund-type dogs, as I carried on talking to Sean inside my head.

He told me that his parents didn't blame me. That he loved me and missed me. And he told me to appreciate being alive.

A part of me suspected that I was making up both sides of the conversation. But the rest of me, most of me, at least most of the time, believed that he was somewhere. A place where he wasn't suffering, but where he didn't want to be. That he hadn't been able to let go of life, or let go of me.

I couldn't help but feel cheated. We hadn't done anything wrong. I'd had to tell his insurance company over and over again that there were no warning signs posted (they'd wanted photos of Haad Rin Nok beach as proof). I'd photocopied the pages of our *Lonely Planet* guidebook to show there was nothing listed under the Dangers & Annoyances section. Assured them that the locals hadn't told us to be cautious. That there were no jellyfish seasons in Thailand.

I'd even taught Sean to shuffle his feet to avoid the stingrays in the warm shallow water there, just the way my grandpa Bob had taught me on the other side of the Pacific Ocean twenty years earlier. But nothing had prepared me for this. There were no waterproof maps for where I had landed.

I continued to walk against the current of the Danube, crossing the Szabadság híd, or Liberty Bridge, to the old castles and churches in the Buda hills. Then back over Margit híd to the flat cityscape of Pest as the color of the river dulled from silver to gray.

Darkness had begun to creep into the far corners of the sky, and I realized I should start thinking about dinner. I'd mostly been surviving on bread, cheese, tomatoes, and Pick Hungarian salami from the central Rákóczi tér market. I decided to treat myself to a sit-down restaurant. The Museum Guest House had recommended the neighborhood Fatál for local home-style food. When I was little and my mum tried to make Hungarian goulash for us for dinner, I'd always thought it sounded like some kind of medieval torture, right up there with thumbscrews and the rack. But as the late autumn temperature began to drop, a thick beef soup with onions, potatoes, and paprika sounded tempting.

I'd spent most of the day walking, so I decided to take the metro. After making my best guess between the four different fares—*vonaljegy* (single ticket), *metrószakaszjegy* (metro section ticket), *metró átszállójegy* (metro transfer ticket), or *metro-szakaszátsz állójegy* (metro section transfer ticket)—I headed down to the underground platform.

As I waited, I pulled a city map from my pocket to double-check the route. A loud smacking sound behind me made me jump and drop the map.

A few feet away, a young couple was wrestling. He was holding her wrists, and noisily kissing the length of her arms. She giggled and twisted, before she ducked and started smacking kisses along the exposed line of his stomach, right above his tracksuit bottoms.

The train pulled into the station, and I moved farther down to another carriage. I'd been surprised by how publicly affectionate Hungarian couples were. I knew I was being overly sensitive. I'd noticed how easily I startled, and I always felt tense and edgy, as if something else terrible was going to happen at any moment.

I got off the red line at Astoria, stepping out of the station into a black night. As I looked up and saw my first star of the evening, I reflexively recited the "Star Light, Star Bright" nursery rhyme from my childhood and wished Sean wasn't dead. Then I realized I'd left my map behind where I'd dropped it. I crossed to the corner and searched for a street name.

"Elnézést." An older woman, with heavy blue eye shadow and thin brows penciled high onto her forehead, approached me.

"Uh . . . English?" The only word I could remember in Hungarian was "Magyar," which, unhelpfully, meant "Hungarian."

"Nem." She shook her head and looked puzzled. Then she held out a map, and spoke in a rapid burst, long vowels and consonants tumbling over each other from somewhere deep in her throat. When she finished, she looked up at me with her eyebrows raised and her finger on the map.

It must have been the fourth or fifth time that day I'd been asked for directions, from both Hungarians and the few other tourists. It seemed odd given my running shoes and detachable daypack. Maybe it was because I was alone. Maybe it was because I didn't look at all threatening. *But did I really look like I knew where I was going?*

I glanced down at the map the woman held, though I knew it would be in a language I couldn't read. The skin on the back of the woman's hand was dry and bruised with purplish spots. I looked from the empty space on her right finger where Hungarians wore their wedding rings to the worry lines on her face. I wondered if she'd ever been married, ever been in love, ever been happy. But the years had pulled at the corners of her mouth, and under the makeup, her eyes were shot with red. Her sketched eyebrows made it look as if she were surprised to find herself here.

"Sorry. *Nem* Magyar," I tried, and shrugged. Then I added, in English because despite the language barrier I thought she might understand, "I'm lost too."

. . .

Although I hardly spoke to anyone else during the five days I spent in Budapest, I still worried about what to say if I did. I didn't want to bring people down on their holiday, but I wasn't sure I could pretend to just be on vacation. *What could I say that wouldn't make me burst into tears? And should I warn other backpackers heading to Thailand? I would have wanted a warning. But then again, I'm not sure we'd have listened. A warning we'd ignored would be worse than no warning at all.*

I still hadn't figured it out by the time I got to Eger. Tucked between wooded hills in the southern Carpathian Mountains, the tiny Baroque town was crowded with churches, a minaret, and a towering castle. But what Eger was really famous for was its Bikavér, or Bull's Blood—a potent, full-bodied red wine.

Michelle, a young New Zealander living and working in London, had taken the same bus from Budapest to Eger and was staying at the same basic Tourist Motel. On a late afternoon, we walked through the city center and past a graveyard, to the Szépasszonyvölgy, or Valley of the Beautiful Women, where dozens of tasting cellars had been carved into the hills.

"Isten hozta." A thin man with white eyebrows and a mustache ushered us through one of the first doorways. His dark cellar was empty except for a few tables and chairs, and a jumbled stack of wooden barrels at the back. We chose a table to the side, where the cold damp seemed to cling to the rough stone walls.

"Egri Bikavér, igen?" With a long glass tube, he siphoned the wine from a barrel before releasing it into two sturdy glasses. A light brown froth skimmed the top of the deep red liquid. He pushed the glasses toward us and waited.

We each took a sip. The wine was strong, oaky, and dry.

"Jó?" The man held up an outstretched thumb.

"Jó," we repeated, with upturned thumbs.

Michelle and I chatted as we drank. She told me about her job at a junior school teaching physical education, and her on-again/off-again boyfriend. I told her about the Australian sea lion pups and Kangaroo Island. Before we'd reached the bottom of our glasses, the cellar owner had refilled them with a wink and without a word.

As we continued talking, an image from that night on the beach at Ko Pha Ngan flashed into my head. The local man pulling Sean's floppy wrist behind his neck. Grabbing him around the waist, and leaning his brown shoulder into Sean's pale half-naked body. Sean's thin legs buckling, his weight sinking toward the wet sand as the man tried to lift him and turn him upside down.

Every day, I spent hours on that beach with Sean's body, replaying the scene over and over to try to find some way to save him.

Back in the cellar, I made an attempt to keep up with the conversation with Michelle. But it began to feel as if every word coming out my mouth were a lie. What I was saying had nothing to do with what I was thinking. I looked down into the dark pool of wine, and realized our glasses had been filled a third time.

"Cheers." Michelle grinned and lifted her wine.

I raised my glass and tried to smile back, but it felt fractured, as if my face had set weeks ago and the now unfamiliar movement had caused my skin to crack and split.

So I told Michelle about Sean. She was sympathetic. I found it difficult to concentrate on her words, but she asked questions and she listened to the answers. She brushed aside her straight blond hair and held my gaze, her light blue eyes looking into mine instead of pulling away.

It was the first time I'd spoken his name out loud since London, and the first time I'd told a stranger. I was surprised when I didn't cry.

Michelle swallowed the last of her wine and stretched her long arms above her head, before reaching into her bag for her wallet. "Where do you reckon we should head for tea? I'm absolutely starving."

· · ·

There's a moment that sometimes comes before drifting off to sleep when you suddenly feel that you're falling. In Hungary, it felt as if I were stuck in that moment and couldn't wake up.

I was directionless and disoriented, unsure and unsteady. I couldn't find my balance or feel the ground beneath my feet. Still too grief-stricken for reflection and certainly not ready for any life lessons, I found I could focus on simple necessities—the distraction and the difficulties of finding food, shelter, and transportation in a language I'd never heard before and an alphabet I didn't even recognize. A girl traveling alone here was a distinct rarity and I was already tired of being constantly stared at, but it was a kind of escape to briefly fixate on hot showers, decent pillows, cheap meals, accurate train schedules, fair exchange rates, and working toilets.

Arriving in Sopron in the northwest corner of the country, I hadn't seen another Westerner since Michelle, though I'd been traveling for almost two weeks. The days had continued to shorten and edge toward winter. I stayed at the budget Jégverem pension, a converted eighteenth-century ice cellar that was as chilly as it sounded.

I spent the crisp, clear afternoons walking around the quiet Old Town, which was still partially surrounded by crumbling medieval walls. Wooded foothills of the Austrian Alps rose up behind the walls, and I hiked for miles through the pine trees on Lővér Hills, and up to the lookout tower at Károly Peak.

But I found it difficult to fill the cold dark nights. Hoping for warmth and to kill time on my last evening in Sopron, I ducked into the ridiculously kitschy and practically empty Papa Joe's Saloon and Steakhouse. After pushing the pistol-shaped door handle, I had to choose between sitting alone at a giant carriage wheel table under an American flag, or on a western saddle barstool. The bartender looked on, expressionless, as I set my bag down on the bar, wiggled my foot into a stirrup, and swung my other leg up and over.

After Bavarian gnocchi with goat cheese and most of Bryan Adams's greatest hits on the stereo, I finally gave up trying to get comfortable. The stirrups were too long for my legs, and the wide leather seats seemed to tip away from the bar, which prompted an awkward reflex of foolishly gripping the saddle horn with one hand while trying to eat, drink, and write in my journal with the other.

Moving on to the nearby Musik Café, I was torn briefly between the draft by the door and the secondhand smoke farther in. There weren't many patrons—a few affectionate, well-heeled couples—but every single one of them had a cigarette. I kept my jacket on, zipped to my chin, and chose a seat near the entrance.

The café was simple and modern. There was a black and white slip of paper on the table with the title *Októberi zenei menu*. On a list of what I could only assume were dates, days of the week, and the lineup of live music, the second to last line read, *25. péntek: JAZZ IN THE NIGHT*.

I ordered a Soproni *világos*, a local lager, as a group of young musicians set up in the corner. They'd certainly dressed the part. The entire band was clad head to toe in too-cool black, complete with turtlenecks or skinny ties, and plastic Wayfarer sunglasses. Even the saxophone player's black felt porkpie hat had been carefully placed at a rakish angle.

At first, I didn't recognize any of the songs. Then I realized . . . the band was playing "Summertime." Although the song was in English, and I knew the lyrics from the Janis Joplin version, the Jazz in the Night singer's accent was so strong that most of the time I couldn't understand the words. It wasn't until he started singing the refrain, *"No no no no, don't you cry,"* that it finally clicked.

The song felt even more foreign because it was supposed to be familiar. The haze of the smoke and the blur from the beers didn't help, but everything seemed wrong. Tomorrow, October 26th, Sean should have turned twenty-six, and here I was, alone in Sopron, surrounded by couples and listening to some wannabe beatnik sing "Summertime" in a thick Hungarian accent while an icy wintertime waited outside in the dark.

I'd been dreading Sean's birthday since his death. Sitting there in the Musik Café that night, I remembered all those musical legends who'd died tragically young: Janis Joplin, Jimi Hendrix, Jim Morrison, Kurt Cobain. Every single one of them had made it to twenty-seven.

. . .

To save money in Győr, near the Slovakian border, I decided to stay at the István Széchenyi Trade School. For three thousand forint, or twelve US dollars, I had my own room for the night with a sink and a toilet. The place definitely felt institutional, but it was clean and only a short walk to town.

The day of October 26th was bright, sunny, and buggy. The warmer weather seemed to have brought out swarms of tiny black flying gnats, especially by the Moson Danube River. As I walked along its banks from the trade school and into the city, I noticed a man twenty feet or so up ahead on the park path. He turned his back to me, his arms moved in front of his body, and his head dropped forward. His jeans sat low and loose around his hips.

It looked like he was peeing, and I was thinking how much I hated it when men took a piss in the streets, when he turned around to face me with his dick in his hands. Staring into my eyes and grinning, he stroked himself rapidly up and down.

My stomach turned, and my skin felt prickly and tight. I looked quickly around, but although it was the middle of the day and there were plenty of people along the riverside, no one was close by.

I spun at a right angle on my heel and headed directly away from the path. Fighting the urge to look over my shoulder to see if the man was following, I walked straight to the nearest couple of people I could see.

But I slowed as I got closer to the two old women sitting and chatting on a park bench. Their white heads were bent together, and one woman was patting the other's knee. They clearly hadn't seen anything, and I was guessing they didn't speak English, so how would I explain? I had a feeling trying to use sign language to mimic a man masturbating would neither be understood nor appreciated.

So I continued toward the city, staying away from the park and sticking close to other people while I kept an eye out for anyone who looked approachable or authoritative, or even just like they might speak English.

I felt I needed to tell someone. By the time I reached Győr's Old Town on the other side of the river, I'd given up.

I'd come to Győr because my guidebook described it as a *picturesque small town, brimming with old residencies of prosperous burghers and clerics*. I'd imagined exploring the *atmospheric old streets*, checking out the Ark of the Covenant statue, and seeing the ceiling frescoes in the seventeenth-century St. Ignatius Loyola Church.

But I hadn't planned on feeling so nauseated, weak, and shaky; I did none of these things. I wasn't sure if it was Sean's birthday, or the beers from the Musik Café the night before, or that asshole by the river. I couldn't stop thinking about him jerking off at me. Years later, I can still picture the leering expression on the man's face.

I decided to sit for a while and have a coffee, but everything in town appeared to be closed. I didn't know if it was a public holiday, or some kind of siesta, or simply a normal Saturday afternoon. After about an hour, I finally found Pálffy on the corner of the Széchenyi tér, and sank down into a seat at an outdoor table. A waiter approached and said something I didn't recognize in Hungarian.

"Uh, cappuccino," I tried.

Two women watching from the table next to mine burst out laughing. Their amusement made me wonder what the waiter had said that I'd replied "cappuccino" to, but he nodded and left.

Moments later, he returned with my cappuccino, served with a shot of carbonated water. The women continued to watch and to whisper and giggle. I pulled the coffee cup closer and took a long bitter sip.

After the coffee, I wandered around Győr's city center until I found a payphone with a black and white arrow, a red target, and the word *"visszahívható"* on the door. According to my *Lonely Planet*, the word meant "call back." This way Sammy, Sean's best mate, could ring me from Australia if my phone card ran out. Luckily I'd bought the card yesterday—1,800 forint for nine minutes—since all the shops still appeared to be shut.

With my thumbnail, I scratched out the code on the back of the card and followed the instructions. There was a rusty-sounding click and a long pause while I held my breath. Then the line started to ring.

"Hello," Sammy answered.

"Hi, Sammy. It's me." I exhaled, and my entire body went limp. I leaned my forehead against the cool metal of the phone box and started to cry.

"Hello," Sammy repeated. I could hear music, loud voices, and clinking glasses on the other end of the line.

"Hi, Sammy." I raised my voice. "Can you hear me? It's me . . . Shannon."

"Helloooooo?" Sammy drew out the last syllable.

"Sammy!" I tried one last time.

"Fucking wanker," Sammy mumbled into the phone, and he hung up.

Exactly, I thought, *fucking wanker.*

I wondered if it was the connection or the background noise that was the problem. I figured Sammy was in a pub for the night with the rest of the boys. But Melbourne was eight hours ahead of Hungary. If I tried much later, he'd probably be wasted, even passed out. I should have called last night when it was Saturday morning in Melbourne, but I'd wanted it to be Sean's birthday for both of us.

I replaced the receiver, then picked up and tried again. A recording at the other end now said that my code was invalid. I double- and triple-checked the code and kept trying, but kept getting the same recording. I tried my parents' number in Davis and my friend Janna in LA. Every time, I was told that my code was invalid. Of course, the only way to call customer service was with a valid code.

I was desperate to talk to someone that Saturday. Anyone. But everything in the city was closed.

With nothing else to do, I wandered up and down the old narrow lanes of Káptalandomb, or Chapter Hill. I passed the cathedral, chapel, and castle without stepping inside. Whenever I saw a payphone, I tried my card again. My code was invalid in every one.

As the sun began to sink, the swarms of black gnats returned. I had only about one and a half hours of daylight left. I'd checked a map earlier to see if there were other routes back to the trade school, and I checked again just in case I'd missed something. I hadn't. The only way to return was through the park and along the river.

I had no idea if there'd be other people on the path after dark, but the streets in the city center had been practically deserted all day. I hadn't seen a single taxi in town, and couldn't call for one with my useless phone card.

I wanted to go for a beer. I wanted to try *halászlé*, or Hungarian fisherman's soup, at Halászcsárad, an inn near the market. I did not want to spend the entire evening of Sean's birthday locked up by myself in a dorm room. I did not want to let that wanker get the better of me.

But it had scared me more than I thought it would, and had shaken my confidence as a woman traveling alone.

Utterly defeated, I grabbed a slice of takeaway pizza to bring back to my room. It was topped with canned mushrooms and cheese, and in typical Eastern European fashion, instead of a tomato sauce base, was smothered with lashings of sickly-sweet ketchup.

I arrived at the dorm well before dark. There had been plenty of people along the Moson Danube, and no sign of the man with the brown wide-set eyes and his dick in his hands.

Then I was stuck for the night. I tried to read, and write in my journal, but I couldn't stop crying. I cried for so long I began to feel as if I were coming down with a cold. I thought about taking a shower, but didn't want to risk bumping into anyone in the hall with such a blotchy red face and ridiculously swollen eyes.

I'd hit my absolute lowest point. I'd always felt most myself when I was traveling, but that night I was frantic, panicky, and nauseated. All I wanted to do was to claw my way out of my body, my situation, my life, that town, that night, and that dorm room.

I didn't see how I could possibly fall any further, though it hardly seemed to matter. I could be in a city like Pécs, which I'd visited earlier in the south of Hungary, where sunny pedestrian streets meandered past fountains and statues, the local Szalon beer was cheap, the central square was lined with outdoor cafés filled with university students and friendly waiters . . . and Sean was still dead.

Or I could be in a place like Győr, where it felt like even the name of the city itself had begun to take on a sinister-sounding edge. Where I'd had a day like today . . . and Sean was still dead.

I could see I was running from his death. Yet I desperately believed Slovakia would be better. It had to be. I hardly knew anything about the country, had never met anyone who'd ever visited, but I was catching the first train there tomorrow. I only hoped there'd be people on the streets, and in the park, that early in the morning.

Sitting cross-legged on my creaky single dorm bed that night, I washed down the greasy pizza slice with a warm bottle of Unicum, a traditional Hungarian digestif. The flavor of the thick brown liquid was herbal and antiseptic, like an alcoholic Ricola cough drop. I raised my eyes and the round green bottle to the ceiling, before bringing it to my lips. *Happy birthday, weasel.*

thirteen

Bled, Gorenjska, SLOVENIA

March 1999

"HAPPY BIRTHDAY, MISS."

Sean winks a blue eye before raising the coconut over his head and lobbing it off our second-floor balcony. The coconut hits the pavement below with a hollow clunk, but without so much as a crack. Cooking chicken satay in Slovenia is proving to be more difficult than we thought.

Slovenia hadn't been on Sean's list. But I was able to talk him into it for my twenty-fifth birthday. We'd spent the day hiking up to the clifftop Bled Castle, and rowing out across the green lake to the church on tiny Bled Island to ring the "bell of wishes."

I'd unwrapped the Jamiroquai CD Sean bought for me, and he'd offered to cook anything I wanted for dinner. Anything I wanted from his short list of staple recipes.

We'd managed to find the peanut butter at the market in Bled. Then Sean had tried to pantomime a Hawaiian hula while pointing over and over to the rows of tinned vegetables. He'd been hoping for canned coconut milk, but it seemed a small miracle when the shopkeeper understood Sean's tropical dance interpretation and produced the real thing. We were running out of cash—ATMs had yet to arrive to Slovenia in 1999—but the coconut felt worth every tolar.

Over an hour later, and we're still trying to get to the milk. We tried a cleaver and a knife, as well as various blunt objects we found around the apartment, before throwing the coconut off our balcony. But that hadn't worked either. We retrieved the coconut and it sat, uncracked, on the counter.

Sean starts emptying the kitchen drawers. He holds up a corkscrew. "At least we can crack open the wine."

He pours out two large glasses of white, and turns up Jamiroquai's "Too Young to Die" on the stereo. We move out onto the balcony and into the spring mountain evening.

I take a long sip. The wine is fruity, with an edge that reflects our budget. It would taste better with food. It would taste better with chicken satay.

"So what did you wish for when you rang the bell today, Miss? Did you wish you were still my age? Only a sprightly twenty-two?" Sean stretches his long legs out in front of him and he grins.

I roll my eyes. There's nowhere else I'd rather be and no one else I'd rather be with, but he knows I've been dreading this birthday. Twenty-five feels desperately old. Especially since I've just been accepted into the PhD program at UC Santa Cruz. No more backpacking around the world teaching scuba diving.

We're interrupted by another low-flying airplane. Planes have been flying overhead from Italy all day. The war in Kosovo is raging and NATO's bombing campaign against Yugoslavia is about to begin.

Sean waits for the rumble of the plane to fade into the distance. "Operation Noble Anvil. Only you Yanks would use a name like that."

"A noble anvil would come in pretty handy right now to bust open this damn coconut."

"I'm thinking of something slightly more subtle." Sean pulls the corkscrew from his pocket and begins to work it through the eye of the coconut. He twists it back out, the tip of the corkscrew dripping with milk, and he winks again. "Who needs a Yankee hammer when a good Aussie screw will do the trick, eh, Miss?"

fourteen

Slovenský Raj, Spiš, SLOVAKIA

October 2002

A s I TRAVELED farther north in Slovakia, I was hoping for snow. I wanted it to be cold. I wanted to be as far away as possible from the heat in Thailand, as far away as possible from the beach at Ko Pha Ngan.

It was almost November, and I was tired of being cooped up alone in overheated rooms after dark. I wanted to be outdoors, away from the dangers of cities and the stares on the streets. I wanted to walk for hours on my own without thinking. I wanted to get lost.

Slovakia in the winter of 2002 turned out to be a good place for getting lost. My pronunciation in Slovak was hopeless, and whenever I tried to ask if someone spoke English—*"Anglicky?"*—it was met with a snarled *"nie."* The few backpackers in Eastern Europe seemed to stick to the capital cities, so I hadn't seen another foreigner for days. Navigating public transportation and finding accommodations had become increasingly difficult.

With a little Slovak and a lot of sign language, I'd managed to buy a train ticket to Poprad. I was in what I hoped was my assigned seat, when an overhead speaker crackled and a muffled voice listed the morning's destinations. I was surprised to hear Spišská Nová Ves immediately after Poprad. I'd thought I had to change trains to get there.

Looking up a few words in my guidebook, I tried to cobble together a request to pay the fare difference on board. I practiced silently while I waited for the conductor to come check my ticket.

"Prosím. Poprad—*nie,* Spišská Nová Ves—*áno.* Koruny?" *Please. Poprad—no, Spišská Nová Ves—yes. Crowns?* It was the best I could do.

"Nie," the conductor grunted, and moved on to the next carriage. I wasn't sure if he'd understood my question, or if his negative response was simply a refusal to try.

The train began to make its way north, and I watched the blurred scenery through the smudged window. We passed tiny towns—red-tiled roofs clustered around a single white church steeple, and yellowed fields of dried wheat and corn. The dark shadows of the Tatry Mountains stretched out into the background under a frost-colored sky.

By the time we reached Poprad, I'd decided to chance it. It was only one more stop. The eighteen minutes seemed to drag for an hour, and I watched nervously for the conductor. But I stepped off at the Spišská Nová Ves station just as a flurry of snow began to fall.

The *turistické informačné centrum* in Spišská Nová Ves wasn't where my guidebook claimed it would be. It wasn't where the maps and signs posted around town indicated either.

After searching in slippery circles on the city's frozen sidewalks, I returned to the station. A bus was pulling out of the parking lot as I arrived. It might, or might not, have been my bus to Čingov. I couldn't make much sense of the posted bus schedule. Each departure was annotated with symbols, and long corresponding explanations in Slovak. Čingov was only ten minutes by bus, so I thought about getting a taxi. But first I wanted to make sure the accommodation near the national park hadn't closed for the winter. So I set off again for tourist information. I finally found it after asking at a three-star hotel, two blocks down and on the opposite side of the street from where my guidebook said it was.

"Nákladný," the woman behind the counter said when I asked about pensions in Čingov. At first, I thought the pensions were closed for the season. But she took out a slip of paper and drew an arrow pointing up next to the letters *Sk* for Slovenská koruna. She shook her dark head, rubbed the pad of her thumb against her forefingers, and raised her heavily shadowed brows.

Using the pen and paper, and tiny scraps of English and Slovak, she suggested a *privát* for 250 Sk, or six US dollars, a night. When she started, it was only a five-minute walk outside Čingov. By the time I had paid and left, it had become twenty.

The woman had counted to four twice on her fingers—*jeden, dva, tri, štyri*—telling me to take bus *štyri* and get off at the *štvrtý* stop. But when I got off bus number four at the fourth stop, it looked nothing like the map she'd drawn for me.

I took off in a few different directions and tried to orient myself. The sun was beginning to drop behind the blackening mountains. There was a dull ache in my spine as the weight of my pack pressed into my hipbones and pulled at my shoulders. I fought against hot, wet tears and was ready to give up. But I couldn't see a single hotel, or even a restaurant. I was surrounded by empty streets and quiet houses.

I finally found a small auto shop with an open garage. A thin, wiry man was leaning down into a car's engine, his head and shoulders blocked by the hood.

"Prosím." I walked to the car and showed him the roughly sketched map. I shrugged my shoulders to my ears, with my open palms held out at my sides.

He pointed to the ground. "Smižany." Which meant I wasn't even in the right town. Maša was where I was supposed to be.

"Prosím," I repeated, and pushed the map toward him.

He wiped his hands on his grease-stained trousers and then ran them through his nonexistent hair. He blew out through his lips for a long time while he looked at the map. Then he pointed in a vague circle somewhere in the middle of the page. He had kind, weather-worn eyes, but they didn't look confident.

"Taxi?" I was grateful that at least that one word was the same in every language. I mimicked holding a phone to my ear. *"Prosím."*

Fifteen minutes and a hundred korún later, I arrived via taxi to my private room. It was four in the afternoon, and would be dark by five. There wasn't enough time to check out the nearby national park, but it was a lot of time to spend cooped up alone in the apartment.

It had taken me the entire day to reach my destination and I'd spent most of it lost. As soon as I locked the apartment door, I broke down crying. But I had succeeded. The next day I could walk outdoors for hours on my own in the snow and the cold without thinking.

I liked the idea of visiting Spiš. There were other reasons I'd come to the Národný Park Slovenský Raj, or Slovak Paradise National Park, but the fact that it was in Spiš held a certain weight. The only souvenirs I bought during my entire trip around Eastern Europe were postcards and maps, but if I'd seen a Spiš T-shirt for sale, I would've gotten one.

Spiš was one of twenty-one tourism regions in Slovakia. It was also what Sean's mates had called him. He'd been called "Spiz" or "Spizza" or "Spizman" for so many years that he couldn't remember for sure how it began. He thought Reilly had become "Rizz," and then "Rizz" became "Spiz." I'd gotten so used to the name, and spent so much time with the boys, that I sometimes called him "Spiz" myself without thinking.

Almost all of the boys had nicknames, and Sean had come up with most of them. Andy was "Jocks," Stephen was "Jacks," Mikey was "Fish," Kevin was "Cobber," and Darren was "Doosh." Even Sammy's real name was Peter. That nickname had started because Peter had the same last name as one of Sean's favorite NBA players, Sam Cassell.

I'd seen that the harder one of the boys fought against a nickname, the more it stuck. So when Sean started calling me "Miss," I'd bitten my lip and said nothing.

But I'd never liked the name. So I finally pointed out that Sean also called his sister-in-law, his two young nieces, even my dog—really anything female—"Miss." I thought he would have to come up with a new term of endearment. Instead, he resolved to stop calling everyone else in his life "Miss," and save it only for me.

I woke up in the apartment in Maša to a heavy silence. Thick powdery snowflakes were coming down in clumps outside my window, swallowing the sounds of the Slovak countryside. It was more than a flurry, but less than a storm. I might have been worried about the possibility of a blizzard, if I hadn't seen the relatively benign weather forecast at tourist information the day before.

I planned on hiking all day in the national park. As long as the temperatures stayed below freezing, at least it would be too cold to rain. And there was the comfort of being inland, of knowing for certain that I couldn't possibly round a bend and be confronted by the enormity of the ocean. I filled my green daypack with all the supplies I had: water, chocolate, oranges, a few extra layers, and the topographic map I'd bought for Slovenský Raj.

Pulling on my gloves and tugging down my beanie, I made my way first to Čingov, which turned out to be more than a forty-minute walk from my *privát*. A hell of a lot longer than twenty minutes, and nowhere near five.

From the park's northern trailheads, I then took the blue trail up to the lookout at Tomášovský Výhľad. I stood at the edge of the cliff, the chalky limestone face dropping sharply away below me, and the valley covered in a dense evergreen forest dusted with white.

The path continued into the Prielom Hornádu, or Hornád River Gorge, my footsteps squeaking as I hiked through the new snow. The steep walls of the canyon narrowed and the river was soon forced into a series of crashing waterfalls. The scenery began to get more dramatic, and the trail became trickier.

Log ladders had been laid down horizontally over the boulder-strewn river. Other metal ladders climbed sheer rock faces a few feet away from icy, tumbling waterfalls. With damp gloves, I clung to freezing chain handholds, and leaped to the next rusted grate platform bolted to the cliffside as the water splashed and rushed past in the opposite direction below me.

After hiking for about three hours, I came to a meadow buried under inches of fresh snow. I hoped it was the Letanovský Mlyn marked on my map, although I couldn't see any sign of a *mlyn*, or mill. But ten minutes later, a green trail broke away from the river and began to climb straight up the Kláštorisko ravine.

As I scrambled uphill, there was a satisfying contrast between the burning muscles in my thighs and the cold air I pulled into my lungs. Stripping off layers, I reached the top of the ravine, and found an abandoned stone monastery and a red *chaty*, or mountain hut. I was surprised the *chaty* was open, since I hadn't seen another hiker all morning. Inside, it was empty, except for a young man listening to music behind the counter who didn't seem at all surprised to see me.

I peered at the squashed foil packets of chips and the ancient-looking candy bars, and pointed to the one hot dish available.

"Bryndzové halušky," said the man, passing over the steaming plate. "Slovensko." He placed his hand on his narrow chest. I smiled; I wasn't sure if he was referring to the dish or to himself. When I ordered a *Zlatý bažant svetlé pivo*, or light beer, he grinned in response and nodded approvingly.

The *bryndzové halušky* turned out to be sticky potato dumplings with sheep's cheese, topped with smoked fatty bacon. It was salty and rich, and I was glad to have the cold bitter beer to wash it down.

As I ate, I studied a poster on the wall of the different animals found in the national park. It seemed to be an optimistic list. There were brown bears, lynx, European wildcats, chamois, deer, otters, martens, foxes, and wolves. I'd figured any bears would be in their winter dens by the end of October, but I hadn't thought about roaming packs of wild wolves. Somehow, Slovak wolves sounded more menacing than American wolves.

The snowfall had stopped while I ate my lunch, and I continued on to the campsite at Podlesok before looping back. Every once in a while,

I'd hear the breath of the wind through the pine trees, or the snap of a dry twig, and I'd try not to think about the wolves. I knew the chances of being attacked were remote, but probabilities now provided the coldest of comforts. Once someone you love falls fatally on the wrong side of statistics, the numbers stop meaning much.

I was hiking along another blue trail that would head back down the ridge toward Čingov when I heard male voices. My heartbeat quickened and I froze in my tracks. It sounded as if there were a number of men, but I couldn't tell which direction the sounds were coming from. I turned in circles, but all I could see were the thick dark stands of fir and spruce. Then the high-pitched grinding of a chainsaw overpowered the voices.

It was too far and too late to turn around and try another trail. I tucked my braids into my hood, hoping I might look like a boy. I walked quickly, trying to keep the weight on my toes to minimize the creaking sounds my boots made through the snow. It felt ridiculous given the noise of the chainsaw. But I found the idea of running into a group of strange lumberjacks in the middle of nowhere unnerving.

I forgot all about the Slovak wolves, as I had to avoid the Slovak lumberjacks twice more throughout the afternoon. Although I could clearly hear the rough-edged sounds of their voices and the mechanical grating of saw blades, I only ever caught shadowy glimpses of their movements. A flash of red clothing between tree trunks far ahead, broken twigs next to large, deep boot prints in the snow. Apparently, national parks in Slovakia didn't provide the protection against loggers I might have expected.

When I finally reached Čingov, it was getting difficult to see in the falling light. I didn't have time to check the restaurants. Instead, I returned alone to my private room in Maša. For dinner, I ate the chocolate and oranges from my pack, and drank bad Slovak *červené stolové víno*, or red table wine. It wasn't until I'd almost reached the end of the bottle that I wrote in my journal: *Had an amazing day—hiking on my own for nine hrs.*

My legs felt shaky and my knees ached, but it was a relief to be physically and not just emotionally exhausted. It was nowhere near happiness. Isolation had its difficulties: negotiating public transport and surly conductors, losing my way in a tiny town like Smižany as darkness fell. It also had its imagined dangers of Slovak wolves and lumberjacks. And no matter how far I'd managed to go to get myself lost, I couldn't stay in the frozen woods forever. But the icy solitude that day had suited me.

fifteen

Huá Shān, Shǎnxī, CHINA

July 2002

I T'S THE BEGINNING of our climb up Huá Shān, the highest of China's five sacred mountains. Stalls line the street leading up to the start of the trek. Vendors call after Sean and me, insisting we need white gloves and red ribbons, at exorbitant prices, for our spiritual journey.

The first ascent gives us an indication of what lies ahead. Qian Chi Zhuang (Thousand Foot Precipice) consists of 370 narrow stone steps carved into the cliff face of Yun Tai Feng (Cloud Stand Peak).

The landscape is starkly beautiful. Only inches from our toes, paper-thin cliff edges plummet into dark valleys. The stony peaks above us are wrapped in mist and fog. Sage-green trees jut out into hazy gray skies, growing at stubborn angles into the relentless wind.

We pass Huixin (Mind Changing Rock), scramble up Tian Ti (Heaven's Ladder), cling to the chain handrails at Yao Zi Fan Shen (Somersault Cliff), skirt Xian Ren Bian (Immortal Needle), and press our bodies into the rock face along Ca Er Yan (Ear Touching Cliff Route). Thousands of Taoist pilgrims have left brass padlocks engraved with their names bolted along the precarious paths and locked into chains at the five towering summits. The padlocks are meant to bring everlasting fortune and love.

By the end of the day, our feet ache and our knees have turned to jelly. Sean's been making a good-natured effort in China to appreciate things that I enjoy, like hiking and sushi when we can find it. But all he wants now is a hot meal and a shower. We find a tiny crumbling inn off the path to Lo-Yiang Feng (Dropping Goose Peak) only to realize how ridiculously unprepared we are. As the sun drops out of view, the temperature plunges and we've only brought T-shirts and shorts. There is no electricity or water. We wash our faces and brush our teeth using a Thermos of warm weak tea. At the inn's faded restaurant, we pay a relative fortune for appalling food. Sean wears my pajama bottoms, many sizes too small, to dinner.

Our descent the next day is even trickier. Huá Shān is often described as the world's most dangerous hiking trail, with an estimated hundred deaths each year. Sean and I are careful, but our legs are tired and wobbly and the wind gusts around our feet. As the path steepens, our steps become more like leaps. Chang Kong Zhan (Floating in Air Road) is where the guardrails disappear. There's just an old wooden plank walkway, less than two feet wide, bolted to the side of the mountain.

Yet it all seems comfortably reckless. We're young and privileged, and feel practically invincible. Not once do I imagine us falling.

part II

SITTING SHIVA

sixteen

Kraków, Małopolska, POLAND

November 2002

"*P*ROSZĘ?*" The woman behind the counter didn't look up as she spoke, but waited with an outstretched finger poised over the ancient cash register. Yellowed-white strands were pressed flat against her head by a hairnet, and she wore a stained apron knotted over her rounded stomach and faded housedress.

"Um, pierogi," I said, choosing the only word I recognized from the menu posted nearby on the wall. "And, uh . . . *fasolka,*" which looked easy enough to pronounce. *"Proszę."* I tried to repeat the Polish for "please." It seemed best not even to attempt *dziękuję,* or thank you.

The woman punched a few keys, held out her open palm, and used her other hand to tap at the top of the register where the numbers were displayed. I handed her a five-złotych coin, a little over one US dollar, and received a numbered ticket and a fistful of change. She turned her back and shuffled into the kitchen, her swollen ankles stuffed into black socks and a pair of worn terrycloth slippers.

I looked down at the number printed on my ticket: seventy-three. My *Lonely Planet* only listed the Polish for numbers one through ten, twenty, one hundred, a thousand, and a million. So I hovered by the pickup counter, hoping to hear something that ended in *"trzy,"* or three, but mostly waiting for a number that none of the other customers responded to.

"*Proszę,*" I tried again, when I finally slid my ticket across the counter in exchange for a steaming bowl of bean stew and a chipped plate piled with dumplings.

At one of the long crowded tables, I found a vacant seat between an elderly woman wrapped in furs and a man in a tattered coat with a blistered, frostbitten nose. Across the table, a group of teenagers laughed and elbowed each other. The girls all looked nearly identical—sticky black lashes framing blue eyes, and blond hair spilling over sharp pinked cheekbones.

The pierogi were pleasantly hot and chewy, filled with a soft, almost sweet cheese and mashed potatoes, and topped with crispy, oily fried onions. I switched back and forth between the dumplings and the saltier, smoky flavors of sausage and bacon in the bean and tomato stew.

We sat and ate in silence, elbow to elbow. The woman in furs stared off into the distance, and the man with the blistered nose concentrated on the bowl in front of him. The teenage girls opposite us chewed, giggled, and whispered together. Someone had drawn hearts and smiley faces onto the fogged-up window behind their chairs, and I watched drops of condensation roll from the bottom of the hearts and the edges of the smiles and wondered what to do next.

The streets outside that morning had been frosty and still. It was the first of November, and apparently the Catholic holiday of Wszystkich Świętych, or All Saints' Day, which meant that everything in and around Kraków was shut for the day: the nearby Auschwitz and Birkenau concentration camps, Wawel Castle and the Wieliczka Salt Mine, the city's museums and most restaurants. Unfortunately, neither the holiday nor the fact that everything else was closed had any effect on my hostel's ten-a.m.-to-five-p.m. lockout policy.

Earlier, I'd spent hours wandering empty cobbled streets through the medieval Old Town before finally finding an Internet café that was open. Checking email provided an excuse to get warm, and it was often my only connection to the outside, English-speaking world. There were four people I'd come to rely on, some of them unexpected, whose messages were always there waiting: Justine, a family friend from Sydney; my cousin Mayhill C; my childhood friend Mary; and, of course, my mum.

Among the other new messages in my inbox was an email from Anna, who had volunteered for me during my fieldwork on Kangaroo Island. We hadn't spoken for a few months, but a mutual friend had told her about Sean. That initial communication with a friend was always the hardest. It was like living through Thailand all over again, experiencing their new shock at his death as if it were the first time for me as well.

I kept wiping at my face, but couldn't stop the tears rolling down my cheeks. I'd almost finished a long reply to my mum when the power cut out. The electric hum from the computers thinned into silence, as if the machines were sighing. The clerk exhaled as well, shrugged his shoulders at me, and stepped through the front door with his cellphone. I waited alone in the dark. After about ten minutes of staring at the blank screen in front of me, I gave up and went outside again.

It was twelve weeks that Friday. The shortest and longest twelve weeks of my life. He was only just here, laughing with me. And I resented each heavy day that took me further away from him. Standing there that bleak midwinter morning on the cobblestone street, I could feel time stretching out on either side, those twelve weeks behind and the weeks that still lay ahead.

That was when I'd noticed the neon blue sign—the capital white letters, BAR MLECZNY, next to a picture of a knife and fork. *Bary mleczne*, or milk bars, were state-subsidized restaurants created by the Communist government to provide food for the poor. They'd also hoped to encourage milk drinking to take advantage of the country's dairy surplus, and as an alternative to vodka.

Although many milk bars had survived the fall of communism in Poland, they'd never managed to replace the vodka. As I sat in the Bar Mleczny next to the man with the blistered nose and ate my pierogi and *fasolka*, I could smell the *wódka* on him. Sour on his breath, but fermented and sweet as it oozed from his pores. He scraped the last bite from his bowl, swallowed a burp, and leaned back in his chair to light a cigarette.

"*Smacznego.*" He grinned at me, exhaling. I smiled in return. I wasn't sure what he'd said, but he looked content and didn't seem to require a response.

When I cleared my space at the table, there was another man waiting by the counter. He held out his hands for my dishes and I thought he must have been an employee. It seemed odd he was wearing a worn-out hat and coat, but the woman who'd taken my order had been wearing slippers.

"Proszę." I tried one more time. It was the only Polish I had any confidence in.

"Dziękuję," he replied. Although I was able to recognize the word, the pronunciation surprised me.

I tried to repeat the sounds of his syllables. *"Jen-koo-yeh."*

But then he leaned in closer and continued. His unfamiliar words came thick and fast and crowded together. I had no idea if he was amused or annoyed, coherent or crazy. As he spoke, he stabbed at the last few dumplings sliding around on my plate and shoved them into his mouth. He then slurped up the rest of my stew, before passing my dishes through the kitchen window.

From the milk bar, I walked to Kraków's main market square, Rynek Główny. The square was lined with shuttered cafés, dark restaurants, and quiet town houses, but the huge open space was teeming with pigeons. The birds circled and bobbed, gurgled and cooed, and scattered as locals crossed through the square. Thin blond girls holding hands, old women wearing handkerchiefs on their heads, and homeless men swigging from bottles and staggering on to the next bench. There were a couple of *obwarzanki* vendors, their rings of poppy-seed-sprinkled bread stacked into piles. But as they pushed their carts past, only the pigeons showed any interest.

I sat on a cold bench with my journal on my lap and watched the square. For weeks, I'd been dreaming Sean was dying, and he'd come to me that one time almost a month ago to tell me he was no good at heaven. But the night before, I'd had my first dreams that Sean was dead.

Keith, Audrey, Eden, and Sean's whole family had come to visit me in my tiny bunkhouse on Kangaroo Island. It felt crowded and comfortable, and I was so relieved. I'd cooked kangaroo-meat fajitas, and as they were getting in the car to leave, Audrey tried to give me a credit card to buy a ticket to Melbourne. She said it would be good for them to have me, that they needed it. And they apologized for not emailing or phoning me back.

In the next dream, I was at the seaside in Santa Cruz with my friends Dorian, Mary, and Kristen. Together, we ran across the kelp-strewn beach and down to the ocean. But as soon as the icy waves of the Pacific touched my feet, I panicked. In that moment, there on the wet sand, I remembered . . . I hadn't touched the water since Sean.

I'd woken up in my bunk bed in Kraków to an aching jaw. It felt as if his death resided somewhere in my throat, just behind my clenched teeth. It caught in my voice and it blocked my breath. I was moving my chin from side to side, still trying to release the tension, when I was distracted by the sound of a single trumpet echoing across Rynek Główny square.

The rounded drawn-out notes seemed to be coming from one of the two brick towers of the Kościół Mariacki, or St. Mary's Church. The music was simple, slow, and direct. But less than a minute after it started, the tune abruptly dropped out.

It wasn't until later that I found out what I'd heard was the Hejnał Mariacki, or St. Mary's Dawn. According to local legend, early one morning in 1241, a lone guard spotted Tatar forces approaching. He played the Hejnał on his trumpet, and woke the inhabitants in time to defend their city. But an arrow pierced the guard's throat and his warning was cut short.

I was only just starting to listen to things like the Hejnał, to take more notice of my surroundings. I began to pay attention to the smells and tastes of Eastern Europe, the emotions, the weather, and the approaching winter.

What I really lost myself in were the stories. Stories here were so different from the ones I'd heard growing up in California—scarier and more honest, less Disney and more Brothers Grimm. In Poland, I found myself in a place where the endings were rarely happy, but the stories were told just the same.

Since I didn't speak the language, it wasn't always easy. I checked the historical sections in my guidebook and read anything written in English at the museums I visited. I looked online for information and answers. Though I would search at smoky Internet cafés as I traveled, sometimes it was years before I found an explanation.

I learned that during World War II, when Poland was under German occupation, Hitler himself had attended a rally in Kraków to celebrate the name change of the main square where I'd sat from Rynek Główny to Adolf Hitler Platz. And that on May 18th in 1944, after four months of fighting, a bugler from the Second Polish Corps had announced Allied victory at the Battle of Monte Cassino by playing the Hejnał.

The square's name was changed back after the war, and by the time I visited, any evidence that it had ever been called Adolf Hitler Platz had long been removed. Yet today in Kraków, the Hejnał continues to be played from the highest tower of St. Mary's Church every hour, cut short as it was 750 years earlier.

The next day's sky was dark and it was pouring rain, which seemed appropriate. It was hard to imagine being in this place under blue skies and in brilliant sunshine. I pulled up my hood and raised the zip on my jacket as I left the redbrick visitors' center.

Walking down the muddy gravel path, I stopped under the infamous wrought iron sign. Beside me, a young Aussie backpacker was using the sleeve of his coat to keep a small video recorder out of the rain. I could just make out the broad familiar accent as he panned along the barbed-wire fence and provided his commentary to the camera.

Winter-stripped trees lined the street leading into Auschwitz. Rain dripped off the branches and onto my hood, splashing into gritty puddles at my feet. Most of the buildings near the entrance were two stories high and built of solid red and orange brick. According to my map, block numbers four, five, and six contained exhibits with titles such as *Extermination*, *Material Evidence of Crime*, and *A Day in the Life of a Prisoner*.

I pushed through the first set of heavy wooden doors. It was colder inside the barracks than out and I shoved my numb fingers deeper into my pockets. I stood in front of glass-walled rooms that were packed with personal possessions from the victims: shaving brushes and toothbrushes, metal kitchenware, artificial limbs and crutches, cold cream container lids, baby sweaters, and prayer shawls. There was a pile of more than eighty thousand shoes, the brightly colored leather of the smallest pairs standing out against the decaying blacks and browns. And another of battered suitcases labeled with names, birth dates, and words like *"waisenkind,"* the German for "orphan."

Bolts of cloth were on display that had been woven from female prisoners' hair. Nearby, a room almost a hundred feet long was filled with braids and clumps of graying locks and curls. On the other side of the glass, my stomach contracted and churned. By the time the Soviets liberated the camp in 1945, most of the hair from Auschwitz's prisoners had already been sent to German factories—to be processed into felt and thread, used to make socks for submarine crews, ignition mechanisms in bombs, as stuffing for mattresses and pillows. Yet the Russian forces still found more than seven tons of human hair stuffed into paper sacks.

Behind another glass wall, there was a tall tangled heap of dusty eyeglasses. A tight lump rose into my chest. For me, Sean's glasses had been such a fundamental part of who he was. His eyes hadn't produced enough tears to use contacts, so he'd worn glasses since he was sixteen. He was always managing to misplace his navy wire frames and would start most mornings by asking me, "Miss, have you seen me specs?"

His glasses had fogged easily in the damp summer heat in China, so he'd played without them during afternoon basketball games with his students. He'd coped surprisingly well, wiping the sweat from his brow and squinting his blue eyes at the ball. Once, I'd told him that I thought his glasses were sexy, and he started making a point of looking at me as he adjusted the frames. He'd raise his eyebrows and nod toward the bedroom, before bursting out laughing.

Now Sean's glasses sat in a box with what I had left of him. A mix tape I'd made when he was working in Ireland and I was in the Caribbean, a paper packet of flu medicine we'd bought in China, a small pot of the Fudge Putty he used for his hair, his favorite blue-checked button-down shirt, silk boxers printed with the Aussie flag, and the dried roses from his casket.

I thought how every single pair of eyeglasses in that glass room had a story like Sean's. How once they'd belonged to someone, someone who had depended on them, someone who'd probably lost them and found them, found them and lost them, over and over again.

The camp was still except for the sound of spattering rain on the rooftops and against the windowpanes as I wandered between exhibits. An empty blue and gray striped uniform hung above the rough wooden clogs the prisoners had been forced to wear. A typical day's ration was displayed in a glass case: a small hunk of black bread and the standard issue rusty-red enamel bowl filled with a thin gray soup. There were architects' sketches for the gas chambers and enormous stacks of used metal canisters of the poison gas Zyklon B. Only seven kilograms could kill fifteen hundred people.

To determine the correct dosage, the Nazis had experimented. First, on two hundred and fifty Roma children at the Buchenwald concentration camp, and then on six hundred Soviet POWs and two hundred and fifty Polish prisoners crammed into the basement of the nearby block number eleven, or Death Block. It had taken more than twenty hours for the POWs and prisoners to die.

The sheer number of photos at Auschwitz was overwhelming. Walls were filled with row upon row of black and white mug shots of prisoners in triplicate: first a profile with the back of their heads placed against a stud in the sidewall, then facing the camera, and finally looking off at an angle to their right while wearing a hat or scarf. The expressions in their eyes were of surprise, terror, pride, confusion, confrontation, and comprehension, sometimes all at the same time.

Many of the shots were labeled with a prisoner number, name, date of birth, occupation, date of arrival into the camp, and the date of death there. But thousands were displayed without even a name.

Different barracks were dedicated to the suffering of different countries. Fresh wreaths had been placed in front of the buildings. I made my way slowly through: *In Memory of 400,000 Hungarian Auschwitz Victims as a Permanent Reminder for the Living, The Tragedy of the Slovak Jews, The Struggle and Martyrdom of the Polish Nation.*

Some of the blocks also displayed information on the victims whose stories were less well known: the mentally ill, Communists, socialists, trade unionists, Freemasons, Jehovah's Witnesses, and homosexuals. Block number thirteen was devoted to another group whose persecution had received little recognition in the history books: *The Destruction of the European Roma.*

The exhibit had opened only the year before, in 2001. As the solitary visitor in the Roma block, I walked through the silent spotless rooms alone. There were rumors in my own family of Spanish Gypsy heritage, which had always sounded exotic and romantic when I was growing up. My mum referred to my love of travel and restless nature as being in my Gypsy blood. But here, I could see why earlier generations might have tried to bury that part of our ancestry.

Apart from the Jews, the Roma were the only other ethnic group targeted for extermination by the Nazis. I read that as many as one and a half million Roma were murdered, and their populations were virtually wiped out in the Netherlands, Luxembourg, Lithuania, Estonia, Croatia, and what is now the Czech Republic. Yet, no Roma were called to testify at the Nuremberg Trials, and no one spoke on their behalf. When reparations were granted to Jewish survivors of the Holocaust, the German government denied any payments to the Roma.

Block number thirteen's exhibit on the medical experiments was particularly shocking. Josef Mengele, otherwise known as the Angel of Death, had been especially interested in Roma children and identical twins. There was documentation of forced sterilizations and castrations, induced hypothermia, and amputations without anesthesia. He sewed siblings together to create conjoined twins, and tried to change eye color with injected chemicals.

But by far the most disturbing photos were the ones without captions. Before and after images in black and white of nameless children turned into ghosts, without any explanations provided. At the end of the experiments, the young victims' dark haunted faces stared into the camera lens while the skeletal shadows of what remained of their naked bodies turned away.

As the dark morning rain that day turned into a dull afternoon drizzle, more and more visitors passed beneath the iron *ARBEIT MACHT FREI* sign and began to wander around the barracks. By the time I reached the Black Wall, or Wall of Death, a small crowd had gathered there.

The wall had been built of logs, and covered with black-painted cork to protect the brick behind it from bullet holes. It stood between block number ten, where the medical experiments were conducted, and block number eleven, the camp prison, or Blok Smierci (Death Block).

At least twenty thousand men and women, mostly Polish political prisoners and members of underground organizations, had been forced to stand naked and barefoot in front of the Black Wall before they were executed. Sand had been laid down at the foot of the wall to absorb their blood. Over fifty years later, as I stood in the dripping rain that second day of November in 2002, bouquets of flowers and lit candles had replaced the blood-soaked sand.

The fresh flowers were wrapped in plastic or tied into bunches with ribbon. Flames flickered in red votive glasses while thin coils of smoke rose from wicks that had extinguished. Crumpled notes and smooth stones were tucked into the cracks of the weathered cork.

People stood a short distance from the wall, elderly women wiping at their eyes with papery hands, and young men in shiny tracksuits struggling with lighters in the rain. I could recognize snatches of Polish from the hushed conversations around me, mostly the words *"dzień dobry"* (good day) and *"tak"* (yes).

It occurred to me that I'd been hearing those same words whispered throughout the day, that most of the visitors appeared to be local. Until

I reached the wall, I'd thought the flowers and candles I'd seen under photos and in the prison cells were a part of the exhibits, memorials placed there and maintained by the museum.

But as I watched a blond couple kneel down on either side of a little boy and point to the wall as they spoke, I realized the candle at their feet had been lit for Dzień Zaduszny, or All Souls' Day. And it had been lit for one soul in particular.

I'd never come across All Saints' or All Souls' days until arriving in Kraków. Raised in a small university town in Northern California, I had parents who believed in education and politics. When it came to religion, they'd wavered somewhere between atheist and agnostic. So I'd looked up the Catholic holiday online the day before when everything else had been shut.

I learned that All Saints' commemorates saints and martyrs, both known and unknown throughout history. All Souls' takes place the following day, on November 2nd, to honor the faithful departed who haven't quite yet made it to heaven. It was a time to remember the dead, and had been widely observed in Poland for centuries. Polish cemeteries would fill with people bringing flowers in the morning and then candles at night, tidying and blessing the graves not only of relatives, but also the old forgotten graves of strangers.

But I hadn't realized that this would be taking place at Auschwitz. I'd ended up there, on that day, entirely by chance. It was the first time since Sean's death when it felt as if I was where I was supposed to be.

The people I'd come across in Eastern Europe could be as cold as the temperatures, which would soon start dropping to fifteen below. We didn't share a common language, or in some cases even an alphabet. But death and mourning were ordinary parts of life here. These were cultures that understood loss.

As the crowd at the Black Wall grew, the flowers began to pile up along the base of the cork. Ink bled from the damp notes pushed into the cracks of the wall. My face was wet from tears and the weather. It was a relief to be able to cry and not have anyone take any notice.

The small stones in the cracks signified a different tradition. The Israeli girls had told me in Thailand that it was a Jewish custom to leave a pebble instead of flowers at a graveside as something more permanent. A token that a soul has not been forgotten.

The blond couple was still holding hands with the little boy in front of the wall. I thought of Sean and me and our son, my future family now only in the past. The woman edged their candle forward into line with the other votive glasses, before they both straightened and crossed themselves. Of the thousands of prisoners shot and killed at the Black Wall, I wondered whose soul they might be praying for. And I wondered if he could hear them.

The other passengers stared out the windows in silence as we rode the shuttle bus for a couple of miles to Auschwitz II, or Birkenau. The network known as Auschwitz had consisted of the *stammlager*, or main camp, from where we'd just come, as well as Birkenau, the Monowitz labor camp, and forty-five smaller satellite camps.

The railway tracks leading to Birkenau passed through a redbrick guard tower, which the prisoners called the Gate of Death. High above this entrance, an enclosed platform looked out over the grounds, giving some perspective of the scale of what had taken place here.

The enormity of it was terrifying. Cold crept along the length of my spine and the hair stood up at the base of my neck as I climbed up to the tower.

Seven villages had been torn down to accommodate the camp: Brzezinka (or Birkenau in German), Babice, Broszkowice, Rajsk, Plawy, Harmeze, and Brzeszcze-Budy. Barbed-wire fences stretched out into the distance enclosing more than four hundred acres. Half the size of Central Park in Manhattan, five times the size of Disneyland in California, almost nine times the size of the main camp at Auschwitz.

I'd spent hours walking around the main camp that day and had left shell-shocked. I didn't think I could take anything more in. But the flat barren wasteland in front of me was shattering.

As much as the size, it was the emptiness. Most of the original structures were gone or in ruins. Of the almost three hundred primitive barracks, only nineteen were still standing in 2002. All that was left of the others were the disembodied brick chimneys, their thin dark stacks spread out over the vast landscape like the charred, skeletal remains of a forest fire.

From the guard tower at the entrance, the train tracks continued for another mile before ending directly in front of the gas chambers. In the spring of 1944, ten thousand prisoners arrived here each day in cattle cars from across Europe. At least 75 percent of them—older men and women, the disabled and the ill, mothers with babies, and children under fourteen—were never even registered. Instead, they rode the railroad tracks from the entrance straight to the gas chambers.

In January of 1945, the Nazis began their retreat. They burned documents, leveled barracks, and dynamited the gas chambers and crematoria at Birkenau. The ruins I stood in front of were just as the fleeing Nazis had left them, mangled piles of brick rubble and fractured concrete. The imposing wreckage of the two largest crematoria, Krema II and Krema III, lay in great broken pieces on either side of the end of the train tracks.

Whereas Auschwitz had been rebuilt as a museum—the barracks restored and exhibits created, even the barbed wire continuously replaced as it rusted—Birkenau was only minimally maintained. All that had been added was a memorial at the end of the railway line.

The memorial was a tall jumble of oddly shaped dark stones. I wasn't sure if the shapes were supposed to represent people or coffins or headstones. I also thought they might have been meant to symbolize the Jewish tradition of leaving pebbles to mark graves, outsized to signify the mass mortalities.

There were words at the foot of the stones: FOR EVER LET THIS PLACE BE A CRY OF DESPAIR AND A WARNING TO HUMANITY. With twenty metal plaques in twenty different languages for the different populations that had been murdered at Auschwitz. Bunches of fresh flowers surrounded the inscriptions in Polish, Russian, Hungarian, Czech, German, French, Greek, Croatian, Italian, Dutch, Norwegian, Romanian, Slovak, Serbian, Ukrainian, Judeo-Spanish, Belorussian, Yiddish, Hebrew, and Romani.

Far more than the memorial, what really struck me that cold November day was the number of candles that had been lit and left along the train tracks. White candles standing alone, simple red votive glasses, and colorful engraved jars were all crowded together along the entire mile. Their tiny beating flames lighting up the same straight path most of the victims had taken.

As I walked back toward the Gate of Death, darkness began to press in along the edges of the barbed-wire fences. The rain fell faster and harder. But the candles continued to burn.

It was difficult to figure out what to do afterward. Nothing felt right after so much cruelty and death. I couldn't imagine going to a movie, and didn't think I could stomach food. Even coffee sounded overwhelming. So I climbed straight onto the bus that would return to Kraków, without seeing anything of the small town of Oświęcim, the town the Germans had called Auschwitz.

The cold from that day had seeped deep into my bones. I shivered as I tried to pull my damp clothes away from my skin. Through the fogged-up bus window, I saw a smudge of wavering light in the blackness and I rubbed a clear circle onto the glass with my fist. The cemetery at Oświęcim was carpeted in a sea of blinking candles. Pulling my journal from my bag, I started to write.

"To help a dead loved one find his way home." A voice from behind me made my pen skip across the page. My heart tensed and pushed against my chest.

I turned toward a scrawny young man with a dark goatee and a backpack sitting behind me on the bus. "Excuse me?"

"The candles," he explained, gesturing out the window and into the dark. "For All Souls'."

"Oh, right . . . They're beautiful."

"I'm Les." He stuck out his hand. "Originally from South Carolina."

"Hi. Shannon. Originally from California."

Les didn't know what to do after Auschwitz either, so he suggested we go for a beer when we got to Kraków. In the Old Town, we found a pub off a narrow cobbled passageway and down a flight of steps in a smoky vaulted cellar.

We took a couple of stools at the bar and waited for the bartender. With long delicate fingers, he was rocking an orange yolk back and forth between two broken pieces of shell. A bowl below the bartender's hands caught the dribbling egg whites.

Looking around the pub, I noticed that the men and the women appeared to be drinking different versions of beer. The women sipped theirs pink-tinged and through lipsticked bendy straws, while the pint the bartender slid in front of the man seated next to me was much larger, filled with a cloudy honey-colored draft and topped with a head of milky foam. The glass rim fogged from the heat of the man's drink and I could smell cinnamon and cloves in the steam.

"*Proszę?*" The bartender wiped down the bar in front of our stools.

I pointed to the drink next to me and held up one finger. The bartender raised his eyebrows and pointed to a woman's beer at the end of the bar.

"*Nie.*" I shook my head and pointed again to the glass next to me. "*Proszę.*" Something hot and spiced sounded much more appealing than something pink. The bartender turned to Les, who held up two fingers.

About ten minutes later, two steaming pints were set down in front of us. The yolky froth at the top was creamy and sweet, while the hot beer below had a bit of a peppery kick. It was an odd, but not unappetizing combination.

As Les reached for his beer, his knuckle grazed the back of my hand and I flinched. After Thailand, I was aware of how physically distant I'd become with people—walking a little farther from friends, avoiding hugs, and pushing away during conversations to create more space.

Les was nice enough. He gave me a pen because mine had run out. I gave him my book, *Fast Food Nation*, which I'd just finished. But I felt remote and disconnected. I didn't talk much and I didn't tell him about Sean.

The bartender returned again and leaned his elbows onto the bar in front of us. *"Dobry?"* he asked, his thumb and forefinger brought together into an okay sign.

"Dobry," Les and I repeated, nodding and smiling.

Pointing to our beers, the bartender spoke slowly: *"Grzane piwo."* And then he pointed again to the woman's smaller glass at the end of the bar and looked directly at me. *"Piwo z sokiem."*

I knew he was trying to tell me something, either about the size or the drink itself. But I was too distracted by how surprisingly similar the Polish for "beer" was to the word Sean had spoken so many times in Mandarin: *piwo* and *píjiŭ*.

Beers with Les that night turned into *tatankas*—Żubrówka, or Bison Grass Vodka, shots with apple juice. I hardly remembered getting a taxi back to my hostel just before the midnight curfew. I woke up with a headache, an empty chocolate wrapper in my pocket, and another bar melted in its package underneath me. And for the first time in months, I couldn't recall my dreams. As awful as the nightmares could be, it felt worse to wake up with nothing.

The memories that could be lost and details forgotten were what really scared me. The stories at Auschwitz had been harrowing, but what I'd found even more upsetting were the stories not told: the prisoner photos without a name, the Roma children turned into ghosts, the thousands of Jews who'd never been registered at Birkenau.

I knew I didn't want to forget anything, not even that night on the beach at Ko Pha Ngan. But I was still trying to work out for myself how I wanted to remember. So I took out my journal and the pen Les had given me, unwrapped the squashed chocolate bar, and started with the word *"píjiŭ."*

Shànghăi, Guìzhōu, CHINA

August 2002

"*Píjiǔ?*" Sean asks. We've stumbled across an expat shop in Shànghăi selling all kinds of foreign foods, and have visions of cold Crown Lager and cheese. But the man behind the counter shakes his head.

For weeks, we've been living on soy sauce, rice, pork, eggplant, the occasional pig intestine, and Chinese beer spiked with formaldehyde. Not ready to completely abandon our dream, we head for the cheese selection at the back of the store. There's a small block of jalapeño jack that costs more yuan than the two tickets we just bought for the Shànghăi Zájì Tuán, or Acrobatic Troupe. We decide it's worth it.

We take the cheese and a box of Australian water crackers to an outdoor pub in the Făguó Zūjiè, or Frenchtown. Pulling two chairs under an umbrella at a rickety table, we squeeze in together out of the blistering midsummer sun. Sean and I are crowded into the small space of shade, my hip tucking comfortably into his, the skin of our thighs touching.

Sean looks up the Mandarin word for "knife." "*Cāndāo?*" He has to try a couple of times before the waiter finally understands.

But Sean's next phrase is much more practiced: "*Bīng de píjiǔ. Bīng de, bīng de.*" We always ask for "ice beer," repeating the words for "ice" in hopes that our drinks one day might actually arrive cold. Sean holds up his index finger: "*Yī.*" By ordering only one to share, Sean figures we can minimize the time our drinks have to warm up before we finish them. Besides, the beers at this pub are ridiculously overpriced, at least for China. Expensive beer to go with our expensive cheese.

The waiter brings a glistening green bottle of Zhujiang beer to our table. It's marvelously cold. But we're less delighted with the knife he presents. The long, chipped blade is covered in rust and streaked with black grease. Most of the wooden handle has broken off. We're glad we haven't ordered food if this is any indication of the kitchen.

Luckily, the cheese has softened in the late afternoon heat and we're able to cut through it with chopsticks. We have no way of knowing that a few hours later, our stomachs will begin to cramp and we'll both be cripplingly ill. Sean will think that after not eating dairy for so long, we might be having trouble digesting the cheese. It will either be that, or the only cold beers we ever got in China.

But for now, we're blissfully unaware. We finish off the entire block of cheese and order another "ice beer," moving our chairs around the table to chase the shade. Sean shields his eyes and squints behind his glasses into the sun as he raises his drink for a toast. "To us, Miss. To China. And to our good fortune together."

eighteen

Haad Rin Nok, Ko Pha Ngan, THAILAND

August 9, 2002

"I LOVE YOU."

My hand rested on Sean's coffin, his body now only a dark shadow beneath the colored glass. After he was locked in, the crowd at the temple seemed to thin. The locals kept their distance, and one of the Israeli girls touched my shoulder before they both backed away, leaving us alone for the moment. I hated the thought of leaving him at the temple, but I couldn't bear to stay there much longer either.

"I love you so much." I raised my voice over the vibrations of the fan's motor and said it one last time. And then one last time, I rode in the front of the truck with the girls. The back of the truck was empty.

The girls and I didn't get back to the Seaview Haadrin until after three a.m. We'd had to wait for hours at the temple for the key, but the girls explained that I needed to be at the police station at eight the next morning. I wasn't sure how they knew this or who had told them.

They said they would come with me. When I tried to politely protest, they insisted. "We will stand outside and wait if you want. But we are going to come."

My initial reaction was relief I wouldn't have to face the police alone. I was privately glad they didn't give me a choice. Still, they had spent most of the night with my shock and Sean's body. If I didn't see them in the morning, I wouldn't wake them. And I wouldn't blame them.

I was, however, adamant that I be alone until then. The girls didn't want me to be on my own; I could stay at their cabana or they could stay at mine. I refused repeatedly. I needed to be by myself. I needed to talk to him, feel him in the room, and not have other people crowding him out.

But as I pulled the flimsy window curtains of cabana 214 shut, there was a knock at the door. A young Canadian girl with unruly gold hair and a maple leaf across her chest. An apple-cheeked boy in a red baseball cap holding her hand. They had heard what had happened; they were worried about me.

"Do you want company?"

"No. Thanks, but no. I really need to be alone." I felt awkward in front of other people, a curiosity. As if, in the course of just one evening, I now came from a country no one else had even heard of. Even the gravity under my feet felt different.

The young couple gave me a flashlight and left. I turned the heavy metal barrel in my hands. *What was I supposed to do with a flashlight?*

I shut and locked the door, but could hear the couple debating outside the window if they should leave or try again. I turned out the lights until the sounds of the ocean covered their fading footsteps.

When I turned the lights on again, Sean's things were spread across the room, casting long shadows on the walls—his T-shirt thrown across the back of a chair, his towel flung over a lamp, his backpack leaning against the side of our bed. My chest was caving in, my heart thudding in my throat, and my stomach churning with acid.

The first thing I did was pack his old purple and turquoise backpack. I couldn't stand to have his stuff everywhere, as if he were still there with me, as if any minute he could walk through the door.

I folded his shirts and boxers, placed his glasses into their case so they wouldn't get scratched, put away his toothbrush, and tucked his passport into the concealed pocket with his plane tickets. I took his cash and put it into my own wallet, feeling oddly guilty. The presents for his family and friends were pushed down toward the bottom. His powdery scent was on everything I folded and packed, and I wondered how long it would be until his smell faded.

I'd been trying to block out the ocean. But the relentless sound of crashing waves and the heavy smell of acrid salt were sinking through the cracks in the walls. After checking the windows to make sure the beach was deserted, I went back in the dark to the spot where Sean had just died. I wrote a message in the wet sand with my finger. *I'm sorry. I love you.*

It must have been after four a.m. Everything was black. The moon only a sliver in the night sky, with no hint the sun would rise again from the water. Broken waves foamed over the sand, blurring and pulling my words out to sea. I turned my back on the ocean.

Inside our cabana, I pulled the thin purple sundress off over my head to take a shower. It dropped into a crumpled heap on the bare wood floor. He had collapsed on the beach while I threw on that dress. I hadn't realized he was dying.

I hated myself for throwing on the dress. Maybe I could have saved him. If I had run to the crowded bar topless. Or started CPR by myself on the beach. Screamed for help instead of running for it. If I had done something, anything, different.

That night, I slept. I surprised myself, and even felt ashamed. I shouldn't have been able to sleep. Not that night. Not in that bed. Not on those clown-printed sheets still smelling of him, and still smelling of us.

Of course, I dreamed of him. We were waiting together at a stoplight. The light was red. The comedian Ali G came up to wait with us. I was trying to tell Ali G how much Sean liked his show, how funny Sean thought he was. But I was too stoned. I couldn't get the words out. The light never changed and we couldn't cross. So we waited.

nineteen

Salamanca, Castilla y León, SPAIN

March 1999

S EAN'S PACK is on our bed, a Gemini MacPac in purple and turquoise. He's told me many times already how much he hates those colors. How he'd thought they were cool in the store, but the moment he left with the pack in his hands, he decided he hated them. Garish, girlish colors. And he hates the small, detachable daypack. It's an uncomfortable shape and an awkward size.

It's early spring, and I can hear the streets of Salamanca below. A clock strikes ten, the church bells clang, and university students flirt and argue with each other on their way to class. Above the city noise, Ben Harper's *The Will to Live* plays on Sean's Discman, projected through tiny travel speakers. The Spanish sunshine spills through the pension's open windows, and onto Sean's things spread out across the sheets.

There's a heavy Picasso desk calendar that was a birthday present from an ex, but is completely blank. A pair of ceramic drums Sean bought in Fes but has never once played. A hand-painted plate from Évora for his mother. A traditional Berber carpet, rolled into a thick duct-taped bundle. And a winter-weight sheepskin jacket I've never seen him wear.

"Whatcha doin', Miss?" Sean walks through our door after showering in the shared bathroom down the hall. I think how sexy he looks with his hair wet and his towel slung low below the scar from his burst appendix. I can smell the Dove soap that we share.

The CD track switches from "Faded" to "Homeless Child" and Sean starts dancing, dropping his towel to the floor and jiggling toward me.

"Unpacking. And we're posting all the stuff you never use home."

"But I might need—"

"To schedule an appointment three weeks from Tuesday?" I ask, and pick up the desk calendar. "Or to busk for spare change on the streets?" I toss him the drums. "Or to travel with your own plate just in case a restaurant runs out?"

"You never know, Miss."

"Seriously. Your pack weighs a ton. Your back is killing you. And we can't afford to keep taking taxis. No more excuses for not walking everywhere."

"Okay, okay, you win." He drops the drums back onto the pile. "But I'll just have heaps more space for presents to bring home." He pulls me down onto the bed and he kisses me.

I taste the mint of our toothpaste, and pull back to look up into his eyes.

"What now, Miss?" His hands are already moving up and under my T-shirt.

In Sintra, Sean had started saying, "There's something I really want to talk to you about. But I'm not sure how you'll take it." I knew what he was getting at, but I hadn't been ready, so I kept changing the subject. We've known each other for less than six weeks. We've both been scared to be the one to say it first. But I take a deep breath. *What is there to be scared of?*

Sean from Australia, age 25.
August 9, 2002. Ko Pha Ngan.

*On August 9, 2002, a 25-year-old Australian male died from
massive leg stings, wading in waist-deep water late in the afternoon off Hat Rin Nok Beach, Koh Pha Ngan Island. He exited
the water, collapsed on the beach, stopped breathing, and was
pulseless within 5 minutes. Despite immediate resuscitation, 15
minutes later in hospital an electrocardiogram (ECG) showed
asystole.*[3]

t w e n t y

Thong Sala, Ko Pha Ngan, THAILAND

August 10, 2002

THE DAY AFTER August 9th, I woke early. In the morning light, Sean's death was inconceivable. Except for the gnawing in the pit of my stomach, the stillness of our cabana, his packed MacPac in the corner, the empty space beside me on those clown-printed sheets.

Under the pillow, my fingers were still closed tight around Sean's ring. There was a faint red mark on my palm where the history of Ireland had been pressed into my skin. I could just make out the curve of the question mark.

The key to our cabana was on the nightstand, attached to a flat block of wood carved with the numbers *214*. The wooden keychain was ridiculously oversized so guests wouldn't lose it at the beach. The night before, I'd clutched at his ring and that stupid piece of wood for hours—at the clinic, in the truck, and at the temple.

"The key is in your shoe." It was the last thing he'd said. The last thing he'd ever say. He'd seemed calm. I wondered if he could possibly have known he was dying when he said it. Or when he realized, if he realized. At the temple, one of the Israeli girls had asked if I wanted her to hold on to the key. But it was the last thing he'd said. I hadn't been able to let it go.

Everything seemed wrong. No one ever died like that in the movies.

No one ever said something like "the key is in your shoe" right before they drew their final breath. He didn't tell me he loved me, or that he would miss me. We didn't have a chance to say goodbye. I would never get to tell him I was sorry. I knew I'd spend the rest of my life outraged at the drama and opportunity of drawn-out Hollywood death scenes.

My throat was raw and my chest sore. I went through the motions of getting dressed and brushing my teeth, before opening our cabana door out onto the spot on the sand where he died.

Low waves collapsed onto the shore in front of my feet, and the briny smell of rotting seaweed hung in the air. I didn't have a clue where the police station was on Ko Pha Ngan, or how I would get there. But when I walked into the open-air lobby of the Seaview Haadrin, the Israeli girls were already waiting.

A local man I didn't recognize was standing with the girls. He nodded at me as one of the girls squeezed my arm and the other rested a hand briefly between my shoulders. We stood without speaking for a few minutes. I was relieved no one said "good morning."

I'd spent hours with the girls the night before, but hadn't realized how beautiful they were, each in her own way. One of them was thin and angular, with big sympathetic eyes, high cheekbones, freckles, and black wavy hair. The other had a Marilyn Monroe–type beauty mark above her lip, hazel eyes, and dark wild curls, lightened just at the edges by the sun.

The thinner girl finally spoke. "Okay." But it was a statement, not a question. "He will drive us to the police. Do you have everything—your passports, Sean's insurance?"

After I'd gone back for the paperwork, we followed the man to a rusting sedan parked behind the cabanas. He drove in silence, watching me through the rearview mirror. I couldn't read the expression in his dark eyes, and my stomach tensed and knotted. I had no idea what to expect from the police, and worse, no longer knew what to be afraid of. I wished I'd thought to check that the marijuana wasn't lying in plain sight directly outside our bathroom window. But any nerves I might have had were crowded out by shock and despair.

The police station was a gray cluster of concrete buildings right outside the dusty port town of Thong Sala. The man stayed by the car while the girls and I were left alone in a corner room. There was a row of plastic seats against the wall, a desk, and a computer that looked to be about twenty years old.

The overhead fluorescent lamps buzzed and crackled while we waited, and I flinched each time the bulbs popped. I'd been crying for the better part of the last twelve hours. My eyes both stung and ached, and I was having trouble focusing. The lights in that room seemed too bright, too white, and too loud. I pushed the heels of my palms against my eyelids until all I could see was black.

When I lifted my head, one of the girls, the one with hazel eyes, reached into her bag and pressed a tiny bottle into my hands.

"Too many tears. These drops are the best."

I glanced at the bottle, but the characters on the label were completely foreign. I tipped my head back and squeezed.

"Thanks." I tried to pass the bottle to her.

"No." She stopped me. "You need it more. You keep it. Please." She closed her fingers around my own.

"Okay. Thanks." With my other hand, I spun Sean's ring loose around my finger and ran my thumb over the little men engraved into the silver— the shepherd and the Viking. "What were you guys doing at the clinic?" It hadn't occurred to me to wonder before.

"We followed you."

"From the beach? To see if Sean was okay?"

They both paused, looking into my eyes. The girl with black wavy hair answered first. "No. To see if you were."

"After the beach, we went back to our cabana and we prayed," the other girl continued. "We prayed for Sean. But then we couldn't just sit. So we walked to the clinic. We had to keep asking for directions. That was why it took us so long. But we needed to see if you were okay. We knew you were alone."

"You knew he was dead?"

It was a minute before one of the girls spoke. "We thought yes."

I nodded. "I think I knew too." Although I'd held on to the tiniest scrap of hope until the doctor at the clinic made it official. But I'd known at the beach. I'd known the moment I realized that the crowd of people surrounding us had stopped watching him, and had started watching me. I'd known when I was kneeling on the wet sand, and they turned him so that his upside-down face was level with mine. I'd known when the Israeli guy looked away while I was giving him mouth-to-mouth in the back of the truck. And I'd known when the Israeli and the local who'd carried him into the clinic didn't wait to hear the doctor's declaration. They'd waited outside, on the other side of the glass door. They'd stood and they'd smoked on that dirt road while they waited to move Sean's body a second time.

The girls and I sat in silence again under the buzzing fluorescent lights. It seemed as if we were waiting for hours, but I could no longer trust my sense of time. Last night alone had lasted a lifetime. Eventually, one of the girls glanced at her watch.

"How long have we been here?" I asked.

"Over one hour."

"Should we tell the driver? Maybe we can call the taxi company when we finish?"

The girls looked at each other, before one of them spoke. "It's not a taxi. He's the hotel manager's brother. He said he would drive us again."

"Again?"

"He's the same driver. From last night. The same man."

"Oh." I'd ridden with him five times the night before, and in the back only the first time. The truck I would have recognized instantly. But I'd never once looked at the driver.

The girls spoke briefly together in Hebrew, and the one with hazel eyes stood. "I'll go see," she said to me. She grabbed a worn bag of tobacco and a packet of papers from her bag and walked outside.

When she returned a while later, it was with a policeman. He wore tan slacks and a short-sleeved shirt and had a cigarette fixed between his teeth. Without a word or a glance in my direction, he sat at the desk and reached for an ashtray. In between drags, he punched at the keyboard. But the computer didn't make as much as a beep and the screen stayed blank.

After ten minutes of this, he picked up a phone and said something in Thai. He then pointed to the computer and shrugged his shoulders. Leaning back in his chair, the cop lit up again and studied me. "We wait," he said, blowing smoke across the room.

twenty-one

Shànghǎi, Guìzhōu, CHINA

July 2002

AFTER A MONTH of disappointing beds, ineffective electric fans, and feeble showers, Sean and I decide to treat ourselves to the midrange Ren Min Hotel in the steamy city center of Shànghǎi. We spend the first morning having sex and dozing in the clean pressed sheets, savoring the cool steady blast of the air conditioner and the quiet morning without crowing roosters, bickering neighbors, or heavy construction. While Sean snoozes, I decide to head out to pick up some dim sum for breakfast. The day before, we'd found a tiny *cha siu bao*, or pork bun, shop down a nearby alley.

At the shop, I notice how much more difficult life is without Sean. His Mandarin is far from fluent, but I struggle to pronounce even the simplest phrases. I smile and nod, stumbling over the words for "sorry": *duì bu qǐ*.

I point to the buns in the glass case and hold up six fingers. *"Xièxie."* I try to say thank you. The girl behind the counter covers her mouth and giggles.

Back at the hotel, Sean wraps himself in a sheet. It looks ridiculous on his lanky body, a cross between a toga and a kimono. He sits on the edge of our bed, and breaks apart a pearly-white bun. The buns are soft and decadent, sticky dough surrounding clumps of savory barbecue pork. Sean pulls me onto his lap and he kisses me.

"Miss, if you'll have me, I want to marry you."

I don't need to answer. I circle my arms around his neck and kiss him back. I can smell the salt on his skin, and taste the surprising sweetness of the bun.

twenty-two

Thong Sala, Ko Pha Ngan, THAILAND

August 10, 2002

THE OFFICER SMOKED and stared as the Israeli girls and I continued to wait under the buzzing fluorescent lights in the corner room at the police station. The early afternoon heat was beginning to kick in, despite a fan creaking overhead, and the backs of my legs stuck to the hard plastic chair.

I shifted in my seat. The policeman's glare was unsettling, but I was too devastated to stay frightened for long. The girls took turns sitting by my side and stepping out for a cigarette, even as his smoke filled the room. One of the girls was rolling the tobacco between her fingers for the third time, when someone finally brought in a battered old typewriter.

It took the officer a couple of tries to get the paper in straight. Then, with two fingers suspended over the metal keys, he looked up.

"Name?"

"My name? Or his name?"

"Him, always. Always him. Okay?"

"Okay." I tried to breathe. "Sean Reilly."

"Spell."

"*S* . . ."

"*F?*"

"No, *S*. As in . . ." But I couldn't think of a single word that started with *S* other than "Sean."

"*S*, as in 'snake,'" one of the girls finished, drawing out the sound of the *S*. "Or 'scream.'" She raised her voice. "Or 'stop.'" She pushed out her palm. "Or 'smoking,'" and she pointed to his cigarette.

"Okay. *S*." He stabbed at the typewriter, and a single key clanged against the page. He looked up again.

"*E*," I continued.

"*G?*"

Each letter took a couple of minutes, with the double letters in Sean's last name causing additional confusion. His date of birth was easier, because I could use my fingers. I held up a two and then a six. In a little over two months, he would have been twenty-six on the twenty-sixth. I'd missed his last birthday because I'd been traveling on my own in Tasmania. If only I'd known it would be his last. That he would always only ever be twenty-five.

"He your friend, yes?" The cop pointed the tip of his burning cigarette at me.

"Fiancé." We'd been engaged for just ten days. We were waiting to tell most of our family and friends in person. I'd been having trouble switching from "boyfriend" to "fiancé." "Fiancé" sounded pretentious. So I was still calling him my boyfriend. Until the moment he died. Then I was desperate to validate what we had. That we were an *us*, not just a *me and him*. "Boyfriend" suddenly sounded trivial, trite. He was more than that. More than a friend.

"Fee-on-say?" The policeman sounded out the word, the syllables thick on his tongue.

"Engaged. We were going to be married."

"But not married?"

"No. Not yet."

"Not now."

"No."

"So friends."

"Almost married. Married soon." I could hear the high-pitched desperation in my own voice. This felt critical. We'd made the decision to spend the rest of our lives together. The fact we hadn't held the wedding seemed an insignificant detail.

"Not married. Friends. Same same but different," the cop decided, and jabbed at the keyboard.

The first time I tried to explain to the officer what had happened on Haad Rin Nok beach, I was crying so hard I had trouble speaking. I struggled to slow my breathing, and control the odd gasping and choking sounds coming from my throat. Then I had to keep repeating myself, searching for words the policeman would understand.

It was as I described turning Sean over that I realized . . . he hadn't inhaled. I'd thought he hadn't been able to breathe with his face in the sand. I'd thought he was unconscious.

But as I was talking, the scene replayed itself again and again in my mind. I can still hear the brief rush of air as his head and shoulders touched the sand. There was something about the cadence that was different from a breath. It was hollow. It was finite. I don't know why I didn't notice the emptiness, the tone, the finality at the beach. But as soon as I started to remember, I knew. It wasn't an inhale. It was the last breath he'd taken being forced out of his body as I'd rolled him over. He was already dead.

Which meant that he had died while I was throwing on a dress. That he had died alone on the beach.

I told the officer everything except the dress. I couldn't be sure how much the cop understood or even listened to. But I couldn't tell him about the dress. I couldn't find the words. And I couldn't tell the Israeli girls, or the manager of the Seaview Haadrin, or Sean's insurance company, or his parents, or my own. It would be more than five years before I would tell anyone about the dress.

Of course I never forgot. The rough gauze against my naked skin just one of many indelible details burned into my memory. The damp and the heat and the salt of that early August evening. The mechanical rise of his chest as I forced my breath into his lungs. The wet sand and his cold, stiff hands.

At the police station, I tried to fit these details into a coherent structure. But the hours dragged on, with the officer questioning and arguing over each sentence, every word. I felt scared and small, worn out and picked apart. By the time the policeman pulled Sean's death certificate from the stack of papers in front of him, I had nothing left. He pointed with a tobacco-stained finger to my slanted signature at the bottom of the page. Then he pointed to my chest.

"You."

It was not a question. But I nodded. I wanted to be helpful. I wanted to be allowed to leave. I was frantic to get out of that room, away from the bright fluorescent lights and away from him.

He brought his yellowed finger to the short jumble of characters the doctor had crossed out. "So drunk drowning." Without looking at us, he turned back to the typewriter and his hands moved to the keys.

"No." Both the Israeli girls spoke at once, fast and loud enough to make me jump.

"Doctor says drunk drowning."

"No." The girl with black hair stood and crossed the room. She pointed to the string of characters the doctor had written next to the thin line. "He was allergic. He was stung."

"Maybe drugs drowning. Same same but different. He take drugs?"

"No," I finally spoke.

"Never drugs?" The cop narrowed his dark eyes.

"Never," I lied. "No drugs."

The policeman stretched out in his chair, grabbed the ashtray, and sucked on his cigarette. He studied us. He exhaled. Then he held up four fingers on his left hand. "Need four male witness."

"What? But no one else was there. It was just me and Sean. No one else was in the water." I thought I must be misunderstanding, or must have misheard. Something must be getting lost in translation.

"Need four male witness." The officer wriggled his four fingers. "Need four men to sign."

"But there was no one else." My stomach turned in on itself. "No one else saw. There were *no* witnesses. Just me."

The officer pushed the phone in my direction. "You call four men."

"There's no one I can call. No one else saw."

"Need four men. Any four men. Four men to sign."

"There's no one to sign. I don't know anyone here. It was just the two of us. Just me and Sean."

"Please call four men. Any four men."

"I can't."

The police officer shrugged. "So drunk drowning."

"No." Both girls spoke again. "He didn't drown," the girl with hazel eyes said.

"He was stung," said the other.

"No men sign. No stung."

I swallowed down on a scream as panic thumped inside my chest. The girls continued to argue with the policeman, their voices steady and strong. They offered him their signatures instead. He refused.

They all began talking at once. Their words washed over me. One of the girls stood and her chair scraped against the wall. The cop flicked a lighter open and closed. The lamps above our heads droned on. I watched the tears drop into my lap. I ran my thumb over the figures carved into Sean's ring. And I stared at the door. Forty minutes passed, maybe an hour, as the girls gesticulated and the policeman smoked cigarette after cigarette.

"Okay," one of the girls said, and the decisiveness of her tone made me look up. "We will sign." I turned to the officer, who pushed a pen toward them on the desk. I had no idea what changed his mind. I didn't care.

The driver had fallen asleep in his car. He drove us back to Haad Rin town, halfway across the narrow peninsula between Haad Rin Nok and Haad Rin Nai, Sunrise and Sunset Beach. We found a restaurant for dinner and the girls were impressed when I ordered something with chili. I remember the textures felt strange in my mouth—I pushed the food around with my tongue as if I'd just lost a tooth—and I couldn't taste a thing. But the nausea reminded me I was pregnant, and I managed to force down a couple of bites before my stomach closed like a fist.

The sun was dropping fast as we walked back to the Seaview Haadrin. The dirt path turned to sand, the air became brackish, and the sound of breaking waves grew a little louder. One of the girls said something in Hebrew.

"She wonders if it's bad to sign our own names," the other girl explained. "Our army. We're not allowed to speak with foreigner police."

"I'm sorry," I said. "Thank you. Really." I stopped walking. "I don't even know your names?"

"Anat." The girl with black hair stopped by my side.

"Talia." The girl with hazel eyes held her palm flat against her chest.

"I'm Shannon."

"We know. It's nice to meet you."

twenty-three

Chángshā, Húnán, CHINA

July 2002

SEAN AND I are weaving our way down an alley in Chángshā crowded with noodle bars, dumpling shops, and vendors selling unidentifiable meat on sticks. Steam spills from the tiny kitchens, carrying smells of cooking oil, chilies, and cigarettes into the heat of the street.

A teenage couple ahead of us stops and stares. Then she reaches into her bag to pull out a camera before approaching us, smiling and nodding.

"Quing?" she asks as she holds up the camera and pretends to take a photo.

"Hǎo." Sean smiles back. I think she wants Sean to take their picture together, so I step away. But the girl slides into my side, threading her arm around mine and leaning her head onto my shoulder.

"Qié zi!" She says "eggplant" instead of "cheese," holding up a peace sign with her other hand and grinning as I smile in surprise. The boy then hands the camera to the girl before standing next to Sean. He stretches on tiptoe to throw his arm around Sean's shoulder and flashes his own peace sign. Sean's used to the attention and he circles his arm back around the boy.

"Qié zi." Sean and the boy say "eggplant" together, squinting into the summer sun.

"Xiexie." The couple thanks us and starts to walk away.

Sean pats the boy on the back as if they were old friends. "See ya, mate." Though of course, we will never see them again. I wonder what they will tell people later when they show the photos: *Here are two white people we met in Chángshā.* They never even asked us our names.

twenty-four

Kiryat Ono, Tel Aviv, ISRAEL

November 2002

"AND HOW DID you meet Ms. Anat Avraham and Ms. Talia Shafir?" The Israeli immigration officer looked up from the piece of paper he was holding in his hands and back to my face.

"In Thailand."

"Hmm. And how long have you known them?"

"Three months. Since August. Since August ninth."

"And you aren't scared to come to Israel because of the security situation?"

I paused. It was the height of the Second Intifada, or second Palestinian uprising. I wasn't sure what the right answer was. "No."

"You have heard about 'the situation' here?"

"Yes."

"And you are not scared?" He raised his eyebrows.

"No," I said again.

His dark eyes studied mine. He handed me back the piece of paper with the girls' names and addresses, and he finally stamped my passport with a *visit permit* in red ink.

"Because you should be." And with that he waved me through.

In fact, I'd started to get a little nervous when I was taken out of line and questioned during the flight's layover in Istanbul. After traveling up and down Poland, and then over to Zagreb, I'd only bought the tickets the day before. The Turkish authorities had checked my US passport, California driver's license, ATM card, credit cards, and student ID. They'd wanted to see my tickets out of Tel Aviv, out of Europe and on to California, and they'd pulled my backpack from the plane's hold to have it X-rayed.

Then I'd been taken out of line again after landing in Tel Aviv and questioned by three different officers there. *Why had my passport been replaced in Ecuador? Did I have copies of all my train tickets through Eastern Europe? Why had I gone to Malaysia the year before? Did I have any Malaysian friends or family? Didn't I know Israelis weren't allowed in Malaysia? How could I afford to travel so much if I was a student? Had I told anyone I was going to Israel?*

I'd first started thinking about going to Israel when I was back in Santa Cruz. But I'd only told a handful of people. My parents were terrified. A couple of backpackers at the hostel in Zagreb thought it was cool. I felt it was something I needed to do.

The only reason I'd waited till the last minute to buy the tickets was that the girls kept changing their minds about how safe it was. The latest email from Talia had said there was a lot of bombing going on, so no, maybe I shouldn't come. Though they were mostly bombing buses, so it might be okay. But she didn't have a car or a driver's license, so it might not. Still, they both really wanted to see me, so yes, maybe I should come.

I was looking forward to being with people who already knew about Sean. It would be such a relief not to have to figure out if, when, or how to tell them. I was looking forward to home-cooked food, doing laundry, and not spending every day entirely alone.

But I'd spent only four days with Anat and Talia on Ko Pha Ngan. They were twenty-one years old. They both had boyfriends. They would be busy with their lives, their families, their friends, and their jobs. They might not even own a washing machine. Really, I was more worried about being in the way than being bombed.

I tightened the straps on my backpack and grabbed the duty-free box of cigarettes I'd bought for the girls. I'd forgotten to ask what brand they liked, so I'd settled for Marlboro Lights, which is what most of Sean's friends seemed to smoke.

Anat and Talia were there waiting on the other side of customs. They were standing together, their dark heads bent down looking at Anat's watch as I approached. Talia blew out a long exhale when she saw me, and they both smiled. Then they each gave me a hug.

"So good you came. We thought of you yesterday. The three months' anniversary."

It hardly felt like three days. But I felt immediately at ease, and touched that they'd remembered. I knew in that moment, I'd been right to come.

After the freezing early winter in Poland, I found the mildly warm weather in Israel in November sweltering. Flat, white sunlight filtered through the car windows as we drove along a quiet dusty highway from the airport back to Talia's family's home. I dug my sunglasses out of the bottom of my pack and stripped off layer after bulky layer until I was down to just a T-shirt and jeans. I'd spent a long cold month in Eastern Europe, and the sunshine on my bare skin made me feel practically naked.

It wasn't just the heat that felt different. Following the intense isolation I'd experienced in Hungary, Slovakia, and Poland, I was surprised how instantly and easily I felt comfortable with Anat and Talia. They knew and understood me in a way no one else in my life could. And at that moment, they were the only two people in the world I wanted to be with.

Talia lived with her parents and her older brother in a small upstairs flat in the leafy suburbs of Kiryat Ono, just outside Tel Aviv. Anat had to return to her job with the military for the afternoon, but Talia was currently looking for work, so she'd arranged for another friend to drive us to Tel Aviv for lunch.

Noa was tall and thin with long, blond corkscrew ringlets, and hardly any English. As soon as we climbed into her rusting car, she checked her watch and turned up the radio. An announcement came on in Hebrew, and Talia turned in her seat to explain.

"Yesterday, our army killed a big Palestinian terrorist leader, so it's going to be bad in Israel." She stopped to roll a cigarette and listen to the broadcast for a moment before continuing. "On the radio each half of an hour, you get the news. And in Israel there is always, always news."

She faced forward again in her seat to pay attention to the last five minutes. "Okay," she said when the announcement ended and the incongruous and apparently inescapable-in-any-country-in-2002 "Ketchup Song" by the Spanish pop group Las Ketchup started to play on the radio—*"an de bugui an de buididipi."* "Right now, Tel Aviv is okay. So we go to Tel Aviv."

But twenty minutes later, as we neared Tel Aviv, both Talia and Noa's phones started to ring. First Anat called, then Talia's brother, and then a couple of different friends. They all wanted to know if we were still in the car. They wanted to make sure that we weren't outside, on the streets, or in the city. They said a Palestinian suicide bomber had escaped from one of the territories, and that he was headed to Tel Aviv.

So Noa turned up the radio again, and after another minute or two, Talia told me that Tel Aviv had been closed.

"Welcome you are here in Israel." Noa winked back at me through the rearview mirror.

Noa started to swing the steering wheel around to head back to Kiryat Ono when both she and Talia recognized a carload of friends driving past. The friends pulled over to the side of the road and rolled down their windows to talk.

As we drove away, Talia translated for me. "They keep going. They said, 'They'll catch him before we get there. If we get bombed, we get bombed.'" Talia shrugged and blew cigarette smoke out the window. "But for you, one traumatic event is enough for just right now."

We hadn't driven far in the other direction before both of their phones rang again, and another announcement came on over the radio. They had caught the bomber and Tel Aviv was open once more. So we turned around a second time and we drove into the city.

When we finally got there, a salty sea breeze blew off the Mediterranean and through the empty streets. Glass, metal, and concrete office buildings towered over abandoned green parks and outdoor cafés. The city was modern, expensive-looking, shiny, and clean, but eerily silent.

Talia and Noa chose a small diner off an alley. We were seated in a brown padded booth and I reflexively picked up the menu, even though the blocky Hebrew dots and characters looked about as intelligible as braille.

"Great. This restaurant is perfect," Talia said, her hazel eyes shining.

"Why? What's good?" I asked, still squinting at the menu and trying to make any sense of the jumble of crowded black lines and letters.

"Everything." Talia reached across the table and gently turned my menu the other way round in my hands. It was only then that I realized I'd been trying to read it left to right . . . or upside down.

"But it is even more perfect because no one else here." She gestured to the vacant room.

"No one else to see me try to read the menu upside down?"

Talia smiled. "No, no suicide bombers."

Talia ordered us plates of crispy fried balls of falafel to share, with rich creamy hummus and *tehina* spreads, warm pita bread, tomato salad, and tiny garlicky dill pickles. Remembering my taste for chilies from Thailand, she also asked for *harif*, a local hot sauce. But when the plate of chunky green sauce arrived, she screwed up her face and pushed it over to my side of the table. "You maybe a little crazy to come to Israel, but you a lot of crazy to eat that."

As we ate, Noa kept slipping back into Hebrew. Each time Talia would protest and point to me.

"English! English! Only English!" Finally Talia gave up. "Okay, I no longer have the power. We teach you Hebrew instead."

There was *shalom* for "hello," *ma* for "what," *ken* for "yes," and *lo* for "no." *Toda* meant "thank you," *bevakasha* "please," and *slicha* "excuse me." And finally, there was *tov* for "good," *saibaba* for "cool," *shekel* was "money," and *l'chaim* was "cheers."

It was so much easier to mimic their pronunciations than to try to guess on my own at the sounds of the unfamiliar words printed at the back of my *Lonely Planet* guidebook. The girls were impressed when I could repeat the throat-clearing *ch* sound in *slicha* and *l'chaim*.

"*Saibaba!* Almost like a true Israeli."

Walking back to Noa's car after lunch, I noticed an abandoned pile of clothing in the middle of the sidewalk. It looked like a long black sweater someone must have accidentally dropped. As we got closer, I started to reach out to pick it up.

"No! Shannon!" Talia's voice was loud, even for an Israeli, and I froze with my arm extended. "Do not touch!"

She pulled me back by my shoulder. "You never know," she said. "It might be a bomb." Talia linked her elbow through mine and pushed me across to the other side of the street. She kept her eyes on the black sweater the entire time.

"You maybe not a true Israeli yet."

That night, the first night I spent in Israel, five Israelis were murdered less than forty miles north of us at Kibbutz Metzer. The gunman shot a woman out walking with her boyfriend, and then he killed the kibbutz secretary who had responded to the shots. After that, the gunman broke into a nearby home where a young mother had rushed into her children's bedroom, trying to protect her two sons. Matan was five and Noam only four when they were shot as they held on to their mother's body from their beds. They found Noam with one pacifier still in his mouth and another balled up in his tiny fist.

I spent seven more days in Israel, and during that week alone twelve more Israelis and sixteen Palestinians were killed. That year, in 2002, forty-seven suicide bombings were carried out, killing 238 people, more than any other year. Almost 1,500 civilians lost their lives. It would turn out to be one of the bloodiest years of the conflict, and for Israelis, the deadliest. Death was a daily part of life there.

I saw how the Israelis, and my two friends, negotiated this. Everywhere we went, there were police and soldiers carrying pistols, rifles, and machine guns. Security checks were required to enter almost any building: banks, cafés, shops, bookstores, bars, and nightclubs. Armed young men or women in olive green uniforms would check the trunk of our car every place we parked, search all of our bags each time we entered, and finally scan everything and everyone from head to toe with a metal detector.

Tel Aviv was closed down at least part of almost every day I was there. We'd be getting ready to go for sushi in the city when Talia's phone would ring, and then military warnings would be issued not to go out. Instead, we'd find ourselves in front of one of the two TVs in the warmth of her family's living room (her parents owned two sets and one pair of headphones so they could view their different programs sitting side by side on the same couch). We'd watch *Fear Factor* and dare each other to imagine leaping out of a twelfth-floor window onto a trapeze, or having to eat sheep eyeballs or live crickets.

When we did go out, there were rules. Don't take public transportation. Never eat at outdoor cafés. Never go to the popular bars or nightclubs, especially in Jerusalem. Avoid crowds.

A suicide bomber was most likely to detonate near an entrance, just before he was caught by security. So instead of waiting in line for the security check, we always gave our names and walked away to wait at a distance. Anat carried a see-through plastic purse to get through quickly. And once we were inside, we never took a table by the door.

Winter was much more dangerous because bulky coats were no longer suspicious. But there were other signs to look out for: a lumbering walk, a large bag, sweating, heavy breathing, nervous tics, vacant stares, and mumbled prayers.

My friends and their friends told and retold stories about suicide bombers the way people back in the United States might talk about the latest *Seinfeld* episode.

There was the bomber in Jerusalem who accidentally exploded himself crossing the street. He didn't kill anyone, but his head sailed through the open window of a fifth-floor apartment.

Then there was the bomber near the university in Tel Aviv. It was the month before I got there, and he'd tried to board a rush-hour bus through the rear doors. The driver didn't see him and closed the doors, trapping him. When passengers yelled that someone was caught, the driver opened the doors again and the bomber fell to the ground unconscious. It wasn't until the driver and other passengers tried to feel for his pulse and administer first aid that they saw the explosives.

Anat, Talia, and I would walk the wide, empty, tree-lined streets of Kiryat Ono in the evening, and they would tell me how alive Tel Aviv used to be. How they hoped it would be again. They were sad to see Israel so quiet, the hotels and cinemas closed, the tourists and crowds gone from the museums, the restaurants, and the white sandy beaches.

The locals the girls introduced me to were all so pleased I had come. They wanted to know what California was like, what I thought of Israel, if I was scared to be there. I wasn't used to being popular because of my passport. A bartender who mixed me a pomegranate mojito one night out in Tel Aviv even told me that George W was their angel.

"We're ready for the next Gulf War," he said, leaning his elbows onto the bar in front of me and cracking his knuckles. "The last one was nothing. When the alarms first started going off, you'd rush to put on your gas mask and run to the room that was specially sealed off with plastic and tape. But then you got so used to the alarms, and you knew you had two to five minutes before impact, so you'd stop and you'd make a sandwich on your way."

The Israelis I met didn't seem hunted or haunted. They were living their lives, going to cafés and clubs, dating and drinking and dancing. They just weren't doing it anywhere near the doors.

One warm sunny afternoon, Anat, Talia, and Talia's boyfriend, Ori, took me to the tank museum at Yad La-Shiryon in Latrun, half an hour by car southeast of Kiryat Ono. The bullet-pockmarked concrete fort was surrounded by dry brown hills and more than a hundred tanks spread out in neat, orderly rows. There were black tanks, white tanks, blue tanks, yellow tanks, green tanks, and camouflage tanks. There was even a tank on top of an old water tower.

As we wandered through the rows, my friends examined the tanks, saying things like "whoa" and "so powerful," or "scary" and "terrifying." Beyond the colors, it was hard for me to see any differences. But with Anat still active in the military, and both Talia and Ori having served their compulsory duty relatively recently, they could appreciate things that I could not.

Near the tank on top of the water tower, there was a long white stone wall engraved with the names of every soldier killed since Israel's War of Independence in 1948 through to the present day. The soldiers were grouped together by the different battles they fought and died in. There were thousands of names, the simple black Hebrew letters lining up column after column after column.

We walked along the wall from right to left, and as we neared the more recent names, Anat, Talia, and Ori began to find people they knew. They stopped talking and put their hands up to the wall, running their fingers over the letters of their fallen friends, fellow soldiers, and ex-boyfriends.

Inside the cool of the museum, at the Gate of Courage, black and white photographs of smiling young men and women put faces to the names. Twenty-four hours a day, their candid snapshots and frozen portraits were continuously projected across a dark wall, the pictures accompanied only by a name, age, and date of death.

The tower in the old fort had been converted to a Tower of Tears. The inside of the tower was lined with metal from damaged and war-torn tanks, the soldered sheets rusting and riddled with bullet holes. Water trickled down these walls and collected in a spring below a glass floor at the base. I'd gotten so used to going to museums by myself in Eastern Europe, it felt almost strange to share the experience with people I knew. It felt even stranger that they each understood what it was like to suddenly lose someone.

The four of us stood together in the tower, silent and still as the drops ran down the battered steel of the walls. We thought of the different people we loved who had died far too young.

. . .

I carried my own photographs of a smiling young man. Anat and Talia had spent hours with Sean's body that night on Ko Pha Ngan—on the beach, at the clinic, and at the temple. But they'd never seen him alive. They wanted to be able to put a face to the name, to see what he looked like before he died. So they'd asked me to bring photos of Sean to Israel.

Sean is in my parents' front yard in California, wearing his favorite blue-checked button-down shirt and his wire glasses. He's burst into a dimpled easy grin and his arm circles my waist as I lean into him, laughing.

The two of us are tumbling onto a hotel bed in Fes in Morocco. Sean's head is thrown back and he's laughing so hard his eyes are squeezed shut. My head is on his chest and I'm giggling into his neck. He's clutching on to me with one hand while with the other he grabs at his hat as it's falling off.

Sean is rowing our tiny wooden boat out to Bled Island in Slovenia. His eyes are hidden behind dark glasses, and he's wearing one of his T-shirts that turned powder blue in a laundry mishap involving navy socks. The shirts eventually faded closer to white with each wash, but for now it's the same shade of blue as the sky that stretches into the distance behind him.

It was a comfort to show the girls these photos, to talk about Sean and about that night in Thailand with the people who'd been there.

Ori had also been on Ko Pha Ngan in August. Talia had met him on the island, their flirtations just beginning when Sean died. And in a bar in Tel Aviv one night, the girls brought me to see Amit, the thin Israeli with the goatee who had helped with the CPR on Haad Rin Nok beach, and then ridden in the truck with us to the Bandon International clinic.

I'd never been introduced to Amit on Ko Pha Ngan, but more than three months later, I recognized his dark brown eyes instantly. He sat at the back of the bar, a worn guitar case on the seat beside him and his long fingers wrapped around a glass of beer. I kept trying to focus on the angles of his face as he spoke to me, but all I could see was the moment he had looked away while I was giving Sean mouth-to-mouth in the back of the truck.

Ori had written a story about Sean's death and Amit had written a song, both in Hebrew. Amit sang the song for me that night in Tel Aviv, but I couldn't understand a word.

It was Anat and Talia who continued to ask me questions about Sean's life. As they had in Thailand, they asked to hear stories about Sean, and about our life together. They listened when I wanted to talk about him—that first time he bounded up the stairs at the hostel in Barcelona, backpacking and eating and drinking through Europe, singing karaoke and scaling sacred cliff faces in China. The girls didn't look away or change the subject when I cried, and they didn't get uncomfortable when I was silent.

After Sean was moved into the back of the truck at the beach, after I'd climbed in and held his head in my lap and tried to keep breathing for him, Anat and Talia had followed us on foot to the clinic. They'd stayed by my side there, and at the temple, and the police station.

I hadn't realized that they were following the rules. Just as there were rules in Israel to avoid death, there were rules to accept it. Although I couldn't bury Sean until I flew his body home to Melbourne, while we were on the island, the girls treated me as if I were sitting shiva.

When I'd later looked up bereavement in Judaism, I learned that "shiva" was a ritualized intense mourning period. Anyone who's lost a parent, a child, a sibling, or spouse sits shiva for seven days. At the funeral, the mourners tear the clothing covering their heart. Then they stay together for a week, usually in the house of the deceased, sitting on low stools or the floor while visitors pay shiva calls. Visitors wait for the mourners to speak first, they bring food, and they come to remember the dead.

On Ko Pha Ngan, Anat and Talia had been following shiva call rules. There'd been no greetings. The girls had let me initiate the conversations, or they'd let me choose to be quiet. They made sure to talk about Sean, to use his name and to say it often. But they never offered platitudes or clichés. They'd brought me food, and encouraged me to keep eating and drinking. And they'd done their best to avoid leaving me alone.

They'd never spoken to me before that night on the beach. I didn't find out until much later that they even changed their flights to stay on the island until I was allowed to leave with Sean's body. These girls could have easily walked away from a tragedy that wasn't their own. Instead, without even telling me, they'd changed their plane tickets and all their plans rather than leave me behind.

In Israel, I slept on a spare mattress on the floor of Talia's room. I still struggled with insomnia and nightmares, and woke up in the middle of most nights clammy and drenched with sweat. Perhaps my body couldn't adjust to the heat there, but I always felt comfortable enough again in the mornings. Then Talia would wake up from across the room, and we'd listen to the news and try to figure out where it would be safe to go that day.

The girls kept trying to take me to visit the Dead Sea in the east. They described the buoyancy of the salt, the year-round sun, the greenish mud, and the dark blue water. I still hadn't touched the ocean since Thailand, and Anat and Talia thought the Dead Sea would be a good first step. It wasn't a true sea, but it was salty. Besides, with no aquatic life there was no danger of jellyfish, and the girls would be right there with me.

But there were other dangers, and every time we tried to go, snipers or suicide bombers from the West Bank made it impossible. I knew they were disappointed, but I never pushed it. Although the macabre sense of poetry appealed to me, I wasn't really ready yet to get back in the water.

"You need to see Jerusalem. We need to get a gun."

"Yes, you cannot come to Israel and not go to Jerusalem. But you cannot go without a gun."

Everyone seemed to agree on these two points. The girls may have been forced to give up on the Dead Sea, but they weren't willing to give up on Jerusalem. Unfortunately, Anat was working and training with her military unit throughout the week (what her specific job was, no one was allowed to say). It took the girls a couple of days to find someone armed and able to accompany Talia and me.

Ari was a close friend of the girls, had a driver's license, and also happened to be one of Prime Minister Ariel Sharon's personal bodyguards. He'd even been assigned to protect Vice President Cheney during his visit to Israel earlier that year.

Ari was always in the papers, always at the edges of the photos. Muscly and dressed in black, he had light red hair buzzed short and freckles hidden behind wraparound mirrored sunglasses. He was currently on light duty after fracturing his hand playing football, so he was free to take us to Jerusalem.

We drove to the ancient city on a cool, clear day. The road from Tel Aviv wound through the Judean Mountains, past rocky terraced valleys dotted with green scrub and threaded with dry riverbeds. As we got closer, I began to see blocky white houses crowded together on hillsides in the distance. All of the buildings in Jerusalem were built from a local pale limestone, in slightly varied shades of cream, sand, pink, and gold. Through the car windows, I'd catch glimpses of bright sunlight reflected off the stone, the bleached roofs and corners packed tightly against each other and set against a deep blue sky. Then we'd round another bend and the shining city would disappear again.

Before driving into the heart of Jerusalem, Ari said he had a special surprise for us. He winked at Talia in the passenger seat and she turned and grinned back at me, her straight white teeth flashing beneath the dark spot of her beauty mark.

He parked the car near the Wohl Rose Garden, and we walked past rows of manicured thorny shrubs and across a wide-open lawn. Opposite us, Talia pointed out the Knesset, or Israeli parliament. It was a large square building draped in blue and white Israeli flags and surrounded by small groups of uniformed men and women wearing black sunglasses and with rifles slung over their shoulders.

Ari checked his watch. "Eleven minutes."

Talia grinned at me again, and I wondered what was about to happen.

Not long after, a number of hulking men in dark suits and dark glasses approached and began to stand around the edges of the lawn. Ari gave a curt nod to the men as they filed past, and the men lifted their chins in return. Then I heard the thrumming beat of a helicopter coming in to land on the grass. The helicopter touched down so close to us, a warm gust of air knocked me back a step and I could feel the thump of the blades echoing inside my chest.

The rotors slowed with a high-pitched whine, and more broad-shouldered men with guns jumped out. In the middle of the group, maybe ten feet away, was a short fat man with a wide waistline and white hair. It was Ariel Sharon.

We watched Sharon walk across the lawn in the opposite direction for a short distance, before he was surrounded completely by his bodyguards. Talia's cheeks flushed pink, and she beamed at me. She was patriotic and proud, but mostly she wanted me to understand I was safe. I was sure many people visited Jerusalem without a gun, much less without one of the prime minister's personal guards. But Talia was doing everything in her power to make sure nothing else happened to me.

Afterward, a few of the guards joined us for lunch at a café a few minutes' drive away. There was hummus, a salty salad of diced cucumbers and juicy tomatoes, smoky grilled eggplant, stuffed olives, lemony fava beans, and sour yogurt drizzled with olive oil.

I'd been dining alone in Eastern Europe for almost a month, pretending not to see the sympathetic or curious stares from other patrons. So I savored the anonymity company provided. It was a relief not to be watched.

At the café in Jerusalem, the bodyguards' biceps were crowded together between the plates of food, the muscles in their square jaws popping as they chewed or told jokes or spoke on their phones. Tucked in among their barrel chests, jostling elbows, and loud discussions of important Israeli officials and daily threats of terror, I felt tiny, quiet, and inconsequential. Yet each time one of the guards started to slip back into

Hebrew, Talia would point to me and yell across the table, slapping her hand down onto the wood.

"English! English! Only English!"

After lunch, Ari, Talia, and I spent the afternoon wandering around Jerusalem. We stopped to watch jugglers and Talia tried to translate the jokes of the street performers. We browsed through open-air markets, but unfortunately none of the stalls sold the one item I was looking for, a new blank journal. I had fewer than ten pages left in the one I'd brought from California, and no idea when I'd find another.

The streets of Jerusalem were bright, noisy, vibrant, and crowded. Men in black hats with bushy beards and ringed sidelocks walked past tanned curvy women wearing green fatigues and lipstick and carrying automatic weapons.

There was a pulsing energy to the city in spite, or perhaps because of the intense political tensions boiling below the surface. Yet underneath it all, there was a serenity or stillness I'd never sensed in other cities. Jerusalem somehow felt centered and calm.

Only a third of a square mile was contained within the Old City walls, but the narrow cobbled alleyways were bursting with color and sound. There were blue-eyed blonds and Africans so black they were almost blue. I saw red and white checked keffiyeh scarves, gauzy white *mandil* veils, long black wool *rekel* coats, and glinting gold crucifixes. Voices rose and fell in more languages than I could count: Hebrew, Arabic, Armenian, Russian, French, Spanish, English, and Ethiopian. There were smells of charcoal, salted fish, floury bread, incense, tobacco, fresh flowers, and sweat. Well-fed cats darted in and out between black-robed legs, and women dragged strings of five or six children behind their long skirts. Yet there was still an inexplicable tranquillity.

Bypassing the Muslim-controlled Temple Mount, we made our way to the Kotel, the Western or Wailing Wall. A group of chubby-kneed schoolchildren hopped and skipped and pushed and giggled just outside the plaza. Their teacher pointed and yelled, trying to get them in line while a man in street clothes carrying a machine gun patrolled the edges of the class.

"School groups always bring a parent with a weapon," Talia explained, lighting a cigarette and inhaling. "There is the hoping that no one tries to take a child hostage if mommy or daddy is there with a gun."

Ari waited outside with his own gun while Talia and I went through the even-more-thorough-than-usual security checks. As we walked into the wide-open stone plaza, the first thing I noticed was that the wall was segregated. I'd gotten used to the sight of armed female soldiers everywhere, and hadn't expected this. Divided by a screen, or *mechitza*, the women's side on the far right was significantly smaller and significantly less crowded. A couple of women stood on chairs next to the screen, peeking over into the action on the men's side. But none of the men took any notice at all of the women's side.

The entire plaza was shaded completely by the high surrounding walls, and the air felt at least a couple of degrees cooler. Pulling a sweatshirt over my head, I was glad I'd had the chance to do laundry at Talia's. Everywhere I looked, huge blocks of chalky honey-colored stone towered over us. Beyond the walls, I could just see the gold-plated Dome of the Rock and the beige, square minaret of the Al-Aqsa Mosque against the blue sky on Temple Mount.

The women on our side were a mix of young and old, dark-skinned and fair, Orthodox women in obvious wigs wearing long sleeves and long skirts, and teenagers in eyeliner and jeans and T-shirts. All were facing the wall. They were either approaching it as we were, stepping backward away from it, or sitting or standing in front of it—chanting quietly, swaying, praying, reading, and pressing their hands and sometimes faces to the stones.

Talia and I paused twenty feet or so away from the wall, and she pulled out two slips of paper and pens from her purse. For hundreds of years, people had been writing down their wishes at the wall, pressing their prayers by the millions into the cracks between the ancient stones.

I hesitated. Every single wish I'd made since Sean had died—on first stars, shooting stars, white horses, lost eyelashes, necklace clasps, blown dandelions, tossed coins, church candles, and holding my breath through tunnels—I'd wished that I could have that one night back and Sean wouldn't be dead. In my darker moments, I just wished that we would be together again, wherever that might be.

But standing there in Israel, I wished for the first time that Sean and I would both find peace. I'm not even sure what made me change my mind. Maybe it was the strength and the resolve of the Israelis I'd met. Maybe it was just Talia standing by my side.

I wrote down my wish and walked up to the wall. The rectangular blocks were large, irregularly sized, and crumbling at the corners. The stone was cool and gritty against my palm. Coming from California, which only became a state in 1850, I found it mind-boggling to be standing in front of something built in 19 BCE. Even the air around the wall felt thick with dust and history.

Every crack and crevice within arm's reach was crammed tight with bits of folded, rolled, and crumpled paper, the edges stained blue where the ink had run. Farther above our heads, large tufts of gray-green grass sprouted in the spaces between the stones. Following Talia's lead, I wedged my wish into a corner against the others and then kissed the wall. I leaned my forehead against the stone and closed my eyes.

But as soon as I started to walk backward away from the wall, I remembered walking backward away from his casket for the last time, and began to regret what I'd written. Of all the places where something crazy could happen, Jerusalem seemed the most likely. I wished that I'd wished for the impossible.

Toward the end of my visit, I was invited to Shabbat dinner with Anat's family. It was Friday, November 15th—fourteen weeks since Sean had died, a month since I'd first flown to Eastern Europe, and two days before I would leave Israel to fly back there alone again.

Talia and I walked from her family's flat to Anat's, less than a minute away and only the next block over in Kiryat Ono. Anat had texted earlier to say that she was running late. Her unit was under sniper fire near Gaza, and she wasn't sure how long she would be. We should start dinner without her.

Anat's family lived in an upstairs flat similar to Talia's, only with more matching white furniture and an additional level. When we arrived, her parents were warm and welcoming, though they hardly spoke English. Her older brother, Shachar, more than made up for it. He was thin and good-looking, charming and funny.

"Oh. My. God. How unbelievably fantastic is the bar scene in Sydney? I'd kill to have a bar scene like that here in Tel Aviv. And you got to live there for a whole year? JEALOUS! I can't believe you left. Though of course, California must be just as fabulous. What I would not give to see San Francisco! If only I could ever get my hands on a tourist visa . . ."

The dining table behind us was already loaded with dishes of food. Just before sunset, Anat's mother was lighting the candles when Anat walked in. Anat's faded green uniform was fitted and somehow neater than the ones I'd seen on the streets. Her black hair was pulled back into a dusty ponytail, freckles scattered across the sharp edges of her cheekbones. She looked beautiful, competent, smart, efficient, and tired.

Her mother held Anat by the shoulders and quickly kissed her. As she spoke, it sounded as if she was scolding Anat, but I guessed it was only the harsh sounds of Hebrew and the Israeli accent. Still, she acted as if Anat had been stuck in traffic instead of under sniper fire.

Anat changed quickly upstairs and then joined us in the dining room. When I was growing up in California, some of my friends had been Jewish, but more in name than in practice, and I'd never been to a Shabbat dinner before. It was filled with songs and stories and shaking hands. Anat's father said the kiddush, blessing the wine and the braided challah bread before breaking the loaves into pieces and passing them around the table.

I couldn't remember the last time I'd eaten so much. I'd lost weight and my appetite since Thailand. But every single dish was tempting that night. Israelis were an interesting mix of people—Anat's mother was from Bulgaria and her father from Iran—and this was reflected in their food.

There was a clear chicken soup with chewy *gondi* dumplings, eggplant stuffed with spicy ground meat and rice, oniony *kofta* meatballs, crispy chicken schnitzel, potatoes, grilled fish, salads, flatbreads, and huge bowls of thick buttery hummus.

Anat's mother was particularly interested in my travels around Eastern Europe. She'd been a small child when her family had fled to Israel after World War II, and she'd never been back. But she was fiercely proud that Bulgaria had managed to save its entire population of forty-eight thousand Jews from the camps.

It was a story I'd never heard before. Later, I looked it up online and read that Bulgaria's government initially acted as a puppet to Nazi Germany, passing anti-Jewish legislation and preparing to comply with demands for deportation. But a few government officials, the Orthodox Church, and a number of ordinary citizens led an enormous national outcry—protesters threatened to block the trains by lying down on the tracks—and persuaded Tsar Boris III to first stall, and then refuse. Although thousands of Jews in the territories of Thrace and Macedonia were deported, every single Jew living in Bulgaria was saved.

The story had been kept secret by the Soviet Union because it didn't want to credit the previous government, the Church, or the king, who were all considered enemies of communism. So it had only come to light after the end of the Cold War.

That night at Shabbat with Anat's family, everything had to be translated back and forth. There was pointing, hand waving, headshaking, people talking over each other in multiple languages, and the clatter of silverware when someone brought their palm down against the table. The flat was warm from Anat's mother's cooking and the family's company, and her face flushed as she asked all about Auschwitz and about every memorial that I'd seen. She wanted to know how World War II and the Shoah, or Holocaust, were remembered in Eastern Europe. And she wanted to know about the food.

"She wants to know if there was anything you ate over there that tasted better than her dinner tonight," Anat explained, laughing.

We held hands around the table, read out prayers in Hebrew, and raised our wineglasses. Despite not understanding most of the words, I still had a sense that night that I belonged. It was the first time since Sean's death that I felt a part of something. There was security and solace in the structure of tradition, even one that wasn't my own.

That feeling shattered a moment after the telephone rang. Anat's mother handed me the receiver, I heard my own mum's voice, and I burst into tears. It took me by surprise as much as it surprised my mum and Anat's family. There was something about the familiarity and the reality, the love, loss, and helplessness in her scratchy voice. Trying to calm down, I walked with the receiver outside into the warm evening and sat down on the concrete front steps. My mum and I had hardly said two words to each other but I couldn't stop crying, and then neither could she.

As we were singing and eating and drinking and telling stories around the table at Anat's, a series of ambushes had begun less than seventy miles away in an area of Hebron that became known as the Alley of Death. The battle lasted for more than four hours. By the end, three Palestinians and twelve Israelis had been killed, including Colonel Dror Weinberg, the highest-ranking Israeli casualty of the Second Intifada. He also happened to be a good friend of Talia's.

When Anat and Talia heard, they were furious. They were particularly outraged, as it was initially reported that the murdered men had been on their way to synagogue.

"Shooting toddlers in their sleep, and killing people trying to worship, is something we would never do," Talia said. "All of their mosques are lit up with bright green lights at night so they don't get bombed. Sometimes I just do not have the power . . ."

I could only imagine what it must be like to have someone to blame. During the brief time I'd spent in Santa Cruz after Sean's funeral, I'd joined an online young widows support group where I'd met Beth, who was close to my age and lived across the country in Albany, New York.

Beth and her husband, Robbie, had a two-year-old son. Since becoming a dad, Robbie rarely had the chance to drive his beloved motorcycle. So one night, he took the motorcycle to Beth's parents' house for dinner while Beth and her son followed behind in their car. It was only a few miles each way.

But on their way home, Beth turned a corner in the road where everything in her life changed. A doctor driving home after a long shift had fallen asleep at the wheel. There were pieces of Robbie's bike strewn everywhere, his body thrown across the road, the shattered glass and crumpled metal of the car where he'd hit it, Beth's own screams in her ears, and her toddler strapped into the backseat behind her.

When I spoke to Beth in the months following Robbie's death, she'd wanted the doctor to lose everything: his driver's license, his medical license, his house, and his freedom. When I was in Israel, I was reminded of Beth's anger on an almost daily basis. I'd been jealous of Beth having her son, but Israel made me realize that not having anyone to blame for Sean's death was something small but significant for which I could be grateful.

"Maybe you make your flight, but maybe you miss it." Talia wrinkled her nose and looked at her watch as Anat drove along the quiet dusty highway back to the airport. "We're not so very late, but you need three hours for flying El Al. And for you, the security will be much worse to leave Israel."

"Worse to leave?" I asked.

"Yes. When you arrive, they're scared you'll protest or do something stupid like hang out in Gaza or West Bank and get yourself killed and make some kind of international incident." Anat's dark eyes met mine in the rearview mirror, a cigarette between her fingers on the steering wheel. "But when you leave, they're afraid you'll give information."

"They're afraid I'll go to Palestine?"

"Shannon, there is no Palestine," Anat said. "Definitely do *not* say that at security."

"But anyway," Talia continued, "it is okay because there is one more flight to Istanbul later in the afternoon. You take that one if you miss the morning. But you should ring your mother." She passed her cellphone to me in the backseat and grinned. "So she knows why you are late when you send the email to say you finally made it okay out of Israel."

Conscious of how much the call would cost to California, and knowing Talia would refuse any cash I offered, I kept the conversation brief. When my mum answered, I told her I was fine but that I had a fifty/fifty chance of missing my flight. Nothing to worry about since I'd just take the later plane. The last time we'd been on the phone, I'd hardly been able to speak, so I told my mum the girls' families had been wonderful and the food had been amazing, and she said she was always relieved to hear from me. After I'd hung up, Anat asked where I was going to go next.

"I'm thinking maybe Bosnia. There was a UN flight leaving for Sarajevo on my way over here. Of course, I'd have to make my own way there."

"Shannon's tour of war-torn countries." Talia laughed and shook her head, before blowing smoke out the window. "You definitely a lot of crazy."

She had a point. There was a part of me that thought I might never come home from this trip. Before Thailand, I probably never would have been daring or stupid enough to go to Bosnia, much less on my own. After, it was hard to see the purpose of being cautious. We hadn't been taking any risks on Ko Pha Ngan. And the worst had already happened.

Still, I'm not sure I would have considered Bosnia if I hadn't come to Israel. Spending time with the girls here had meant everything to me. I felt tougher and braver. The rules and rituals of their country and culture had provided strength and solidarity. The traditions for grieving in Judaism had made sense. Anat and Talia never tried to distract me, cheer me up, or calm me down, and the pain of Sean's death felt acknowledged in a way it never had in the United States or Australia. It had been exactly what I needed, and the girls had been exactly who I needed.

But it was harder to talk to Sean with other people around. I was ready to be alone again. According to my *Lonely Planet*, during the relatively recent Siege of Sarajevo, the city's only access to the outside world was via a one-kilometer tunnel under the airport. I'd never met anyone who'd even considered visiting Bosnia. It seemed like a place to be alone.

At the Ben Gurion Airport, I made it through the heavily armed guards at check-in, the luggage searches, and the extended interviews with security officials just in time to make my original flight. I arrived late via Turkey and into a cold night in Croatia, where the only available accommodation was a single hotel room. I didn't often have a TV in the cheap hostels and pensions where I usually stayed, and I'd gotten used to constantly listening to the news with the girls, so I flipped on the set as I got ready for bed. The first bulletin was out of Israel, and I stopped in my tracks with my toothbrush caught between my teeth and toothpaste dribbling down my chin. El Al Flight 581, the afternoon flight from Tel Aviv to Istanbul, had been hijacked.

twenty-five

Perth, Western Australia, AUSTRALIA

January 2002

S EAN POURS TWO more glasses of cold white wine, hands me the world news section of *The West Australian*, and leans back in his chair with the sports pages. I scan the international headlines. Another Palestinian suicide bomber has blown himself up at a mall in Tel Aviv. Daniel Pearl is still missing in Pakistan. The Enron hearings and the trial of John Walker Lindh have just begun.

Sean's left his job at Cadbury Schweppes but hasn't yet left for China, and we're at the end of a spur-of-the-moment vacation in Perth. We've spent the hot summer week swimming in the sea and at the pool of our hotel, snorkeling and cycling around Rottnest Island, drinking Crown Lager at the harbors in Freemantle, and eating the crispiest, most succulent, delicate, feathery fried calamari either of us had ever tasted.

After our return flight to Melbourne was delayed, we'd headed back into town for one last boozy lunch over a newspaper. I'm noticing how much thinner my stack of world news is compared to Sean's sports section, when I realize there are a few pages missing.

"Do you have the article on Bush's No Child Left Behind?" I ask him.

"I've hid the more *disturbing* pages, Miss. The ones with the initials GW. You'll only get upset, and we're still on holiday." Sean winks and raises his glass.

"How 'bout instead of reading about Dubya"—he smooths down the front of his worn blue-checked button-down shirt, creases his paper, and sets it to the side—"we talk about moving in together? Chapter Three. Once I'm back from China, I'm thinking Carlton North. We'll be able to walk to the pubs on Brunswick Street and the cafés on Lygon, and you'll be right by Melbourne Uni."

His hand slides under the hem of my shorts and up my thigh, and he leans in to kiss me. I taste waxy ChapStick and the ripe sweetness of Riesling.

"So when we finally get to live with each other, and after it's been a while, what do you think will eventually annoy you?" I ask. Sean and I have traveled together for months at a time, at last count through ten different countries, and I stay over often at the house he shares with three of his mates on Albion Street. But we haven't had the chance yet to spend much ordinary day-after-day life with each other.

"That newspaper thing of yours," he says, glancing at the crumpled pile of world news to my left. "You never put a paper back together properly. And what about me, Miss? What endearing quality of mine will eventually drive you to tears?"

"How you never put the cap back on the toothpaste. And then it dribbles down the side and gets stuck all over the counter." I don't think of myself as particular, but the bathroom at the boys' house in Melbourne is disgusting.

"Aren't you a lucky girl that toothpaste is all you can come up with?" Sean tops up both of our wineglasses. "I reckon we'll be right then, Miss. You just need to learn how to refold a newspaper . . . and how to get over a silly ol' cap. And then we're laughing."

twenty-six

Haad Rin, Ko Pha Ngan, THAILAND

August 10, 2002

B Y THE TIME Anat, Talia, and I reached the Seaview Haadrin, the late summer sun had sunk behind the cabanas. I'd only just met the two girls, but they'd spent the entire day with me at the police station.

The officer had been evasive about when Sean's body would be released. I had no idea when we'd be allowed to leave the island. I only knew I couldn't stay another night in cabana 214—the window, the door, and the porch all opening up onto the spot on the sand where he died.

"So you stay with us." Anat pointed to the block of concrete rooms behind the restaurant.

"Yes," Talia said. "You will take my bed and I share with Anat."

"No. Thank you. It's okay. I'll get my own room."

"Please. Our room is much too big."

I looked at the row of doors squashed together and doubted it.

"Really. Thanks. But I need some time alone."

"Maybe no more rooms, maybe fully booked." Anat raised her eyebrows and shrugged her thin shoulders.

But when I went to ask at reception, the manager of the Seaview Haadrin smiled and extended her hand. "No problem."

The manager was tall and thin, with straight black hair pulled into a low braid. Her tawny skin was burnished and smooth, but her eyes were tired. When we'd first arrived on Ko Pha Ngan, I'd thought of her as old. She was probably only in her midthirties.

"No problem," she said again, still smiling and stretching her hand out farther. In my fist, I held on to the flat block of wood carved with the numbers *214*. I uncurled my fingers and finally let go.

She reached for a new key, to a cheaper smaller cabana set back away from the beach. A single bed. No sea view. She pressed the key into my palm and she grinned. "Everything okay now?"

When we'd first arrived four days earlier, Sean had gone through his usual hopeless flirtations for an upgrade. But at the Seaview Haadrin, it had worked. He'd winked and he'd laughed his way to cabana 214. I'd left him joking with the manager, and was making my way to the beachfront, when he had her lean from the window and shout out to me that I was lucky. Then he'd caught up to me on the sandy path, shouldering both of our packs.

"Did you hear what she said, Miss? She said you were lucky. Lucky to have a man like me."

"I heard her, weasel. You know that I heard. And I know that I'm lucky."

I had been lucky then. Now, standing in the lobby the night after he died, I couldn't think of a single response to the manager's question, "Everything okay now?"

The inside of my new cabana was musty and dim. The first thing I noticed was the bed, the sagging narrow frame and the clownless sheets. The new plain white sheets were all too similar to the ones they'd wrapped his body in only yesterday. Only yesterday he'd woken up by my side, sprawled out in the bright morning sunshine on the double bed in 214, our bodies wrapped together in those clown-printed sheets.

Yesterday I'd woken up restless. I was starting to get bored on Ko Pha Ngan and was ready to move on. Sean wasn't in any rush. He enjoyed life at a slower pace than I did. He'd tried to slow me down that morning, but I hadn't been in the mood. So he'd hopped out of the double bed and strode his bare skinny butt to the shower, calling back to me and laughing over his shoulder.

"Miss, how 'bout you get naked, get on the button, and work yourself up into a lather for when I get out?"

Which I hadn't exactly done. But after Sean's shower, he kissed me. It was long and hard and soft and slow. And the next thing I knew, I was giving in and getting turned on in spite of myself. Of course we had no idea it would be the last time. Our last time. His last time.

Now I felt an odd kind of satisfaction that at least I'd changed my mind. That we'd somehow unknowingly made the most of our last few hours together. That I hadn't been too stubborn or too moody. That we both came.

The new single cabana felt as if it were miles away from 214. It took me two trips to drag both of our packs over. The black shapes of palm trees bent over the sandy path, the new August moon a white splinter in the sky. I locked the door and pulled the curtains shut before unpacking his things to make a pile of what I might need.

I set aside shorts and his favorite blue-checked button-down shirt to dress him if I got the chance. I cringed each time I thought of him in only his boxers. It wasn't as if Sean had ever been modest. Even in his shared house on Albion Street, he'd stroll stark naked down the long hallway to the bathroom, with his towel slung over his shoulder.

Yet I was desperate to cover him now. I wasn't sure how much longer the rigor mortis would last, or if I would be able to move his limbs. I didn't know if he'd be too heavy for me, if he would have started to smell or to swell, or if I would be able to do it at all. I didn't even know whom to ask for a key to the refrigerated glass box he was locked in at the temple. But I was worried about what his parents would think if they found out that I let him be transported and viewed in his underwear.

I'd spoken to our families briefly after the temple, and again after the police station. My mum and Sean's father had both been out of town the night he died, but I'd finally gotten through to my dad in California and an uncle of Sean's I'd never met before in Melbourne. Sean's mother had stopped answering after that first call. So I talked to a different relative each time I rang. I never spoke to her on the phone again.

It also seemed as if I would never stop telling the story of how he died. I'd explained it to the doctor at the clinic, my dad, and Sean's uncle, then to the police, the hotel manager, my mum, Sean's oldest brother, and his father. Tomorrow morning, I'd have to tell it again to his insurance company, the Australian consulate, maybe the airlines. If the Thai police weren't finished with me, then I'd have to try to talk to my consulate as well. I pulled out Sean's passport and plane tickets to add to the pile, along with his insurance paperwork and his *Lonely Planet* for Thailand.

It wasn't satisfaction so much as relief I felt that Thailand hadn't been my idea. Sean had bought the *Lonely Planet* in China, and started campaigning for it as a holiday destination over email back in April. *Just think, Miss. Sex, beach, beer, sun, smoke, sea, sex = Thailand.* I'd wanted to go to Vietnam. But flights from Shànghǎi to Hanoi were twice the price as tickets to Bangkok. And Sean had wanted us to have a break from traveling around China—somewhere less intense, somewhere easy and relaxing. Even Ko Pha Ngan had been his idea. Wrestling on the beach the night before, his idea.

But after we'd wrestled, he'd followed me out into the water. He'd followed me out to where I stood in the ocean, and he'd held me and he'd kissed me and he'd died.

For the hundredth time in the last twenty-four hours, an image of the welts around Sean's calves flashed before my eyes. The web of deep red lines had seemed almost alive, coiling and circling and choking his thin white legs.

Then, for one last time, I packed Sean's old purple and turquoise backpack. I did it slowly, lingering over the slippery texture of his silk boxers, the powdery smell of his T-shirts. I talked to him as I folded his clothes, telling him how sorry I was and how much I loved him and how I would give anything for him not to be dead. His death felt like something that could still be fixed if I could figure out what to trade it for—my life, my health, my happiness, my heart. I offered them all. Then I took the bar of Dove soap and the sticky tube of toothpaste that we shared and tucked them into my own bag. I pushed his pack into a far corner of the new cabana, and spent the rest of the week trying not to look at it.

Later that night, I was startled awake by a staccato burst of chirps and squeaks. A solitary gecko was trapped within the four walls of my cabana. It called on and off for hours in the dark, and I wondered if it was trying to attract a mate or scare off a predator. But each time I turned on the light, I was all alone and there was nothing there.

twenty-seven

Essaouira, Marrakech-Tensift-El Haouz, MOROCCO

February 1999

I SLIDE MY HAND into Sean's, our fingers curling comfortably together. There's a strong brackish wind coming off the ocean, but Sean's palms are soft and warm.

We walk along the crumbling sand-colored brick fortifications of Skala du Port, in Essaouira on Morocco's west coast. We've only just started holding hands. It's barely been a few weeks since our first meeting and our first kiss in Barcelona. We haven't slept together yet. But we're ready to be recognized as a couple.

Sean's hands are much bigger than mine, so I hold on to his pinkie and ring finger. I've never held hands with anyone like this before, but it feels easy and secure.

I can practically swallow the salt in the air as we walk past whitecaps off the rocky Atlantic coast. Seagulls chatter and swoop through the updrafts in the blue skies overhead. I relax into Sean's side. Ever since the summers I spent growing up in San Diego, a west coast feels like home. I use the ocean to orient myself, finding north with the water to my left and telling time as the sun drops into the sea. An east coast has always felt a little foreign to me, a sunrise over the ocean a little wrong.

We make our way to the harbor, where a sunbaked mustached fisherman untangles a couple of surprisingly large lobsters from a netted basket stiff with salt. He boils and cracks them, before spreading out our lunch on a makeshift table of crates and barrels. We sit and eat next to his wooden boat, the brightly colored paint peeling off the hull in long strips. He serves the lobster with lemon and salt, but it doesn't need either. The flesh is tender, creamy, and sweet, with an ocean tang as seawater drips from the broken red-orange shell onto the meat inside.

As we're wiping the briny juices from our fingers, a dark-skinned young man in a Western-style fleece jacket and baseball cap approaches, leading two russet-colored camels.

"Français?" he calls out.

Sean shakes his head.

"English? Where from? London?"

Behind him, the camels blink their ridiculously long eyelashes and chew from side to side. Over their humps, they wear large saddles covered in patterned quilts and bits of multicolored rags. It doesn't take long for the man to persuade us to climb up into the saddles; we have no plans for the afternoon and there isn't a cloud in the sky.

The camels first kneel in the sand and we clamber on with a boost from our guide. As the camels pad along the beach, we do our best to stay on top of them as they roll, sway, and lumber along.

The guide leads the camels to Jimi Hendrix's old commune—a group of ruined concrete buildings—talking all the way of famous jam sessions Jimi had with the locals, all-night bonfires on the beach, and outrageous rock-star parties that lasted for days. He then takes us to the inspiration for Hendrix's song "Castles Made of Sand." In the eighteenth century, Bourj El Baroud was a watchtower. Now the stone castle is disintegrating—worn away by hundreds of years of waves, half-buried in the sand, and slowly collapsing into the sea.

"And so castles made of sand, fall in the sea, eventually," the guide sings in a heavy North African accent as he turns the camels to lead them back. "A beautiful Moroccan girl, she helped Jimi write this." He winks to Sean over his shoulder. It's a romantic tale, and one we want to believe in. So we're disappointed years later, when we find out Hendrix in fact wrote the song two years before visiting Morocco, and the guide's stories themselves begin to crumble.

twenty-eight

Haad Rin, Ko Pha Ngan, THAILAND

August 11, 2002

THE FIRST MORNING I woke up in the new single cabana at the Seaview Haadrin, it took a moment to remember where I was. The dank smell of wood that has never had enough air or sunlight, the sounds of the ocean muffled by groves of whispering palm trees, the shadowy outline of Sean's bulging pack in the corner.

The events of the last two days flooded over me as a physical sensation more than anything else. A rush of cold that began at my toes and crept up my body to press on my chest.

I hadn't been awake long when there was a knock at the door. I stiffened, before hearing Talia's low voice call out, "Hallo."

The girls stood, smoking together on my doorstep. Without another word, Anat pressed a warm banana muffin and a cold bottle of water into my hands. I looked down at the muffin and the water and started to cry. The girls didn't even know I was pregnant, but they kept making me eat and drink.

"Thank you. Thank you so much. Really. I cannot thank you guys enough. For everything. But you honestly don't have to . . ."

"Please," Anat said, and placed her hands on top of the muffin and water, her long fingers wrapping around mine. "It is only what anyone would do."

"But I know you guys are on holiday. Today, I can go by myself. It's okay. You don't have to come . . ."

"Please." Talia held up both of her hands to stop me again. "You do not need to say thank you anymore. It is nothing. You would do this. Anyone would do this."

I knew they were wrong. I knew what they were doing was far above and beyond what anyone would do. But I'd spent enough time with both of them to know there was no point in arguing. Beyond that, I didn't really want to face the morning of phone calls on my own.

We walked together to "Chicken Corner," an intersection in the center of Haad Rin town where a couple of shacks sold Thai-style grilled chicken sandwiches and shady-looking young men on scooters slipped folded dime bags of marijuana to customers in the alleys. From there, the girls and I made our way to a small shop with an advertisement in the window: *FONE! FAX! FOTOCOPY! YOUR FRIEND HERE!*

We pushed open the door and a young girl with a chubby face looked up from behind the counter.

"We need to make calls international," Talia said.

"Where you want to call?" the young girl asked, looking back and forth between us.

"Australia."

The girl's brown eyes widened as her gaze rested on my face. She grinned between a matching set of dimples. "Oooh, I heard about you? You're the girl whose boyfriend died! You're famous!"

Anat placed her hand on my arm. Talia cleared her throat, and repeated herself, "Australia. Please."

"No problem!" The girl turned the phone around on the desk to face me and waited, still smiling and dimpled, with her chin in her hands.

I looked up the number for Sean's parents. As they had done the night Sean died, Anat and Talia urged me to consider what I would say before dialing. But once again, there was nothing I could think of that would make this any less painful.

After checking in with Sean's father and my own parents, I rang SOS travel insurance in Melbourne. Sean hadn't planned on travel insurance for his move to China, but his parents had bought the policy for him at the last minute. On the back of a receipt, I jotted down a list of what the agent, Samuel, said they'd need: my firsthand account of how Sean died, photographs of Haad Rin Nok beach to show there were no posted signs warning of jellyfish, photocopies of both his passport and the Dangers & Annoyances section in our *Lonely Planet*.

The photocopier was behind the counter, so I hung up and handed Sean's passport to the girl. Then I thumbed through the guidebook to the Dangers & Annoyances listed for Ko Pha Ngan. The short section was limited to drugs and mostly concerned the hazards of *tôn lamphong*, a local relative of nightshade. Travelers had been turned into *wandering zombies—stumbling down streets and clawing at thin air—oblivious to anything but their own hallucinations, which they try to follow and grasp*. A bad trip ending at the island's psychiatric hospital seemed pale in comparison with the surreality of my own last few days.

"Whoa." The first photocopy slid from the machine, and the girl behind the counter reached down to retrieve it. Her back was to us, the piece of paper in her hands. "Too much scary."

She turned and placed the sheet on the counter. The photo page of Sean's passport had printed as a negative. One side of his face was washed out by light, his pupils white dots, and his left eye almost blown out completely. His dark forehead was framed by white eyebrows and a cloud of colorless hair. He looked dead, like a death mask or one of those postmortem portraits from the nineteenth century. Like a skeleton, or a ghost.

"Maybe better you go," the girl behind the counter said. "I think breaking machine. You maybe go now."

I looked down, at the goose bumps on the girl's bare arms and at the image in front of her, the bleached-out letters of Sean's name across the page. There was something about the negative—the black ink of his skin, the blank circles in his eyes—that seemed to make his death irreversible. I hadn't been able to see his body since that night at the temple. His passport didn't expire for another six years. But he was gone.

"Maybe better you go," she said again. I could tell the girl was spooked, and we were done at the shop anyway. Taking the photocopy and a clean notebook, we left and found an empty table in the shade at an outdoor café. Anat and Talia rolled a couple of cigarettes and said they'd come back later to check on me. I needed to be alone to try to write down everything I could remember from August 9th.

After we'd had sex on the clown-printed sheets, Sean and I had gone for breakfast. We'd sat outside on the restaurant's deck overlooking the beach at the Seaview Haadrin. The umbrella at our table had blown over in the wind. Sean had his usual: soft-boiled eggs, bacon, toast, a mango shake, and a grilled cheese sandwich. I ordered eggs and toast and a banana yogurt shake.

When our food arrived, Sean proclaimed the meal a logistical nightmare. The small pats of butter were nearly frozen, and he'd had to warm the foil packets between his hands before being able to spread his toast. Yet the eggs were so hot, we burned our fingers trying to break into the shells. Sean had to open mine for me. Then we were surprised to find the yolks hard-cooked, but the egg whites still runny and raw.

We'd spent the day under blue skies at Haad Rin Nok beach. I got a cheap coconut-oil massage on a beach towel, but Sean was too sun-burned. He said he'd get one tomorrow. He smoked a joint or two and we'd read on our porch. I'd picked up *Kite Strings of the Southern Cross* at a Friendship store in Shànghǎi and Sean had only just started *Into Thin Air*.

I snapped a few photos: of the beach, our cabana, and the view. I even changed rolls of film. But I didn't take a single shot of either of us.

In the afternoon, we'd gone for a swim. Sean hated stepping on the rocks underwater, the slippery sensation of seaweed and tiny slimy creatures he couldn't see. So we walked to the northernmost end of the beach where there was a passageway of bare sand between the pebbles. The tide was so low that we had to wade quite a distance out into the ocean to get deep enough to submerge.

We'd had a late lunch in town at Orchid Restaurant, splitting a hot chili salami pizza and a green salad while *Spider-Man* played on a large screen at the back of the bar.

On our way back to Haad Rin Nok beach, Sean wanted to check

email. I did not. For me, email was work. Each time I got online, there would be something that had to be dealt with for my PhD. And I was on vacation. At the moment, I just wanted a break from the permit applications, grant reports, teaching assignments, conference talks, and committee meetings.

"I'll be quick, Miss," he'd said.

"I'll wait."

"I'll send your mum a message from you." He winked as he went inside.

As we'd traveled through Asia that summer, I often got so bogged down with university work online that Sean would finish his own email and start in on mine. He'd log into my Hotmail account, pretend to be me, and write to my mum. I'd thought he was just telling her what we'd seen in China and Thailand, giving my family travel updates and assuring them we were okay. I didn't know he was also writing about how easy he was to travel with, how patient and kind and understanding. *I find myself falling more and more in love with Sean.* My mum hadn't realized the messages weren't from me.

Sean sat down at a terminal in the Internet shop while I waited outside on the dusky streets of Haad Rin town. I danced for him through the windows, a little bit dirty, turning around and shaking my ass. The shopkeeper stared and Sean cracked up. I loved how easy it was to make him laugh.

He motioned for me to come into the store. I shook my head, but Sean persisted. There was a message from Stevie D he wanted me to read. Megan had dumped Stevie again, it was raining in Melbourne, and Stevie wanted Sean to come home. At first I thought Sean wanted me to hear the news. It was their second breakup in weeks. It wasn't until later that I realized . . . it was because Stevie wanted him home. Sean loved to be needed. He poured himself into his friendships, and he wanted me to savor this with him.

As we were leaving the shop, Sean told me he'd sent me a message as well. "Short and sweet and waiting in your inbox, Miss." He winked again and reached for my hand.

We'd walked back to cabana 214 along Haad Rin Nok beach. The tall palm trees lining the edge of the shore were motionless. The sea was calm. Darkness was starting to fall, though it was still warm and sticky. It was like every other evening on Ko Pha Ngan.

Outside our cabana, we'd wrestled. I lost, threw sand at him, and walked into the ocean. Everything that happened next I wrote down in the notebook for SOS insurance, sitting alone two days later at the table in the shade at the outdoor café. Dark blue ink stained the tips of my fingers as I filled the pages with my cramped handwritten account. All I really wanted to say was, *This wasn't our fault.*

I spent the rest of the afternoon of August 11th taking photos of the beach for the insurance company, sending off faxes, and making phone calls. Filling out the forms and carrying around the paperwork made me almost forget about the emptiness itching in my palms. What I missed more than anything was just holding his hand. I could practically feel the ghosts of Sean's fingers wrapping around my own.

I met Anat and Talia early in the evening, and they insisted we have something to eat and drink. They chose a quiet restaurant on the outskirts of town, away from the sea.

Our food arrived and I forced down a few bites. I kept forgetting I was pregnant until I tried to eat. Then my stomach tightened and I felt the acid rise into my throat. I pushed my plate to the side and focused on the glass of water in front of me.

"There's one thing we need to talk to you about." Anat twisted her long black hair into a bun and leaned closer over the table.

"It's time for you guys to leave. It's okay. I know you're traveling. They have to let Sean and me go soon, right? But you don't need to stay. You've done enough."

"No, no, no. We are staying with you until you can leave. That's not what we need to say. There was another girl. She was stung."

"Oh my God." My chest heaved, and I choked on a sob. I felt nauseated and cold and dizzy. I covered my mouth with my hands and my eyes filled with tears.

"She was stung here yesterday. The same beach as Sean. She was screaming and slapping the water. But only a very small sting on the face." Anat held her index finger and thumb an inch or two apart, next to the freckles on her own cheek.

"Because of Sean"—Talia touched my shoulder—"they took her with a speedboat to Ko Samui. To a bigger island. To a bigger hospital."

I fought to breathe. *Because of Sean.*

"But, Shannon." Anat paused and looked at me. "Today she died."

A hundred thoughts seemed to race through my mind at once. Everyone—the doctor, the police, the hotel manager—had said that Sean was the first to die in decades from a jellyfish in Thailand. They all said he was allergic. It had seemed like the only explanation.

But if it wasn't an allergic reaction, then he'd been stung by something that could have killed me as well. How had I not been stung? He was holding me in the water, my legs wrapped around his waist, when the tentacles wrapped around his legs below me.

Then he'd dropped me. Dropped me in the water in the exact spot where he'd been stung.

If Sean and I had both been stung, they would have called our deaths drunk drownings. That is what they would have told our parents. Our parents never would have known. They would have spent the rest of their lives believing we'd both been drunk and drowned.

Most importantly, if this other girl had not died, if this bigger hospital had helped her live, then it would have meant that maybe Sean could have survived.

But I couldn't speak. I couldn't say any of these things out loud. Instead, I sat there, silent and staring and sobbing. Anat and Talia waited for what felt like a long time. Finally I asked, "How old was she?"

"She was twenty-three," Talia said. "Her name was Mounya."

"I am so sorry," Anat continued. "But, Shannon, it is not your fault she died. There is nothing you could have done to save her."

"That is not why she is crying," Talia said, not even glancing at Anat. Talia's hazel eyes looked across the table and straight into mine as she spoke. "She is crying because she knows now there is nothing she could have done to save him."

Mounya Dena from Switzerland, age 23.
August 10, 2002. Ko Pha Ngan.

The next day, August 10, 2002, a 23-year-old Swiss female was stung on chest, arms, body, and legs off a beach on Koh Pha Ngan. She collapsed within minutes and received immediate resuscitation but arrested twice more during transfer to hospital at nearby Koh Samui, before succumbing some 12 hours postenvenomation.[4]

twenty-nine

Běijīng, CHINA

July 2002

S EAN AND I are pushing through a noisy, crowded platform onto a subway in Běijīng. The midsummer humidity below the streets is insufferable. At six foot two, Sean stands above the throng. But I'm little, even in China, and my face is pressed into the soggy back of someone's T-shirt.

Sweat runs down my legs as Sean squeezes us past uniformed school-children. The older students try to climb over the little ones. Teenagers attempt to hurl themselves on board. We dodge sharp elbows thrown by cagey old women. The people still standing on the platform begin to protest, their voices rising in angry anticipation of being left behind.

We've arranged beforehand which stop we'll get off at if one of us doesn't make it. That doesn't prevent a small panic from catching in my chest as I'm shoved backward to the platform. The doors are about to shut, and I can't see Sean. But at the last moment, he reaches through the mob to grab my hand and pull me on board.

part III

S U N S E T

thirty

Sarajevo, BOSNIA and HERZEGOVINA

November 2002

THE WOMAN WAS STALKING the payphones in the parking lot when we arrived, circling the phone booths and darting her hands into the silver slots to search for forgotten coins. I watched her through the window as we pulled into Sarajevo's bus station. Her hair was tied back under a dirty handkerchief, but straw-colored strands had escaped and stuck out at odd angles.

She turned to scan the faces of the passengers. Her gaze settled on me—the only foreigner, but possibly the only person who was also watching her. I looked away.

We all piled out of the bus and crowded around the luggage compartments. Clouds of breath rose and disappeared above our heads as we waited. People lit cigarettes, rubbed their hands, and stomped their feet to keep warm. The driver pulled out bag after bag from the base of the bus. Most of them were identical—cheap square woven-plastic totes, in either plaid or stripes of white, red, and blue, sometimes called refugee bags and ubiquitous in developing countries. But there were also cardboard boxes, falling apart at the seams and held together with twine. By the time the driver reached my lone backpack, the woman with straw-colored hair was at my side. Her breath suspended in the air between us.

"I know a good pension. I take you," she offered. I was surprised.

I'd been traveling around Eastern Europe for well over a month and had been met only once by a woman offering a room. I certainly hadn't expected it in Bosnia. And this woman spoke English. And she spoke it well.

"No thank you. I'm okay." But she followed me back to the phone booths.

I pulled the door shut, trying to ignore her as she resumed her circling. I blew warm air onto my frozen fingers and took out my *Lonely Planet* guide to check the numbers for pensions in the city center. As I opened the book, a phrase near the Dangers & Annoyances section caught my eye: *Make sure that your medical insurance plan includes evacuation from Bosnia-Hercegovina.*

I turned the page and lifted the telephone receiver, but couldn't get a dial tone. I leaned over to look into the booth next to mine. The rusted cord dangled limply from the phone box, frayed at the end that should have been attached to a handset.

The woman knocked on the glass. I unfolded the door and she held out her hand with her palm facing up. Twice, she closed and opened her fingers. I assumed she was begging and I didn't have any local currency yet, so I shook my head. "Sorry."

But her hand remained outstretched into my booth. She pointed to the book. "Can I look?" I handed over the guidebook.

She ran her finger down the list of pensions. "These are all full of Turks. Very bad. I know a good place. No Turks. No snipers." As she said the word "snipers," she ducked, as if involuntarily, and then straightened.

"That's all right. I'm okay," I said again.

"We take a taxi. You can say no if you don't like. Snipers very bad in Sarajevo." She ducked again. "Post-traumatic stress problems. But I know a good place. No snipers. We take a taxi." She glanced sideways and wiped her nose on the sleeve of her dark green wool coat. The cuffs of the coat were frayed and a split seam gaped above her elbow. In the confined space of the phone booth, she smelled sickly sweet, like bruised fruit.

I scanned the empty parking lot. The other passengers had all left. It was late November, and the light was beginning to fade even though it wasn't even four thirty in the afternoon. She was obviously crazy, but I didn't see many other options.

"Snipers very bad here. Post-traumatic stress problems. We go?"

We went.

The woman with straw-colored hair had immediately jumped into the passenger seat of the only cab near the bus station. The driver seemed to be waiting for her. I'd thrown my pack onto the cracked plastic upholstery in the back and climbed in after. She continued to twitch and duck as we pulled away. "Good place. No snipers."

Maybe at that point in my life I didn't mind being around crazy people. Maybe by the time I'd reached Sarajevo, it was a relief to be with someone who was so clearly crazier than I was. Maybe I sympathized with her because she seemed damaged, like me, like Bosnia. Maybe she was what I expected of Sarajevo, even what I wanted.

My emotions had plummeted since leaving Israel. Anat and Talia had provided a kind of temporary reprieve from the intense grief, loneliness, and guilt that I was carrying.

After landing in Croatia, I'd stayed only a few nights. I'd zigzagged from Zagreb to Plitvice to Split, making up the itinerary as I went along, making up my mind about Sarajevo. Roberto and Guadalupe, a couple I met in Plitvice, said Bosnia was a bad idea, especially on my own. They were close to my parents' age, with grown children only a little younger than me, and they already worried about me traveling in Croatia alone. I wrote in my journal that I wished I had someone to go with. But I didn't. And I wasn't ready to face the long Croatian coastline and the Adriatic Sea.

The bus to Bosnia went inland. After crossing the border, we'd rolled past rocky mountains and dark valleys threaded with milky-green rivers. The landscape was dotted with debris. Charred, rusting cars missing doors and wheels had been abandoned at the edges of the road, their sunken bodies surrounded by pieces of broken glass. Bombed-out buildings remained vacant, the walls covered with pockmarks from bullets and shrapnel. A few new houses with fresh paint were scattered among the splintered structures. So far, the country was living up to my expectations.

I'd really come to Sarajevo because I thought it would match my mood. I expected the capital to be as devastated as I felt. Grim, destroyed, dark, depressed, limping along, barely surviving. Possibly even angry, resentful, and bitter.

So I went with the crazy traumatized woman from the bus station. And she took me to a small cluttered shop in the center of the city, opened the front door, and pushed me inside.

Inside the shop, a thin man with a thick mustache stood behind a glass counter displaying pipes and packets of cigarettes alongside piles of sticky, clumped tobacco in shades of auburn, chocolate, and coffee. He was neatly dressed, in a short-sleeved checked shirt tucked tightly into khaki trousers. The shelves were packed with brightly colored hookahs and coiled rubber hoses. The air was damp and thick with the smell of burned coffee and smoke. Two older men sat behind me at a table, inhaling from skinny crooked cigarettes and sipping from miniature white cups.

"Is there hot water?" I hadn't had a hot shower since Israel.

"After *minuit*." He tapped the number twelve on the cracked glass face of his wristwatch. "*Sonnez.*" Three times, he tapped the air in front of him and then pointed to a doorbell on the other side of the front door, his outstretched index finger stained a dark shade of amber.

"No, is there hot water?" I tried to pantomime a shower.

"*Oui, abondance* Americans here." He pointed his stained index finger to the ground as he said the word "here." "*De* Washington, DC . . ."

I waited for the list of American hometowns to continue, but his voice trailed off after just the capital. He blinked at me expectantly and pulled on a corner of his black mustache.

The woman who'd brought me to the shop/café/pension paced on the other side of the front door, whispering to herself. What she lacked in sound, she made up for in movement—chaotic gestures that used her entire body and filled the small area of the doorstep. At times, her voice would rise. She'd clap a hand over her mouth and cast a startled glance in our direction. The men didn't seem to notice.

I gave up on hot water. Using a combination of broken English, French, Spanish, and sign language, we managed to negotiate a room. As I descended the dimly lit stairs, I heard the man leave the shop to join the woman on the porch.

Later that night, I went to dinner at the nearby restaurant Ragusa Taverna, overlooking a dark square. The wooden tables were scattered with foreign businessmen and diplomat-types in suits. The restaurant didn't have the first dish I requested, so I pointed to *zeljanica* on the menu, and waited to see what would arrive. It turned out to be a thick, layered pastry filled with oily spinach and salty, crumbly cheese.

As I sat alone and ate, I studied a charcoal sketch of a classic young nude on the wall beside me. She sat in front of a mirror, brushing hair that cascaded down her back in dark waves, as bombs exploded in the background outside her bedroom window. One of her legs had been blown off below the knee.

When I returned to my own windowless room below the street, I realized I was the only guest. The basement was dank, dark, cold, and empty. I'd expected to find other people staying at the pension. I'd expected a room door with a lock.

But this place wasn't anything like a hotel. It certainly wasn't listed in my guidebook, and no one, apart from the crazy woman at the bus station and the man upstairs, knew I was there. I should have emailed my family, should have told someone. No one even knew I was in Bosnia; I hadn't wanted my parents to panic. Now I was stuck for the night in a basement below a shop with a strange man, no window to escape through, no telephone to call for help, and I couldn't even lock my own room. What had seemed a somewhat reasonable decision in the light of the late afternoon now seemed to be an incredibly bad idea. *This is why everyone told me not to come.*

All I could think to do was to shove the second empty bed up against the door. I forced the bedframe just below the doorknob as a barricade and blockaded myself inside.

That night, I dreamed of Eden. I was holding her hand, her small sticky fingers wrapped tightly around my own. I was telling someone that even though Sean had died, Eden, his four-year-old niece, would always be in my life. But as I woke the next morning, sliding back to reality and landing heavily in Sarajevo, I knew it wasn't true.

I hadn't heard anything back from Sean's oldest brother, Michael, Eden's father. Or from his aunt Susan or uncle Josh. I knew Sean's parents didn't email, but thought they might send messages through his other brother, Kevin, which was how they'd always communicated with Sean when he was traveling. They should have received my postcard from Hungary by now.

The air was briefly thick with silence. Then a jackhammer started up. I turned to look at the pink alarm clock Sean and I had bought a few months ago in China. I resented this cheap piece of plastic, still ticking loud and insistent after Sean's own heart had stopped. Some nights, I had to bury the clock deep in my pack so I couldn't hear its relentless beating, tracking the minutes he'd been gone. But I couldn't bear to throw the clock away either.

I tried to cling to Eden, tried to sink back down, between the knotted lumps of pillow stuffing. But there was no escaping. Each morning grief would arrive again, creeping up like a tide or knocking me over with the force of a wave. I had to get out of bed, away from the windowless room, through the door I'd barricaded the night before. Otherwise I would just think think think.

I was anxious, even excited to explore Sarajevo. I usually went sightseeing as a distraction or out of some odd sense of duty to visit the important monuments and museums. But something had shifted in Poland and Israel. I realized I had a vested interest in how Bosnia had recovered.

I wanted to see what survival looked like.

• • •

The landscape outside was gray, the sky bruised with blue-black clouds. A few scattered trees had bare branches. Decaying leaves and garbage lay in the gutters. Crumbling concrete buildings were riddled with bullet holes. Eden faded, further and further away.

Although it was early on an icy dark Wednesday, the streets were teeming with Stabilization Forces, or SFOR. NATO still had around twenty thousand peacekeepers in Bosnia, and most of them seemed to be in the capital. There were uniformed men from Germany, Greece, the United States, Denmark, Norway, the Netherlands. The Italian soldiers wore a long, curved black feather in their hats. The feathers looked ridiculous, and every time I saw them, the tune "Yankee Doodle Dandy" would run through my head for hours.

Scrawny children shouted and chased each other up and down cobblestone alleys, slipping around frosted corners. A young man missing a leg leaned on a wooden crutch, smoking a cigarette. He winked and smiled as I passed.

"Lost?" A cloud of exhaled smoke formed an ashy ghost in the cold air between us.

"No, thanks. I'm fine."

"Directions," he offered. "Where?"

"I'm okay. Vijećnica," I tried, but the word felt broken on my tongue. "National Library," I conceded, pointing down the street toward the burned-out shell.

"Ah. We Sarajevans." He spoke slowly, the hand with the cigarette laid flat against his chest. "We remember the day, the ashes of books flying above the city. Like black snow." He raised and tapped his cigarette, watching the ashes fall to the sidewalk. He winked again, this time without smiling, and nodded in the direction I'd pointed.

I followed the shallow olive-green River Miljacka until I stood in front of the skeletal National Library. Its stone face was streaked with soot and charcoal, blackened window frames staring out like empty eyes.

Through the holes, I could see piles of rubble and debris: singed pebbles, cracked bricks, and larger blocks the color of bone.

The National Library was destroyed August 25, 1992—exactly one hundred years after construction began. The Serbian army hit the building with fifty incendiary grenades and it began burning shortly before midnight. Continuous shelling kept the fire going for three days and thwarted attempts to rescue the books. Firefighters were specifically targeted; mortar rounds were aimed at the crews and machine guns shredded the water hoses.

Despite the dangers, volunteers formed a human chain to rescue manuscripts. Aida Buturovic, a librarian, was shot and killed by a sniper while trying to save books from the flames.

By the time the fire died, the building was gutted. Over two million books, manuscripts, newspapers, and periodicals were gone. The written history of the city turned to dust.

As I read the National Library section in my guide, watery sunlight filled the hollow structure. The building had become a symbol of the city. Segments shot for foreign television often began with the demolished stained-glass dome in the ceiling, cameramen turning in circles underneath to capture shafts of light filtered through splinters of colored glass.

But the building also became a symbol for the locals. The wrecked interior was turned into a place to celebrate Bosnian culture. The library became a venue for concerts, performances, and art exhibitions held throughout the siege. Musicians, actors, artists, and audiences risked their lives to participate. I'd seen a black and white poster earlier that day advertising a music festival held in the winter of 1993. A lone cello player with a dark, droopy mustache, wearing a tuxedo and sitting in the scorched ruin, heaps of flint and chalk-colored stones behind him. Playing his cello with one hand and using the other hand to cover his eyes.

That first morning in Sarajevo, I felt like walking. I spent most days in Eastern Europe walking: to avoid the hassles of public transportation in

Cyrillic, to explore, to observe, to keep warm, to talk to Sean, or to keep from thinking.

But my guidebook warned about venturing off the asphalt, advising to *regard every centimeter of ground as suspicious.* In 2002, Bosnia was the most heavily mined country in Europe. Since the war's end in 1996, almost fifteen hundred people had been killed or injured by mines.

With my back to the National Library, I looked out across the River Miljacka to the surrounding rocky hills of black fir trees and dull green pines. In the city's suburbs alone, there were almost two thousand recorded minefields. And half of Bosnia's minefields remained in locations that had been deliberately left unrecorded.

Since I had to stick to the pavement, I decided to walk through the city to the other side of town. There was something oddly reassuring about staying within the boundaries of the old blockades and trenches. My body felt stiff from the long journey into Bosnia, but my daypack was a welcome relief compared to the weight of my full pack. I raised the zip of my jacket against the cold and shoved my hands deeper into the wool-lined pockets.

Squeezed beside the ever-present bombed-out shops, there were packed cafés filled with the smells of brewing coffee and burning tobacco. I ducked into what I hoped was a bookstore. The faded sign *Šahinpašić* meant nothing to me, but underneath the lettering in the window were piles of English-language newspapers, magazines, and paperbacks.

Hiding behind the sagging shelves at the back, I hoped to browse on my own and avoid a lengthy round of charades. I'd already filled the pages of my journal, writing in a cramped hand now on the inside covers to make it last as long as possible. I needed a new one and hadn't had any luck so far. But in a stack of dusty volumes in a corner, I found a shamrock-green notebook, filled with graph-paper-lined pages.

I took the notebook to the cashier, a young man dressed in black with his chin in his hand as he read a book spread out across the glass counter. A silvery scar shadowed one eye, running from the bridge of his nose, under his cheekbone, then back up to his ear, like a crescent moon tipped onto its back.

"*Zdravo,*" he said without looking up.

"*Zdravo,*" I tried to mimic, and slid the green notebook across. He looked up at me with a crooked grin that twisted away from the scar.

"Where you from?" he asked.

"California."

"California girls?!"

"Yup." I silently cursed the Beach Boys.

He looked me up and down. "You want the map?"

"Excuse me?"

"The map. Made during the war." He reached under the counter and, sweeping his book and my notebook aside, spread out a large, glossy, colorful poster.

"The map," he said, folding his arms in front of his thin chest. I leaned over the counter. A bright pink banner at the top said *Sarajevo*, with the years of the siege: *1992, 1993, 1994, 1995.* Comic-strip-style tanks and cannons surrounded the city, facing inward behind a thick red line and every single one poised to fire. Sniper Alley was labeled, in English, and various trucks, vans, tanks, and buildings were marked *UN* in block letters. Most of the buildings had been bombed; huge chunks were collapsed or missing. Gold exploding stars, red circles, and target crosshairs were scattered over the map.

And everywhere, tiny cartoon people ran. They ran across bridges and streets, through parks, down alleys, past corners, along the river, and sometimes through the snipers' crosshairs.

I looked up at the cashier. He was grinning. "The map," he repeated, and with a flourish, turned it over. The back was filled with text, again in English, beside colorful comics with headings such as *SNIPERS, SHELLS, TRENCHES, DANGEROUS ZONES, CEMETERIES,* and *THE TOBACCO FACTORY.* It was an uncomfortable but intriguing mix. A childlike drawing of occupation and destruction, whimsical cartoon characters caught in the snipers' sights, cheerful colors depicting a disturbing topography of life and death.

"How much?"

"For you, California girl . . . *deset*, ten marks."

I paid for it and my notebook. On the sidewalk, I pulled out the *Survival Map.* The price tag was labeled in smudged black ink: ten marks.

• • •

The map was one of those designed to betray foreigners. The only way to look at it was to unfold it completely, arms spread wide and crowding out the locals on the sidewalk. But I'd given up hope of blending in weeks ago. The section under *DANGEROUS ZONES* read:

> . . . *the most dangerous zones were those directly in the line of fire. Bridges, crossroads and streets exposed to the mountains. Those were the places where the possibility of getting shot was somewhat lessened if one was a fast runner. Such places also seemed less terrifying than other parts of town where one was never sure whether one should walk fast or slow. Would the shell land where you are or in front of you?*

"Dobar dan," a voice said behind the map. An elderly man with paper-white hair leaned on crutches held together by rags and string. The left leg of his rumpled suit was rolled tightly and pinned just below his groin. He smiled and reached up to tip his hat. I moved out of the way, smiling and mumbling. I couldn't remember the Bosnian for "sorry" or "excuse me."

"Dobar dan," I finally replied. He tipped his hat again and smiled one more time before moving deftly past, his crutches swinging with practiced precision.

It had been ten years since the beginning of the assault on the city of Sarajevo, but only six since it ended, making it the longest siege in modern history. Of the 100,000 people killed during the Bosnian war, 13,952 died in Sarajevo—1,601 of them children.

As I walked through the city, I passed makeshift graveyards crowded around churches and mosques, in school yards, gardens, and parks. Bright silk flowers and plastic toys were piled next to white stones, and crosses were placed almost on top of each other. Four thousand people were thought to be buried in improvised graves. I read on the *Survival Map* that of Sarajevo's two cemeteries, one had become part of occupied territory and the other the front line. So people buried their loved ones where they could, usually late at night to avoid shelling. Sometimes, gravediggers working in the dark would be killed by a sniper and end up buried in the hole they'd dug for someone else.

Graves replaced the benches, fences, and trees as everything combustible was uprooted for fuel and heat. Ironically, the first parks in Sarajevo had originally been converted from old Muslim cemeteries. Throughout the siege, ethnic Bosniaks were killed in far greater numbers than any other group and Muslim graves crept in again, reclaiming these public green spaces.

I thought of Sean's grave, grave number 102, back in Northern Memorial Park in Melbourne. The luxury of manicured apple-green grass and orderly spaced rows. The long black hearse that had carried him there, the ornate wooden coffin from Thailand, the spray of fresh roses dripping over the sides of his casket—these would have seemed like extravagances, even absurdities during the Bosnian War. But they did nothing to prevent the desperate panic that caught in my chest as they lowered him into the ground.

I can still feel the sensation today. He'd been dead for ten days, and I'd spent hours with his body, taking him from Ko Pha Ngan to Bangkok to Melbourne. But the finality of watching his coffin descend was unbearable, to lose physical possession of him for the last time.

The young girls in Bosnia who'd lost lovers must also see the long years ahead, stretching and unfolding in front of them. Like me, they'll visit his grave on anniversaries and birthdays, bringing purple irises because he always loved van Gogh's painting of the drooping flowers, and two bottles of Crown Lager, his favorite celebratory beer. They'll share the beer with the ground where he lies. They'll continue to talk to him even when they can no longer recall the cadence of his voice. And they'll try not to think about what is happening to his body below.

. . .

Benches were still noticeably absent in Sarajevo. I'd been walking all morning. My back ached and my toes were numb from the cold. I decided to find somewhere warm where I could just sit for a while.

I went into the first café I found. Mismatched tables were crammed together, most of them filled with men drinking, smoking, talking. Trying to be as unobtrusive as possible, I weaved my way through the smoke toward the back, sank into a chair at one of the few empty tables, and shrugged off my daypack. A waiter approached, dressed in black with a stained apron around his slender waist.

"Coffee?" I tried to give the word what I imagined might be a Bosnian lilt. He nodded and left, which seemed like a good sign.

When he reappeared, he was balancing a copper tray covered in intricate relief. Placing the tray in front of me, he pointed to a steaming long-handled copper pot.

"Džezva." He then pointed to a miniature white coffee cup without handles. *"Fildžan."* He raised the *džezva* high above the *fildžan.* And poured thick, dark coffee from the burnished pot. *"Kahva."*

"Hvala," I replied, hoping it was the right word for "thank you."

Ignoring the looks from the men surrounding me, I focused on the little cup at my table—the warmth of the liquid and the rich, bitter flavor.

"Razgovoruša." A man with a wild black beard streaked with gray leaned in close. He sat at the next table with three other men with beards. They watched.

"Sorry." I shrugged my shoulders and shook my head, resolving to later look up how to apologize in Bosnian.

"Razgovarati means 'to talk.' *Razgovoruša* is the coffee we drink late in the morning with friends. Talking."

"Ah."

He scraped his chair closer to mine and clamped his hand around my wrist. His lips were cracked and dry. "You must be very lonely."

"Excuse me?" I swallowed hard, forcing down emotions rising to the surface. I would not cry.

"There is a saying in Bosnia. If someone is truly alone, they say they have no one with whom they can drink coffee."

I looked away. I felt my face flush and a wet heat behind my eyes. I tried to clear my throat, and swallowed again.

I wasn't sure how to read this man. He might be friendly. He might be flirting. But there was an aggression in his voice and his grip. In my own culture and country, it might have been easier to understand, but then again, it might not have been. I felt like I'd lost the ability to interpret social situations. I was always so close to tears, it made it hard to guess the intentions of other people. It would be years before I stopped flinching in everyday conversations.

"We never drink coffee alone," the man continued. "We can't afford it. And we can't afford to eat in restaurants. There's no work. So we buy one cup of coffee and make it last for hours each day with our friends."

"Mmm." I nodded, moving my arm out of his grasp by reaching for my cup and simultaneously sliding my chair away from him.

He picked up one of the sugar cubes I'd ignored on my tray. "You don't want to make life a little sweeter?" I could smell the saccharine acidity of his breath.

"I don't really like sugar."

He studied me with a smile twitching at the corners of his chapped lips. Without taking his eyes off me, he reached behind to grab his cup from his table. After dipping the sugar, he popped the coffee-soaked cube into his mouth and drained his cup. He smiled again, the stained cube clenched between his teeth. Then, still watching me, he tapped a white packet of cigarettes against the inside of his thigh before extending his arm. I recognized the black lettering of the local brand, Drina.

"No thanks, I don't smoke."

"Tsk, tsk, tsk. No one to have coffee with, no sugar, no smoke. When did you quit?"

"I've never smoked."

"Well, you want one for later? When you stop quitting?"

. . .

THE TOBACCO FACTORY

There is the cult of the cigarette in Sarajevo . . . For a pack of cigarettes one could get several tins of humanitarian food. Due to the lack of paper cigarettes were rolled into various textbooks, books and official documents. You couldn't read on them warnings about health hazards but you could learn, for instance, about the process of producing copper. The citizens were often telling the story about how Sarajevo would have surrendered had the cigarettes disappeared.

I spent three days in Sarajevo, learning to navigate my way through the city using signs from the siege. Sniper Alley led from the Stari Grad, or Old Town, into the commercial center, narrow cobblestone lanes giving way to wide boulevards of high-rises. As the buildings became taller and more modern, the devastation was more extensive and complete.

Although the street was officially named Zmaja od Bosne, or Dragon of Bosnia, everyone still referred to it as Sniper Alley. There wasn't a single structure without scars from the war. Men tried to fish in the trickle of the Miljacka by the torched post office. The Parliament building was a tall silver wreck, the facade blown off and split open. The only hotel open during the siege, the Holiday Inn, looked as if it had been dragged through barbed wire, its trademark bright yellow paint peppered with gashes and scratches. According to the cartoon *Survival Map, it was one of the few hotels in which the most prized rooms were those without a view. A view of the mountains meant a view of the snipers' nest . . . If you see him, he sees you.*

There were faded posters everywhere. The National Library smothered in white flames, black smoke pouring from its windows with the words *Not fiction... ...it is fact.* A wavy black and white imitation of Munch's *The Scream*—the openmouthed man holding his head on the bridge, the black river flowing toward a city of minarets, towers, and cathedrals. The caption at the bottom read: *Sarajevo 1993.*

Another, a bluish-tinted black and white image of a line of leggy women with big hair, a banner held daintily above their stilettos: *Don't let them kill us.* The photo was from the Miss Sarajevo Under Siege pageant in 1993. It'd been held in a basement due to constant sniper attacks. The contestants wrapped themselves in plastic from humanitarian aid packages and posed with assault rifles.

There were Sarajevo roses. Artillery shelling throughout the siege had left skeletal handlike scars in the pavement and on walls across the city. Fatal explosions were marked by filling the scars with red resin. A red rose left at the site of each deadly blast.

One night, I came across a sidewalk covered in roses. Sarajevo had been hit with an average of 329 shells every day for almost four years. From where I stood, there were more red spatters clustered together than I could count. It was difficult to negotiate a path without stepping on a rose, which I'd heard you weren't supposed to do. One rose was off all on its own—the shrapnel scar so tiny, it seemed to represent the death of a baby or toddler. I felt an emptiness in the pit of my stomach and the cold air creep up the back of my neck. In the dark, the red resin looked exactly like dried blood.

There was graffiti, splattered on the sides of the wrecked buildings and walls, on sidewalks and abandoned cars. The only Bosnian I recognized was *Pazi—Snajper!*, which I was pretty sure meant "Watch out—Sniper!" This message seemed to be on every corner.

I was surprised by how much of the graffiti was in English: STAND YOUR GROUND OLD TOWN, *Welcome to hell!*, *Hellcome to Sarajevo*, *Why?*, *Fuck the war*, *Help Bosnia Now!*, and DON'T FORGET SREBRENICA scrawled next to a large detailed drawing of a skull. There were two painted lines I could never get out of my head: *People of the world help us. Stop killing children.*

And wherever I walked, there were tight packs of SFOR soldiers. Always with their fellow countrymen, never mixing with other nationalities. They wore sunglasses, wolf-whistled at women wearing short skirts, and took photos of each other in front of shattered landmarks, two fingers raised and spread as peace signs.

...

My second day in Bosnia, I headed to Zelena Pijaca Markale, the city's main market at the edge of the Old Town. On the *Survival Map*, I read how the markets had stayed open throughout the siege, selling edible and less edible plants, homegrown teas, and humanitarian aid such as *Truman eggs (the powdered eggs which had been stored since WWII)*. Although there wasn't a market in Sarajevo that hadn't seen a massacre, Markale was the location of two of the most significant ones.

The first, on February 5, 1994, was the single bloodiest attack during the siege. The crowded market was bombed shortly after noon. Sixty-eight people were killed and two hundred wounded. I'd been nineteen years old, a sophomore at UC San Diego, and remembered seeing the footage of mangled bodies and severed limbs scattered around the bloodstained stalls as the attack made news reports around the world.

But the siege continued and the market was bombed again the following year, on August 28, 1995. At around eleven a.m., five grenades were fired into Markale, killing forty-three and wounding ninety.

On my way to the market in 2002, I passed old splashes of graffiti with the warning *Snajper!* and painted arrows pointing to the hills. But as I wandered through the covered stalls, there was no evidence the massacres had ever taken place. The produce on offer seemed exhausted, the winter harvest heaped into small piles of shrunken apples, wrinkled potatoes, and weary cucumbers. Yet the vendors waved and nodded and smiled, and the streets surrounding the market were buzzing.

Outside in the weak November sunlight, men sat at sidewalk cafés drinking muddy coffee and nibbling on soft powdered squares of Turkish delight—smoking and talking and staring. The soul of the capital was here in the Old Town, the city's pulse throbbing strongest in the maze of tangled cobblestone lanes of Baščaršija, the old bazaar.

Each alley in Baščaršija was dedicated to a different trade. I passed cluttered shops selling leather, jewelry, pottery. The sides of ul Kazandžiluk were stacked with traditional copperware and some more modern metalwork: Turkish coffee sets, elaborately decorated plates, chess sets, hookahs, and engraved shell casings with etchings of the ruined National Library and slogans like *Welcome to Sarajevo*.

I found Hodžić on a block wedged in with other *ćevabdžinicas*, or traditional grills. The open doorways poured onto the street, filling the cramped lane with the sounds of brittle Slavic consonants, white smoke, and the smell of grilled meat.

Inside, it was dark, warm, and busy. I grabbed a table at the window and ordered *ćevapi*, the national dish. Moments later, a sizzling plate was set down in front of me. A puddle of plain yogurt, a pile of chopped raw onions, juicy blackened sausages the size of my thumb, and *somun*, a thick chewy flatbread. The bite of the onions was mellowed by the sour yogurt and peppery sausages, the spongy *somun* soaking up the savory flavors. I was easy to please. It was freezing outside, I was starving, I'd been surviving on salami and cheese since Israel, and hadn't been eating or sleeping well for some time. But the *ćevapi* was simply delicious.

After lunch at Hodžić, I found myself once again with my back to the National Library. Rusting Yugo cars rattled along, spewing blue clouds of exhaust. I could see Princip's Bridge crossing over the Miljacka to the west. Four simple arches with two distinctive circles cut through the gypsum and stone, the openings blinking in the faint sunshine as the river bubbled past.

I made my way along the river and arrived at Princip's corner, where on a hot summer day in June 1914, the nineteen-year-old Bosnian Serb student Gavrilo Princip fired the fatal shots that would eventually take over fifteen million lives.

On that day, Archduke Franz Ferdinand, heir to the Austro-Hungarian throne, and his wife, Sophie, were visiting Sarajevo in hopes of easing Serbian tensions. But a nationalist secret society, Crna Ruka (Black Hand), had planted seven young assassins and Princip was among them.

He shot the archduke and his wife when their car made a wrong turn in front of a deli.

Eighty-eight years later, I stood alone in the cold at Princip's corner, checking my map to make sure I was in the right place. There was nothing to mark the assassinations that eventually led to not only the First World War, but also the Second.

It hadn't always been that way. According to what I read online, on the exact spot in June 1917 the Austrians dedicated a massive monument—stone columns thirty feet tall surrounding an enormous medallion engraved with images of the assassinated archduke and his wife. But when the Serbs, Croats, and Slovenes took over in 1918, the monument was dismantled.

In 1930, Yugoslavia placed a simple black plaque above the street: *Princip proclaimed freedom on Vidovdan (28) June 1914.* Nazis removed the plaque during the first days of their occupation of Sarajevo in 1941. It was presented to Adolf Hitler for his fifty-second birthday.

Following the city's liberation in 1945, a new plaque was placed at the assassination site: *The youth of Bosnia and Herzegovina dedicate this plaque as a symbol of eternal gratitude to Gavrilo Princip and his comrades, to fighters against the Germanic conquerors.*

Street names were changed to honor everyone involved in the assassination. In 1953, the Museum of Gavrilo Princip and Young Bosnia was established. Princip's footsteps were etched into the concrete in the exact place where he'd stood, with another plaque: *expressing with his shot the national protest against tyranny and our people's centuries-long aspiration for freedom.*

During the Siege of Sarajevo, those street names were removed, the museum was closed, and the plaque and Princip's footprints were ripped out of the pavement. Serbian nationalism was not something the city felt like celebrating.

Although the siege had ended more than six years ago, nothing had replaced Princip's footsteps on the corner. It felt strange to be standing at the location where a single violent act had taken place that shaped the modern world, and yet have no formal recognition of it.

The total lack of official monuments in Sarajevo in 2002 was striking.

The only testament to the most recent war was on the faces of the city's buildings and the bodies of its inhabitants. Was the tragedy of it all still too close, too painful? Were they still too focused on immediate survival? Was it a lack of funding? At the time, unemployment in Bosnia was 40 percent. Or had the wasted buildings intentionally been left as memorials?

I wondered if it wasn't also that Sarajevans couldn't agree on how to remember. Just as the Austrians, Serbs, Croats, Slovenes, Yugoslavians, and Nazis had disagreed on how to memorialize the assassinations of 1914, how could the siege's aggressors and victims agree on any kind of official tribute to the many lives lost? Bosnia's government was now a so-called consociational democracy, three rotating presidents representing three ethnicities (Bosniaks, Croats, and Serbs) and two entities (the Federation of Bosnia and Herzegovina, and the Republika Srpska), each with their own constitution.

Months later, Stevie D emailed me a photo when Sean's headstone was placed onto his grave. I thought again of Princip's plaques, and the difficulty in agreeing on how someone should be remembered. Sean's parents had chosen a simple engraving:

Sean Patrick Brian Reilly
1976–2002
Son, Brother, Uncle,
Brother-in-Law, Mate

By oversight or intention, I was not included. My mum tried to tell me that I had been his mate, a biological mate, not a buddy. That the word "mate" did include me. But I knew that this was how his family had chosen to remember Sean, as their son, brother, and even brother-in-law, but not as my lover or fiancé.

Their memorial had included a Catholic funeral—a portly priest who'd never met Sean, friends and family kneeling at a wooden altar before reading passages from the Bible. His father had handed out the wallet-sized memorial cards in front of the church, with a moving tribute he'd written printed inside—remembering Sean's smile; his tuneless whistle; his zest for life; his honesty, integrity, and generosity; his love for his family and friends; the way he loved his mum.

I'd agonized over whether to take the communion. I'd never been baptized (and had become much more superstitious since Sean's death), but wanted to take part in every aspect of the service. In the end, I took the tasteless white host on my tongue, but felt neither damned nor saved.

Then Sean had been buried in a family plot. This was who he was to them, how they chose to remember him. It wasn't wrong.

But if they'd asked me, I would have told them that Sean hadn't wanted to be buried. He'd said to me once that he didn't want his loved ones worrying about caring for his grave, or feeling guilty if they didn't visit the cemetery. And that Sean was agnostic. But he could never quite remember the right term, so he'd always ask me, "What am I again, Miss—agnostic or atheist?"

If they'd asked me, I would have told them about how he'd interrupt a story I was telling to say that he loved me. Or how if he was broke, he would ask me to hand over all my cash in the parking lot so that he could be the one to shout the meal for his family or buy the rounds of drinks for his friends. How he always had to have the side of the bed farthest from the wall. And how when he was really stoned, he would make me sleep with the light on. On the inside of the card, I might have written about how the first thing he would say to me in the mornings was either "Can I steal a morning kiss?" or "I love you." Or how when he first died, the thing I missed most was just holding his hand.

Sarajevo is surrounded by mountains, and the city's days slipped away quickly. But despite the chill of winter, the streets came alive after dark: Roma kids begging for coins, teenagers kicking half-deflated soccer balls, stunning women with cheap orange-blond dye in their hair, SFOR soldiers drinking bottles of imported water and beer.

There didn't seem to be many bars. But toward the end of my second day in the capital, I spotted The Bar, on one of the broad graffitied boulevards near Sniper Alley. Inside, it was filled with smoke and SFOR. Coldplay's new album, *A Rush of Blood to the Head*, buzzed over the speakers. I ordered a Sarajevsko *pivo* and sank deep into a sagging couch in a corner.

A Western-looking guy in dingy jeans wandered over. The few other foreigners I'd come across traveling in Eastern Europe were almost always young male backpackers. Matt was from Brisbane, the lazy twang of his accent instantly familiar. He said he'd noticed me earlier in the day. I wondered briefly if I'd been crying.

"I reckon we must be the only two backpackers in all of Bosnia," he crowed, raising his tall glass. He drained the last of his beer and asked if I wanted another round.

A couple minutes later, Matt returned, beaming, with two large beers. "Cheers! To Sarajevo!" His eyes were glassy and his cheeks ruddy from the warmth of the bar and the booze. The smell of his drugstore aftershave intensified with his rising body heat, cheap scents of musk and cloves steaming from his skin. Although he was the same age as Anat and Talia, he seemed a decade younger. "Another round?" he asked, a slight slur at the end of his sentence.

I'd hardly touched my beer and his was finished. But it was my turn, and I wanted to talk to the bartender anyway.

Tempted to head to Yugoslavia next, I'd checked my guidebook but visitors needed *an invitation from an official body or a pre-arranged itinerary with booked hotels—all in writing*. I'd heard you could just show up in Belgrade and try your luck for a visa, but luck hadn't been on my side lately. So I thought I'd try Croatia again, before traveling around Yugoslavia to Romania. Except the only bus from Sarajevo to Dubrovnik left at 7:15 a.m. Sunrise wasn't until seven.

I hated early-morning journeys. Not because I minded waking up, though I'd never been a morning person, but because I hated being on the deserted streets before dawn. Cities in those quiet early hours felt ominous. At least late at night, bars would be emptying, their drunken clientele pouring onto the streets and trickling down sidewalks toward home.

Death didn't scare me anymore. It was rape I was terrified of. So I ordered two bottles of Tuzlanksi, the most interesting name of the local brands on offer, and asked one of the bartenders at The Bar about being on the streets that early. I asked if I should book a cab in advance, hoping he might offer his phone and his Bosnian to order one.

"No, no problem," was his reply. "No problem that early. No problem finding a cab. No problem, no problem."

I cringed and stumbled back a step, my hands sticking to a tacky patch at the bar. I hated those two words. The night Sean died, the Thai receptionist at the clinic had kept saying "no problem." "No problem" as they shoved long tubes down Sean's throat and up his nose. "No problem" as they leaned onto his limp body, compressing his chest. "No problem" as they plunged thick, dripping needles of adrenaline into his heart. And "no problem" right before the doctor told me there was nothing more he could do.

That night at the clinic I'd wanted to scream at the receptionist to stop saying "no problem." I'd wanted to yell that this was a fucking un-believable problem. That it was far beyond the worst thing I could ever even fucking imagine.

I knew her English was bad. I knew she couldn't communicate well. Maybe she didn't even really understand what she was saying. But every time she said it, the pain those words caused was profound and physical. After that night, whenever I heard those words, I wanted to scream all over again.

Taking the two glasses of Tuzlanski beer, I returned from the bar to the couch in the corner. Matt raised a toast again to Sarajevo, and I watched his dark curls above the rim of his pint glass. While he remained cheerfully determined to drink, my thoughts were stuck somewhere else.

Matt was reveling in the idea of being somewhere sketchy, some-where that would frighten his parents, somewhere that would impress his friends. Yet he didn't really expect anything truly terrible to happen, even pushing the odds. Maybe he'd come away with a good story.

Sean and I had been the same. We hadn't even expected a good story from Thailand. Sean had been more likely to die from a snakebite or scorpion sting, from falling out of bed or being hit by a falling coconut, from being struck by lightning or choking on a hot dog, than being killed by a jellyfish. One in a million only means something to the other 999,999.

After the rounds with Matt at The Bar, I needed something to do next. I wasn't hungry, but decided on dinner as a distraction.

The restaurant I chose, To Be or Not to Be, back in Baščaršija turned out to be the wrong kind of place to try to stop thinking about a dead lover. It was down a quiet alley, tiny and intimate, with only two tables on the ground floor and three more up a creaking narrow staircase. Dining couples leaned in close, sharing private jokes and bottles of Herzegovinian red wine. But the waiter had already acknowledged me at the top of the stairs and was bringing over a menu. I sat down at a candlelit table alone.

The menu he placed on my table was in English. I hadn't opened my mouth, but it must have been obvious. In the small space of the restaurant, I could hear snatches of conversations in English and French from the other two tables.

The restaurant's specialty, chili chocolate chicken, sounded too rich and heavy, so I pointed to the grilled fish.

"Ne," the waiter said, frowning.

But I'd expected this, and had a backup order ready. I pointed and tried again. "Steak?"

"Ne," he repeated, shaking his head and still frowning. This I wasn't prepared for. I scanned the menu, looking for something simple and settled on chili pasta.

"Da." His frown eased into a grin.

"Um . . . vino?" I pointed to the bottles of red on the neighboring tables, but motioned a smaller shape with my hands, hoping for a glass.

"Da." His grin relaxed into a wider smile. *"Crno vino?"*

"Da." I thought this was the Bosnian for black, or red wine. If I was wrong, I'd be fine with whatever he brought.

When the glass of red was placed on my table, I was grateful to have something to do with my hands. I tried to concentrate on the Miles Davis playing in the background, the aromas of garlic, dill, mint, and fennel drifting in from the kitchen, the warm smokiness of my wine. But surrounded by couples and candlelight, I felt that the coziness of the restaurant became claustrophobic. I missed Sean, but I also missed Anat and Talia and the camouflage of their company. One of the diners bent to whisper, and her partner turned in his seat to stare. They cast long, concerned looks in the direction of my table.

Pretending not to notice, I took out my old journal. I still had a little bit of room left. Two extended Miles Davis tracks later, the waiter returned with a gigantic mound of spaghetti that he placed next to my pages. *"Prijatno."*

I didn't recognize the word and wasn't sure if it required a response, so I smiled up at him. *"Hvala . . ."* I ventured, grateful to remember "thank you." He nodded and left.

The spaghetti was appetizingly uncomplicated—just olive oil, garlic, and chili flakes. But even that reminded me of Sean. The pleasant burn in my mouth made me think about how we'd try to eat chili peppers without the other noticing, before leaning in for a kiss. Passing the surprise of the heat back and forth on our tongues.

As I was leaving, I noticed the restaurant's dark wooden sign hanging over the alley. The words "or not" had been crossed out. Apparently, during the siege the owners had slashed through the white lettering with a thick red line. "Not to be" was not an option.

The last afternoon I spent in Sarajevo was sunny and cold. On the way to my second Turkish coffee for the day, I was distracted by a crowd gathered in a park. A group of men stood in a kind of circle—shouting, smoking, laughing. Unsure whether I'd be welcome, or even noticed, I hesitated at the edge. There were men with thick white hair, balding men with silvery beards—some with their hands thrust deep into coat pockets, others yelling and pointing, a burning cigarette pinched between their outstretched fingers. I skirted the group until I could get a glimpse in between elbows.

A man wearing a brown beret and missing an arm was lifting an enormous chess piece, a black knight the size of a small child. He paused, the knight against his hip, and surveyed the other pieces arranged on the pavement. The spectators' voices grew louder. A few of the men stepped in close, pointing out possible countermoves and arguing tactics.

Sean had taught me how to play chess. At a market in Fes, he'd been offered a chess set he wasn't interested in. The vendor had followed us, dogged and persistent. Finally, Sean suggested a sum so far below the asking price, he thought the man would give up and walk away. But the vendor accepted and Sean was stuck with the heavy handmade set. He carried it in his pack and we played through North Africa and Western Europe. As soon as I started winning in Austria, Sean seemed to lose interest in the game.

In Sarajevo, scattered among the more polished classic figures, there were improvised pieces—slender metal columns of various sizes, covered in flaking black or white paint. It'd been almost four years since I'd last played with Sean in Salzburg and I couldn't work out what the new pieces represented. Later, I learned the men had been playing with spent shell casings.

As I turned to leave, a stocky handkerchiefed woman approached and grabbed my arm. She spun my body to face hers and took hold of both my hands. Her fingers were coarse and callused.

"Dobro došli. Dobro došli. Dobro došli." I looked around to see if anyone else was watching, checking my jacket's inner pocket with the inside of my elbow for my wallet.

She clasped one hand to her sagging breast, and with the other tightened her grip around my knuckles. *"Hvala, hvala."*

It was the only word I recognized. Women rarely approached me in Eastern Europe. When they did, it was to offer meals or trinkets, or to beg for spare coins. But she seemed friendly. I smiled, hoping it would be an innocuous exchange.

"*Dobro došli u Sarajevo.*" She beamed, squeezing my fingers with a surprising strength.

With her free arm, she pulled on the elbow of a man passing by. She spoke to him in rapid Bosnian, the crisp sounds of her words stacking on top of each other. Taking his hat in his hands, the man turned to me.

"*Zdravo. Da li govorite Bosanki?*"

Clueless, I shrugged my shoulders. "English?"

"*Russkiy?*"

"*¿Español?*" I was grasping at my last straw. Spanish was my only other language.

"*Français?*"

I shook my head.

"Okay, okay . . ." Speaking carefully, he pointed to the woman still clutching my hands. "*Elle dit, bienvenue. Merci de venir à Sarajevo.*"

The words were similar enough in Spanish that I understood. "*De nada,*" I said, hoping he would understand as well.

The woman watched the conversation back and forth between us. Over her shoulder, I noticed a crumpled poster on a corner. A white dove bound in barbed wire with the title *Sarajevo witness*. "*Hvala,*" the woman said to me again, and smiled.

"*Hvala,*" I replied. She sighed, finally dropping my hands. Flexing my wrists as sensation started to return to my fingers, I turned to the man. "*Hvala,*" I said as he replaced his hat and returned to the chess game. "*Merci.*"

Across from the park, I found a busy café. Next door was a souvenir shop selling ballpoint pens made from bullet casings, spent shells turned into shining coffeepots. A rack of postcards caught my eye.

Instead of the usual touristy advertisements for a city, the racks held bright photos of the wasted Parliament building, glossy pictures of the torched National Library, and colorful images of minefield warning signs—*Od mine se gine!* I picked up a commemorative postcard, printed that year, with a caption under the photo: *1992 SARAJEVO 2002*. It was a contemporary black and white shot of a young boy sitting and reading while perched on the roof of a dilapidated, sunken car. The doors hung loosely from the frame, the tires had collapsed, the windows and head-lights were missing.

I'd never been to a country with such recent, visible scars of war. Israel was in the midst of fierce conflict, and the streets felt abandoned and empty. But places in Israel where bombs exploded were cleaned up quickly. I'd seen where the bomb had gone off in the discotheque a couple years ago, and even the café only a few months before. The damage had been fixed, the destruction removed, and the blood washed away. There was no indication anything violent had ever happened. Even updates on the El Al flight I'd narrowly missed out of Tel Aviv had been difficult to find. I'd read the suspected hijacker had been overpowered by security guards and none of the 170 passengers were hurt. But it was almost as if the news itself had been swept out of sight.

In Sarajevo, the streets, parks, and cafés were crowded, with all the evidence out in the open. There were wounded people and buildings on every corner. Sarajevans might not be able to rebuild their city the way Israelis could, but they'd adapted. Signs of the siege had become part of their landscape, the death and wreckage absorbed into their daily lives instead of swept away.

There was an intensity in the capital here, but also an unexpected sense of humor. Locals had a glint in their eyes, and a macabre wit when it came to anything regarding the war.

Everyone had told me not to come. Yet men who'd been torn to pieces from landmines smiled and tipped their hats as I walked past. Not once had I felt threatened. Sarajevo was one of the most alive places I'd ever visited. It was like a city waking up after a long nightmare—so relieved that it's finally over, she can't stop smiling.

. . .

I stood at the edge of the city once more, against the former barricades and looking out into the blackening hills as the sun sank lower into the sky. It was the end of my last day in Sarajevo. Turning, I headed toward the main pedestrian street, Ferhadija, and what was left of the light.

At the World War II memorial, the Vječna vatra, or Eternal flame, locals were huddled in a tight circle. The green metal wreath at their feet was filled with a dancing fire. They rubbed their hands together over the warmth, lit their cigarettes from the flames, and turned to toast their backsides. I squeezed past to look at the inscription carved into the white stone alcove behind the fire. It was in Bosnian, but later I looked up the translation:

> *With Courage and the Jointly Spilled Blood . . . with the Joint Efforts and Sacrifices of Sarajevan Patriots, Serbs, Muslims and Croats on the 6th of April 1945 Sarajevo, the Capital City of the People's Republic of Bosnia and Herzegovina, was liberated.*

Other wreaths had been placed at the base of the alcove: mostly dried, some plastic, and one or two with fresh flowers. Framed portraits and loose snapshots were scattered among the wreaths. The photos were warped from the cold and the wet.

But something wasn't right about the images. They were too bright, too modern, too candid to be from the 1940s. The pictures could have been taken from my own albums, my own life: professors I'd had at university, boys I'd had crushes on as a teenager, young girls I'd competed with in gymnastics, and toddlers I'd babysat for extra cash. There was a print of a schoolgirl with blond bangs and braids who could have been my best friend. An older woman with bright eyes and a short dark haircut who looked like my grandmother. And another of a bookishly handsome young man in glasses, dates penned in a careful cursive script along the bottom of his photo: 1970–1995 . . . who'd also only been twenty-five.

My chest constricted. I gave up trying not to cry. I felt a compulsive need to pay attention to every detail, examine each smile, memorize the age at every death. Just as I studied photos of Sean, trying to capture each curve, line, and angle of his face. There were things I was already losing: his smell when he first woke up in the morning, the sound of his laugh, the way he looked when he was sleeping. But it seemed if I concentrated hard enough, and looked long enough, I could at least hold on to an image. Finally, wiping at my eyes and my nose, I turned back toward the street.

The old man was missing most of his teeth, all of his hair, and both of his legs. When he saw my tears, he gave an exaggerated cartoonish pout, before using his index fingers to push up the corners of his lips toward his ears. His hands dropped back onto the rims of his crude wheelchair, but the broad toothless grin stayed on his wrinkled face. The stretch of his smile seemed to hint at madness, but his eyes were focused and lucid. Had he lost everything, and then his mind? Or had he found some kind of clarity in knowing what had mattered most to him?

The wheels of his chair rested near a red spatter in the concrete. A single Sarajevo rose.

I saw then, that in the absence of official monuments, the survivors here had found their own ways to remember—in the spontaneity and chaos of the unplanned graveyards and Sarajevo roses, the impulsiveness and anger of their graffiti, the independence and even humor of their map, posters, and postcards.

Maybe that was why I was traveling. Maybe I was trying to create my own memorial to Sean and the life we would have had together in the blank spaces of an Eastern European winter.

I left the legless man still beaming. A sharp wind swept down from the mountains as the sky began to darken. From a minaret, the muezzin began the Adhān—his haunting call for sunset prayer resonating over the red-tile roofs of Sarajevo.

Only minutes after the Adhān had faded, the sounds of shouting, laughter, buzzing trumpets, and pounding drums came up from Ferhadija behind me. I wiped at my eyes and nose again as a parade of clowns and musicians turned the corner.

Cherry reds, mint greens, and lemon-pie yellows against the gray winter city backdrop. Waving, yelling, singing, and passing out bright plastic clown noses. I was struck dumb for a moment, then moved to the side to let them pass, their knees bouncing high in an animated marching step. A noisy blur of baggy checked pants, big shoes, blue wigs, and smeared greasepaint.

Kids sitting at the edge of the sidewalk begging with their mothers ran to join the parade. They donned bright red noses and giggled and danced with the clowns. They fell into step behind the musicians and mimicked their movements. Even a sullen group of preadolescents—skulking and smoking in a dark doorway—got swept up into the commotion, turning briefly back into children as they jostled with the clowns.

The parade was gone as quickly as it had come. I might have wondered if I'd imagined it; I sometimes felt my grip on sanity was slippery. But for the rest of that night, each time I turned a corner, there were laughing kids wearing bright red clown noses.

The next morning, a washed-out sun was just cresting the tops of the mountains as the bus I'd boarded eased away from the Sarajevo station. I settled in for the six-hour journey to Dubrovnik. A movie crackled to life on the overhead monitor. *Conspiracy Theory*, which of course, I'd seen with Sean in Chángshā. The picture jumped and the track skipped.

I stared out the smudged window at the countryside and tried to block out the jolting dialogue of the film. The landscape was rocky—broken by deep gorges, cloudy rivers, and steep hills cloaked in elm and pine. There were the now-familiar shattered buildings and empty homes. Fragments of wood and steel washed down rivers and piled onto sloping gritty shores.

Pulling out my new shamrock-green journal, I wrote Sean's full name on the inside cover as I always did, and the dates of his short life. Turning over the first page, I began to write about Sarajevo.

I started with the posters. The nude with her leg blown off brushing her hair in front of a mirror. The cellist covering his eyes. The National

Library engulfed in flames, the Sarajevan *Scream*, and Miss Besieged Sarajevo. The white dove bound in barbed wire. The cartoon *Survival Map*. I couldn't communicate with most of the locals, but the posters were a language I understood.

On the bus, *Runaway Bride* replaced *Conspiracy Theory* on the overhead screen. The track didn't skip, but the picture and sound were distorted into wavy psychedelic tones.

At the border, the driver collected our passports and his cigarettes before walking over to a guard's hut. Most of the passengers also drifted off the bus with foil packets in hand, taking the opportunity to chain-smoke while we waited. A tall gaunt teenager paced next to me. He managed to smoke four Drina cigarettes before the driver emerged from the hut.

Winter storm clouds crept across the sky and the wind began to howl. Heavy drops of rain splashed around our feet and we hurried back onto the bus.

As the surreal colors and sounds of *Runaway Bride* danced on the television, we approached the green valleys and fields of Croatia. It was a startling change in scenery. The intact houses with no pockmarks, the plum and olive orchards, grazing goats, and orderly row upon row of meticulously tethered grapevines.

But we'd left someone at the border. Another passenger informed the driver and we turned around to head back toward Bosnia. In all the years I'd been traveling, that had never happened on a bus I'd been on before. *Funny*, I wrote down in my journal as the bus rumbled along. *I'd always been afraid of being the one left behind.*

thirty-one

Kangaroo Island, South Australia, AUSTRALIA

November 2001

MY CELLPHONE BEGINS to buzz in the passenger seat, and I glance down to see Sean's name on the screen. I leave the phone on vibrate to keep it from startling the sea lions. I reach for the turn signal, but flick the windshield wipers instead. I've been driving on the left in Australia for almost six months, but still do this every single time. Without another car in sight on Kangaroo Island's South Coast Road, I decide not to bother and pull over onto the red dirt beneath the eucalyptus trees.

"Morning, Miss." Sean's voice crackles through the static. "How's life on 'the Rock' today?"

And then he's gone. I try to move my body back into the exact position where I'd had a signal seconds before. When that doesn't work, I climb out and stand on the trunk of my old white '87 Mitsubishi Magna. "Sean?"

"Miss, I'm here." I freeze, and then allow myself to exhale. It's always good to hear his voice. I love my research on Australian sea lions, but it's not without its challenges. I'd started fieldwork in the dead of winter, spending countless long days alone outside in the cold and the rain. The wind is the worst, as it seems to put the sea lions in a foul mood. Just yesterday, I'd been chased by three different SAMs (subadult males) during a storm. I'd had to run as fast as I possibly could with a backpack full of gear, and tore my waterproof pants on a tea tree bush.

But over the months, the pups have grown used to my presence. I'd hidden out in a cave once with a few to wait out the rain. Another time, right after a capture, the pup just climbed onto my feet and sniffed at my hands. And I never tire of watching the chubby young sea lions splashing and playing in the shallows.

"It's done, Miss. I've quit bubbles and am moving to China. And only three sleeps until your next visit." He sounds happier than I've heard him in weeks.

"Three sleeps. I can't wait." My only physical contact on the island is with the sea lions, and I ache for Sean in Melbourne. "I'm proud of you, Sean. Seriously. We'll be fine. It's only for five months. And I'll definitely come visit you in China."

A breeze rattles through the eucalyptus and I get a whiff of sea lions and L'Oréal bleach. No matter how many times I shower, or how hard I scrub under my nails, I can't seem to completely get rid of the smell. I'm looking forward to a weekend off, to restaurants and bars and stoplights and Sean.

Then he's gone again, and there's only silence on the other end.

I hold the phone up over my head, waving it around and trying to find a signal bar. When I finally glance at my watch, it's later than I want it to be, so I climb back into my car. It's not like the sea lions at Seal Bay are going to wait for me.

t h i r t y - t w o

Dubrovnik, Dalmacija, CROATIA

November 2002

I USED TO HOLD my breath with him, waiting for him to inhale. Sean's sleep apnea would wake me in the middle of the night and I'd lie beside him in bed, counting the silent drawn-out seconds between his exhales and inhales. I always had to gulp for air before he did. Now, fifteen Fridays since his death, and it felt as if I were still holding my breath with him, waiting for him to inhale.

That Friday, my first night in Dubrovnik on the southern tip of Croatia, I tossed and turned as usual. My feet got caught in the mysterious slit all duvet covers had in Eastern Europe, straight across and halfway down the underside. My arms tangled in one of Sean's old T-shirts. His scent was already fading and the cloth had begun to smell, inexplicably and disconcertingly, more and more like dust. I hesitated before pulling his shirt off over my head. I'd been lucky to avoid bedbugs at the hostel in Zagreb. But my single room in Dubrovnik was spotless, with clean towels and a door I could lock.

After Israel and Bosnia, Croatia seemed safe and peaceful and mellow. The temperatures were relatively mild, and there'd even been a crowd of women at the Gruž bus station offering *sobe*, or rooms. More surprising, one of the women had been holding a small cardboard sign with my name, backward and misspelled—*Flower Shanon*—the inked letters smeared from the afternoon rain.

"*Zdravo*. You stay *sobe* with my sister in Split. She tells me you go Bosna *i* Hercegovina three days and then to come here."

I'd no idea her sister would pass along this information. The sister had hardly spoken two words of English, and it wasn't often I guessed right how long I might stay somewhere. But the room in Dubrovnik was perfect—close to the Old Town and the Lapad Peninsula for sixty-five kuna, or less than nine US dollars a night.

What I'd seen of Dubrovnik so far had been breathtaking. Even in the pouring rain, each corner I turned I found myself thinking, *Oh my God*. White houses with honey-red tiled roofs were packed together on verdant hillsides and perched on rocky tumbling cliffs, surrounded by orchards of orange, lemon, and olive trees.

Within the medieval walls of the Stari Grad, or Old Town, no cars were allowed. Quiet cobblestone streets wound around steep narrow stairways and marbled squares, past palaces, towers, fountains, and statues. Enormous plants dripped from museum roof corners and bright green tendrils climbed the walls of ancient stone churches.

Walking along the top of the old city walls that cold, wet November afternoon, at times eighty feet above the ground, I couldn't imagine myself doing anything else. Dubrovnik was the most beautiful town I'd ever seen, and it was impossible not to appreciate my surroundings.

Yet it also reminded me of another walled city by the sea. Essaouira was where Sean and I had first started to spend time alone as a couple, away from our other traveling companions. We'd held hands and drunk red wine together on the rooftop of Hôtel Smara, watching the sun drop into the Atlantic Ocean.

Standing on top of Dubrovnik's stone walls, I could see the sun beginning to sink in the storm-colored sky. My grandpa Bob and grandma Joy had taught me to look for a green flash the moment before the sun slips below the horizon. But I knew there was no chance with the clouds in the sky that day. And as the sun made its way down into the Adriatic Sea, I felt a panic climb into my throat.

I didn't know how I was going to go home after this. My return flight to California was booked for January, and in February, I was supposed to be back in my PhD program in marine biology, as a visiting academic at Melbourne University. I'd need to find a place to live on my own, without Sean, and return to my fieldwork at Seal Bay on Kangaroo Island. I'd see Sean's friends and family in Melbourne, and drive by the pubs where we drank, the cafés where we ate, and the funeral home where I last saw his body.

Off Croatia's Dalmatian coast, the ocean swallowed the sun and began to darken. I thought of how the light would be spat out again over Haad Rin Nok. It felt completely wrong that Sean's life had ended on Sunrise Beach, a place where dawn began. We'd never even made it to the other side of the island's narrow peninsula, to Haad Rin Nai, to watch the sun set.

The next morning, I bought a ticket to the Akvarij Dubrovnik, a small dimly lit aquarium tucked away in one of the medieval forts within the city walls. It seemed like a manageable first step if I was ever going to try to confront the ocean.

Inside, the fort's limestone ceiling arched high above me, the brick walls and floor were worn smooth, and the air confined within felt damp and cool. I was the only visitor, and once I'd bought my ticket, I never saw another staff member. In the empty space, the bubbling sounds of water filtration systems reverberated off the blocks of stone.

I peered into the pools of frowning grouper and circling amberjacks. The gaping moray eels had always been one of my favorites, ever since I'd gotten to know a couple of friendly California morays while learning to scuba dive in the cold rocky reefs off La Jolla Cove in San Diego. But these were territorial solitary creatures, and there were far too many of them crowded into one tank at the aquarium in Dubrovnik.

Moving on to the tank with the common octopus, I thought back to the summer I'd spent at the Bodega Bay Marine Lab. Ripley, a giant Pacific octopus, had been brought into the lab after being caught in a crab trap. She weighed over forty pounds, had an arm span of almost fifteen feet, and was considerably stronger than I was.

As I'd studied Ripley's learning behavior that summer, she began to recognize me. When I walked into the room, she would crawl up to the trapdoor at the top of her huge tank and reach out a tentacle, her suckers sticking and gripping and tasting the length of my arm.

In turn, I began to recognize her moods and corresponding colors and textures. Her skin turned white and rippled when she was frightened, red and spiky when she was angry or frustrated, and she flushed a deep smooth purple when she was content, usually after a meal. I used to watch what I swore was dreaming—wedged into a corner with her eyes narrowed into slits, her eight arms piled into loose coils around her body as she pulsed from pink to camouflage to brown. After we released her back into the ocean, I was never able to stomach the sight of the scalloped purple tentacles of a *tako* sushi roll again.

In Dubrovnik, the wan, washed-out octopus might have been a different color in a bigger tank with more hiding places. But it was the sallow-green loggerhead turtle that really broke my heart that day. This was an animal known to travel eight thousand miles across the entire North Atlantic Ocean, yet here it had been stuck in a tiny cement pool since 1953.

There was a faint smell of rust and decay, and I wasn't sure whether it was coming from the turtle's tank or her own shell. She should have been migrating across ocean basins, hunting flying fish, squid, and even jellyfish. In almost fifty years in the wild, she might have laid more than ten thousand eggs, spawned three generations of endangered hatchlings. Instead, she would continue to be trapped in that dark tank, surrounded by only a few algae-encrusted rocks and tossed coins, for another nine years, until her death in 2011.

Of course there was no way of knowing this when I visited in 2002. All I knew was that I couldn't bear to watch as she swam head-on straight into the concrete side of her pool over and over and over again. I continued to hear the dull underwater thuds long after I walked away.

• • •

With a knot in my chest, I finally went to the last wall of tanks. Lying on the pebbled bottom close to the glass, there was a large ugly mottled brown lump.

It was a poisonous scorpionfish, and it was the first and only venomous creature I'd seen that day. It lay motionless. Its mouth was dropped open, its spines slack, and a few loose white scales hung from its skin. I bent my face down, and inches away, one dull black eye rolled back.

I was surprised to feel no animosity or anger, separated from its toxic spines by only a thick pane of glass. Yet I didn't stay looking at it for long. And as I neared the exit, I felt nothing but immense relief that there hadn't been any jellyfish.

Then I found I wasn't quite ready to leave. I could still hear that poor turtle banging her head against the side of her tank, the deadened sounds echoing across the empty building. I went back one more time and leaned out over the murky water.

"Jesus." I resisted the urge to reach out to her. "God. I am so, so sorry."

After the darkness in the aquarium, I stood for a while, blinking back the tears on the streets of the Old Town. Winter sunlight reflected off the cobbled lanes and the sides of the nearby houses, cathedral, and palace, all the buildings cut from the same creamy-white stone.

It was hard to believe that eleven years ago, these same streets had been under siege, the city itself an early casualty of the Yugoslav Wars. The wars—a series of ethnic battles caused by the breakup of Yugoslavia— lasted more than a decade and took more than 140,000 lives, making it Europe's deadliest conflict since World War II. It first raged across Croatia and Slovenia, then Bosnia and Kosovo, only ending in Serbia and Montenegro a year prior.

The only sign of the months of bombardment in Dubrovnik were the newer, slightly mismatched, slightly brighter roof tiles—creating a patchwork of red when viewed from on top of the city walls. That, and the small plaques posted at the city gates documenting the destruction. These plaques told the story in five languages, showing the roofs damaged by direct impact and by shrapnel, the direct impacts to the pavement, and the buildings burned by fire. The plaques' map of the Old Town was covered in corresponding black and white triangles, black circles, and red squares. The ground right where I stood had been hit and the cathedral in front of me bombed twice.

Reconstruction efforts had begun even as the shelling continued. By the time I visited, the historic walled city had been practically restored.

Just across the rugged Dinaric Alps, immaculate Dubrovnik couldn't have felt more different from the graffiti, rubble, and red resin roses of Sarajevo.

Time and resources were certainly factors. The siege in Croatia had ended just as the long siege of Bosnia's capital was beginning. It had lasted almost eight months instead of nearly four years. The repairs in Dubrovnik's Old Town, a World Heritage Site, had followed UNESCO guidelines. And there were sure to be many more complicated and varied issues I would never begin to understand.

But it was as if Dubrovnik's inhabitants had had the ability and the means to make a conscious decision. They'd match the red tiles of their broken roofs as closely as they could, rebuild, and try to move forward. It was astonishing, even a little discombobulating, to see such a perfect example of the shattered pieces of a city put back together again.

As I walked that afternoon along the Placa or Stradun, the main pedestrian promenade in Dubrovnik's Old Town, the shiny polished stones felt slippery beneath my feet. I turned toward the clock tower in the sun at one end of the street, and then toward the huge brick-domed Onofrio Fountain in the shade at the other.

As ridiculous as it sounded, I knew part of what I'd really been doing in Eastern Europe was looking for Sean. I'd half-expected to see him around every corner, that he'd take a seat on the empty barstool beside me and order a Jack and Coke. I knew it was crazy, but I caught myself scanning visitors' books looking for his name, checking the hometowns for someone from Essendon. As if I only had to travel long enough, go somewhere far enough away, and I'd find him. As if I would look up and he'd be right there in front of me, checking his Hotmail account in some dusty long-forgotten Internet café. Or eating a hot chili salami slice in a pizza joint in the middle of nowhere. That as long as I kept moving, kept chasing him, we would meet again. And it would be just like that night on January 31st in 1999, at that cheap hostel off Plaça Sant Miquel in Barcelona. And we could start all over.

"Shannon!"

I jumped and looked up to see Roberto and Guadalupe, the older couple I'd met in Plitvice, waving and smiling to me from across Dubrovnik's Placa. Crossing over, Guadalupe tucked a dark brown wisp behind her ear and took my arm.

"*¡Buenos días!* We were hoping to see you here. Please tell me you have decided not to go to Bosnia."

"I already went. I just got back. It was . . ." I couldn't think of how to even begin to describe Sarajevo in a word or two.

"*Ay ay ay*, Shannon. So. We'll buy you a cappuccino and a cake and you tell us all about it. *Vámonos.*" Taller than both of us by at least a foot, Roberto began to steer Guadalupe and me by the shoulders toward a nearby café.

Roberto was from Argentina and worked as a translator, and Guadalupe was from Mexico, so we spoke in a combination of English and Spanish.

Last week we'd been strangers, standing together on the side of the road outside Hotel Jezero in the Plitvička Jezera National Park. The hotel staff had said a bus to Split would come at 2:30 p.m., and another at five thirty. Sometime after three, a bus marked *Turistički* had slowed to flash its headlights but refused to stop. By the time a bus with a sign to Split pulled over at four, I'd told Roberto and Guadalupe about Sean.

They'd insisted on paying for my bus ticket and buying me dinner at a rest stop along the way. They'd even wanted to get me a cab to my hotel in Split, but it was easier to decline since I hadn't figured out where I was going to stay.

I'd run into them a couple of times in Split. We'd always stopped for a coffee or a chat, and they continued to fuss and fret over me. Running into each other again in Dubrovnik, we caught up at the café and then spent hours wandering and exploring the Old Town together. As the cooler evening approached, we decided to head for a pizza and beer at Mea Culpa. But first, Guadalupe wanted to check out one last church, Crkva Sveti Vlaho, or the Church of St. Blaise.

We climbed the wide, weather-worn steps and entered the Baroque eighteenth-century church. According to the plaques posted at the city gates, St. Blaise's had been shelled five times during the siege. Yet even though I was looking for it, I still couldn't see any evidence of Croatia's recent devastation.

Inside, white stone columns stretched above the glossy tile floor. At the front of the church, the ornate altar was surrounded by gilt-framed oil paintings, marble statues, and a towering gold organ.

Guadalupe made the sign of the cross and took a seat on one of the red-cushioned wooden pews. She dipped her head, closed her brown eyes, and folded her hands. As Roberto ducked into the alcoves to take photos, I made my way toward the table of prayer candles off to one side. Slipping a few coins into the slot of the metal collection box, I selected the longest yellow candle I could find.

In the company of other people, it was harder to imagine I might look up and find Sean in the gilded corner of some ancient church. Just as his smell was beginning to fade from his old T-shirts, it seemed as if he were starting to fade as well. Although I still spoke to him often, I couldn't feel him as strongly or hear him as clearly. In many ways, it felt as if I were losing him all over again.

I dipped the wick of my candle into the nearby flame of another, told Sean I loved him, and made a new wish. Instead of looking back, I tried to look forward. But wherever Sean was—still wandering the earth, up in heaven, or stuck somewhere in between—I wanted us to be able to move forward together. So all I asked that evening was that both of us would learn to accept his death at the same time.

Since I had to travel around Yugoslavia to get to Romania, the next day I decided to take the ferry back up to Split, before hopping on a bus to Zagreb and then taking a train to Budapest and then another across the border. It was a ludicrous journey, with many opportunities for mistakes and delays, but I couldn't see any other way to get to where I wanted to be.

The last time I'd taken a ferry had been in Thailand. Sean and I had ridden together on our way to Ko Pha Ngan. I remembered the blistering heat and the exhaust fumes as we sat on deck in the sun—drinking warm beer, eating strange shrimp-flavored potato chips, playing cards, and laughing. Thinking we were going to paradise. One week later, I rode the same ferry back to the mainland alone.

The Jadrolinija ferry waiting at the concrete wharf in Dubrovnik was far bigger and more modern than the rusting, sputtering bucket we'd taken to Ko Pha Ngan. Cinching the belt of my old green backpack tighter around my hips and adjusting the weight on my shoulders, I tried to take a deep breath. Then I boarded and found an empty seat by the window.

As the ferry pulled away, I leaned my forehead against the glass and watched the changing scenery. In the warm, early-morning sunshine, clouds tracked across the blue sky and jagged cliffs plunged into the sea. The colors of the Dalmatian coast seemed about to pop: the white stone walls wrapped around red pointed roofs, hillsides dotted with green clusters of orange groves and yellowed rows of vineyards, rocky islets, leafy islands, and the ocean itself a shocking turquoise.

Maybe it was the surprising shade of the water. Maybe it helped that it was a different ocean. A different ocean than the one I'd first fallen in love with twenty years ago, and a different ocean than had taken the one I loved three and a half months earlier. It was still hard for me. I was nowhere near being ready to touch the water, and I wondered if the sea would ever remind me of Sean, instead of reminding me of Sean's death. But that morning, I couldn't take my eyes off the ocean.

For hours, I stared out the window, my shamrock-green journal lying open in my lap, a pen loose in my fingers. The water churned white along the ship's sides, but was so clear farther out I could see all the way down to the sandy bottom. There were dark blue shadows in the depths, and it was difficult to tell if they were rocky reefs or just the reflections of clouds in the water. And there was a moment—the aqua Adriatic Sea stretched out before me—when I realized that the ocean could be beautiful again.

Before, I would have been out on deck. Breathing in the ocean spray, bracing against the wind, and searching the surface for the dorsal fins and blows of bottlenose dolphins, common dolphins, striped dolphins, and Risso's dolphins. Maybe even hoping to spot a fin whale.

Instead, I curled up in my seat and settled in for the nine-hour crossing to Split. Sea salt spattered against the windowpane, and I was closer to the ocean than I'd been since Thailand. For just right then, that felt close enough.

thirty-three

Xī'ān, Shǎnxī, CHINA

July 2002

S EAN AND I are chatting with a young university student on a train. It's sweltering, but she's focused on us. Thick black braids hang down her back as she perches on the edge of her seat. We exchange pleasantries, and then she points to Sean's nose and says in a serious tone, "Big nose."

"Yes." Sean winks a blue eye and his answer makes her smile. "To keep my glasses on."

The student tells us she can see that we will be very happy together. And that I am just like a funny chicken. I have no idea what she means by this, but she is insistent on both points.

When we arrive in sunbaked Xī'ān, we spend the first day, as usual, trying to sort out our train tickets to leave. We ask first at the train station, though by this stage we already know what their reply will be. Our destination is sold out for weeks and there is nothing they can do.

We begin to make the rounds, visiting the various travel agencies in the city. We linger in the ones with functioning air conditioning, gulping down cold water from their coolers. We know eventually we'll find a travel agent who will give us a wink and a sly grin. "I can get you tickets. No problem. For a small fee. I have a friend." But no one will tell us which shop to go to or where this friend is.

Sean insists we book our ongoing journey before exploring the city or visiting the Bīngmǎ Yǒng, or Terracotta Warriors. Instead of one day, it takes us two. One young man behind a counter tells us there are no train tickets, but he can get us a good price on an apartment. Of course, he has a friend.

"Not to worry, is very nice apartment. But both you can never, ever leave. You will have to live here in Xi'ān." A gap-toothed grin spreads across the young man's face, and he reaches over to pat my hand. "You live here together. Forever."

Moa Bergman from Sweden, age 11.
April 3, 2008. Ko Lanta.

On April 3, 2008, around 10 am, an 11-year-old Swedish female died after being stung by jellyfish on Klong Dao Beach, Koh Lanta. She and three other girls (similar ages) were paddling and playing in water 1m deep, about 20m from the beach. The girls screamed, attracting the attention of hotel staff, who ran into the water to assist. The girl was pulled from the water but was blue and pulseless some 4 minutes postenvenomation despite CPR and application of vinegar and a locally obtained salve.[5]

thirty-four

Suceava, Moldova, ROMANIA

November 2002

"WHY?" the guards on the train asked when they checked my passport at the border. "Why you want to come to Romania?"

It had already been an incredibly long journey. The train carriage was filled with cigarette smoke and stiflingly hot. Despite the fact that, when no one was looking, I'd pulled the thermostat lever as hard as I could to the left, from the red-filled thermometer to the thermometer with only a thin blue line. I couldn't stop sweating. The locals didn't seem to notice the heat. Many of them hadn't even removed their scarves, gloves, or shabby winter coats.

I regretted getting a window seat, which was always next to the heater. There was nothing to see anyway, since the Crişana countryside had turned pitch-black hours ago. I'd been cramped now in ferry seats, bus seats, and train seats for almost two days.

So when the guards asked why I had come, I didn't have an easy answer. I'd hardly planned any part of this trip. My guidebook had tempted me with its introduction: *In a country where mass tourism means you, a horse and cart and a handful of farmers, Romania is the Wild West of Eastern Europe.* So I told them that I'd come to see the medieval villages and the wild landscapes. The guards looked at me. Then they bent down to look out the blackened train windows, shook their heads, and snorted with laughter.

I also didn't have an easy answer when a girl about my age asked what I was reading on the train. I'd bought Jared Diamond's *Guns, Germs, and Steel: The Fates of Human Societies* back in Poland. The selection of English-language books had been limited, and after I'd burned through the four *Harry Potter*s, it was increasingly difficult to find books without love or near-death. Besides, I'd figured *Guns, Germs, and Steel*, at 539 densely typed pages, would last me a while.

"Um, it's about why some countries and cultures succeed while others fail."

"Mmm," the girl replied, twisting a lock of black hair around one finger. I had no idea if she'd understood a word I'd said. But then she leaned forward in her seat, and her dark brown eyes focused on my face.

"So like the USA and Romania. You are from the USA, no?"

At that moment, a couple of scrawny young men rejoined our carriage. They greeted the girl, who then explained to me that the men had hitch-hiked across the border to avoid paying the international supplement.

It turned out that Andrea was fluent not only in English and Romanian, but also in Hungarian, French, and German. After working as a nanny in France and Germany, she'd just managed to get a five-year working visa in the United States, where she was going to waitress on a cruise ship out of Miami. She was excited and nervous about moving to the other side of the world, and I told her a little about my plans to move to Melbourne.

"So lucky," she said. "For you to live in the USA *and* Australia. Two beautiful places where most of the world wants to live and never gets to."

I knew she was right. I knew I needed to hear things like this right now.

And I was lucky that night, despite arriving into icy Cluj-Napoca alone at midnight without a reservation or a single Romanian leu. The train station seemed surprisingly safe at that hour, with plenty of people around—one girl even asked if I needed any help, and the hotel across the road was open. It had been forty-one hours since I boarded the ferry back in sunny Dubrovnik. A chilly single room, a tepid shower, a lumpy bed, and breakfast the next morning felt like godsends. And as I brushed my teeth and watched the news—China was using genetic engineering to try to save the giant panda—I was grateful when Israel wasn't mentioned.

I didn't stay in Cluj long. Breakfast ended up being four pink hot dogs, dry bread, and tea with so much sugar it set my teeth on edge. The city streets surrounding the hotel were industrial and polluted. By the time I finally found an ATM, and had crammed a bricklike wad of nine million lei into my wallet, I was ready to leave. I thought I'd head to Suceava, in the Carpathian Mountains of the northeast, to see the countryside and the *exotic painted Orthodox monasteries of Moldavia*.

In the freezing cold light of day, the train station at Cluj looked ragged and run-down. The entrance was crowded with starving stray dogs and beggars: shriveled old men limping on twisted feet and Roma women with dirty faces and tangled black hair clutching tiny babies to their breasts.

None of the station platforms were marked, and I couldn't find a single clock. I missed the first train because I hadn't realized Romania was one hour ahead. So for the second train, I dug the pink alarm clock from China out of the bottom of my pack. It would have been easier to wear a watch, but I was still wearing the same jewelry I'd had on when Sean died, the same simple silver rings and earrings. I hadn't been wearing a watch that night. Besides, I couldn't stand to be so constantly aware of time passing without him.

Pink alarm clock in hand, I counted out the station platforms and hoped for the best. I kept trying to check my ticket, but couldn't make much sense of the tiny brown cardboard stub. When a train finally rattled to a stop in front of me, I climbed on board. The racks above the seats were so high, I had to aim and throw my pack into the air.

The train creaked back out of the station and it wasn't long before we'd left the grit and grime of the city behind. We passed knotted woodlands and forests of fir trees such a deep green they were almost black. In the shadows of snow-covered mountains, horse-drawn carts began to out-number the cars—the wooden wagons filled with hay, women wearing kerchiefs on their heads, and men in their mustaches and tall furry hats.

When the train conductor came by to check my ticket, and without a word punched a small hole through the cardboard, I began to relax. Ever since Sean died, I always had this nagging worry I might not be where I was supposed to be. Scared I was in the wrong seat, on the wrong train, heading to the wrong place.

Arriving into Suceava, seven hours later and well after dark, I found myself wondering again if I was in the right place. The train station was nowhere near where my guidebook map indicated, and there was no sign of either the ticket kiosk or the trolleybuses that were supposed to help me *easily reach* the city center.

Instead, I grabbed a *caşcarabeta* or maxi-taxi (a kind of shared mini-bus) for five thousand lei (about fifteen US cents) and found a room at the Hotel Gloria for 370,000 lei (about eleven US dollars). I briefly considered searching out a cheaper room or a restaurant for dinner or even checking email or seeing a movie, decided against it, and then slept for thirteen hours.

The next day was bright and bitterly cold. I pulled on a thermal top and bottoms, followed by a grubby shirt and jeans, my turtleneck, sweater, wool-lined jacket, beanie, scarf, and gloves.

Outside, massive concrete buildings scraped against the faded blue sky. The stink of sulfur hung in the air. Stepping around a gaping hole in the sidewalk and turning a corner, I realized the smell was coming from a paper mill. The rusting compound of brick and steel stood at the edge of the city, white smoke pouring from its giant factory stacks.

Most of Suceava's buildings were in various stages of disrepair. A number of inhabited apartment blocks looked more like abandoned construction sites. Many of the residents also seemed to be in a state of disintegration. There were people with frostbite, goiters, crossed eyes, and cleft palates.

Romania's megalomaniac president Nicolae Ceauşescu's twenty-five-year reign had ended with the 1989 revolution and his own execution, but the country was still on a long path to recovery. Thirteen years later, annual inflation was 24 percent, the average yearly salary was less than a thousand US dollars, and more than 30 percent of the population lived well below the poverty line.

Withered gardens took up the corner plots, alleys, balconies, and windowsills. Scattered patches of earth crowded with the brown-edged vines of tomatoes, potatoes, and pumpkins. I could hear chickens clucking from the few cramped backyards.

I'd been wandering for some time when it occurred to me that I hadn't seen a single restaurant. With that, I realized it had been about twenty-four hours since I'd last eaten. I was immediately starving.

I pulled out my *Lonely Planet* and looked up Places to Eat. The guide conceded that dining options in the city were *rather limited*. It suggested the chicken *kievskaia* at the nearby Restaurant Suceava. But when I arrived at the address, it was yet another Communist Bloc–era apartment complex, with no indication anything else had ever been there. The only other restaurant listed was Country Pizza, outside the city center.

With my guidebook open to the glossary at the back, I approached a thin man with dark hooded eyes and a long worn coat. *"Scuzaţi-mă,"* I started, reading from the page. *"Unde este . . ."*

It seemed a bad sign that the Romanian translation for "restaurant" wasn't included. So I tried in Spanish: *"¿ . . . restaurante?"* and motioned a forkful of food to my mouth.

The man's black-olive eyes widened for a second, before he broke into a grin. *"Da, da."* He turned around and pointed: *"Drept înainte."* I didn't have a clue what he'd said and couldn't see anything resembling a restaurant. But he gestured for me to walk with him, back in the direction he'd come from, *"Vă rog."*

I checked the page again for the word for "thank you." *"Mulțumesc,"* I tried, tripping over the brittle foreignness of the diacritical mark.

We started across Suceava's main square, Piaţa 22 Decembrie. Hundreds of brown dirty windows looked down onto the bedraggled trees and hedges. As we walked, the man glanced sideways and caught my eye. He made a large sweeping motion, taking in our cement surroundings.

"Romania bun?" He held both his thumbs up in front of his chest and smiled broadly. *"Sau . . . rău?"* He spun his thumbs down to the ground and stuck out his lower lip in an overstated pout.

"Bun, bun." I smiled back with both thumbs up. We paused at the edge of the square and I saw it.

"Un restaurant bun." He beamed and pointed. *"Cam scump."* He rubbed his thumb against his forefingers, before patting down his pockets.

"Mulțumesc," I tried again, placing my hand on my chest. Then I turned and walked into the McDonald's.

After lunch, a Big Mac meal number two, I arranged for a tour of Moldavia's painted monasteries. During the 1500s, in an attempt to educate the illiterate peasants, the walls of these Eastern Orthodox churches were covered with colorful paintings depicting biblical stories.

Five centuries later, at the Bucovina Estur travel agency, the receptionist and I attempted our own communication using drawings and scribbles. When pen and paper didn't work, we resorted to pantomimes and the few phrases I could pretend to say in Romanian, though the words always came out sounding more Spanish and less Slavic than I intended.

My driver for the afternoon was in his early forties. He was tall and lean, with dark circles under his eyes. He nodded to me, we climbed into his boxy old car, and he lit up a cigarette and turned up the heat.

We drove in a comfortable silence through the foothills of the Car-

pathian Mountains. Farms with mud-packed houses and cottages with
dull tin roofs were surrounded by dense forests. The journey was bumpy
and slow as the driver maneuvered around frozen ruts and puddles,
donkey-led wagons, plows pulled by bony-hipped oxen, and indecisive
flocks of sheep.

At the first monastery, Mănăstirea Humor, the driver pulled up onto
an empty patch of gravel. He lit another cigarette, reclined his seat back,
and motioned for me to go on ahead.

The wintry mountain air stung my face as I climbed out of the car. It
reminded me of scuba diving through a thermocline—how I'd feel the
sudden drop in temperature on my face and any other exposed skin as I
descended and hit the layer of cold, deep water. The cold water, denser
than warm water, sinks far below the surface mixed by wind and waves.
There's less light, less oxygen, and less life below the thermocline, so there's
also a sudden increase in water clarity. Sometimes the demarcation would
be so distinct, I could see the edges of the thermocline below me, like
wrinkled glass, before plunging into the clear cold void.

Back in the Romanian mountains, I zipped up my jacket and pulled
on my hat and gloves. I could smell woodsmoke and wet straw, and felt
the chill pull down into my lungs.

I spent the next few hours in the quiet and the cold, standing in
front of vibrantly painted scenes of martyrdom, the Siege of Constan-
tinople, the Parable of the Prodigal Son, the Last Supper, and the Last
Judgment. Winged angels rolled up the signs of the zodiac to signify
the end of time, and the sins of mankind were weighed on an oversized
scale. The believers' heads were all encased in large halos, burnished gold
circles that reminded me of old-fashioned scuba-diving helmets. While
the nonbelievers, mostly wearing Turkish-style turbans, were swept away
in a river the color of dried blood.

Many of the walls were covered in rich gory detail. Black bears and
yellow lions clutched ragged pink hands and legs in their teeth as the
graves gave up their dead for resurrection. Yet other walls had been completely eroded, the flecks of paint and color worn down to bare stone with
only the ghostly outlines of figures to suggest what had once been there.

I wandered the monasteries alone that late November afternoon, the solitary visitor. At Humor, a lone elderly nun had approached. Bringing her right hand to her temple, she'd mimicked a camera shutter and pointed to a handwritten sign: *Fotografii—5000 lei.* I'd smiled, shaken my head, and spread my empty hands. But she'd followed on my heels, leaning forward every time I made a move toward my daypack.

Then at Mănăstirea Voroneţ, a young nun in full habit padded up behind me and motioned for me to follow her into the church. In the dim light, surrounded by carved wooden statues, Cyrillic inscriptions, crucifixes, and candelabras, the nun beckoned me over with a crook of her finger. Her white face stared into mine, and she clasped her hands to her chest before opening her palms out to me. She repeated this gesture a couple of times, and then reached behind her back and brought out a giant, lime-green stuffed turtle.

"No, no. I mean . . . *nu, nu.*" I shook my head and tried to refuse as she pressed the soft toy into my hands. I was wondering how old she thought I was, when I noticed the glint in her eyes and the new pink flush in her cheeks. She could hardly have been a teenager.

She glanced over her shoulder at the church door, and pointed to my daypack. I slid the bag down my arm, and before I could object, she'd unzipped it and stuffed the turtle inside. It was the size of a small beach ball and not an easy fit. Her fingers fumbled as she quickly rezipped the pack. Then, her grin stretching to the sides of her black wimple, she winked, brought her index finger to her lips, and widened her eyes.

The young nun didn't say one word my entire visit. She didn't know my name, where I was from, or a single thing about me. Yet when I was ready to leave, she raised her finger again to her lips, linked her arm through mine, and walked with me in the cold to the edge of the monastery.

It seemed important to find the turtle a home. On our way back to Suceava, I tried to give my driver first a tip and then the turtle. He wouldn't take either, gesturing that his children were too big. So I started asking if anyone had kids at Hotel Gloria and at the Assist Internet Café. Since I didn't know the Romanian for "child," I tried rocking an imaginary infant in my arms. Finally, back at the Bucovina Estur office, I found a new father who was happy to take the toy.

Then I felt I could go. The next day, Thursday, November 28th, was Thanksgiving. And although I had no intention of celebrating, I thought I'd spend it taking a train to either Braşov or Sighişoara in Transylvania, instead of spending it at McDonald's.

I was at least thankful Sean hadn't celebrated the holiday. I'd been planning on introducing him to our family's traditions: my aunt Mayhill's sweet squash rolls and caramelized candied yams, Aunt Chris's rich pumpkin pie, and my mum's tart apple one. Local wines from Napa and Sonoma, and whichever cousins were currently in California all laughing and teasing each other around the large wooden table at my uncle Jim's house on the hill in Oakland.

Now it was just one in a long line of dates and holidays to dread. Soon it would be December 9th and the four-month anniversary of his death, then Christmas, New Year's, Valentine's, my twenty-ninth birthday in March, the baby's due date in April . . . Compared with these, avoiding Thanksgiving in Transylvania would be easy.

When I woke the next morning, the early light was still a stony gray. I packed my bag and grabbed a *caşcarabeta* back to the train station.

"Gara Suceava Nord." The other passengers looked up as soon as I spoke to the driver.

I took a seat behind two men with matching bad teeth and tall fur hats. A ruddy-cheeked woman wrapped in a ragged coat leaned across the aisle and patted my thigh. Smiling, she held up her hand with three knobby fingers pointing up and her thumb folded into her palm. But since most of her index finger was missing, the stub pinched off at the first knuckle like a sausage casing, I wasn't sure if she was trying to tell me three stops or four.

When we got to the next stop, the two men twisted around in their seats. They shook their heads, and one of them held up his hands with his palms flat. They did this at every stop while the woman counted down on her fingers, nodding to me each time.

"*Trei.*" "*Doi.*" "*Unu.*" When we reached the train station, they all turned to grin.

"*Noroc!*" one of the men called out as I grabbed my pack and stepped onto the street. I turned around, and he brought both his thumbs up to the window.

Bolstered, I approached the ticket office and raised one finger. "*Unu.* Braşov."

But the man behind the counter only shrugged his shoulders and looked at me with his black eyebrows knitted together. "*Nu înţeleg.*"

I had no idea what he'd said and didn't know what I'd said wrong. Romanian had just enough similarities to Spanish, Italian, and French to give me a false confidence. Yet with a harsher, slightly stilted Eastern European edge, it lacked the familiar rhythm and seduction of the other tongues. A Latin language without the romance.

With that, the gaunt old man behind in line pushed past me and stepped up to the ticket counter. Although this happened many times on my trip, I hadn't figured out an appropriate response. Locals seemed to ignore anyone who cut ahead, except I still needed a ticket. But before I could push back, protest, laugh, or cry, the man turned to me.

"Braşov, *da?*"

I nodded, and he turned back to the counter. Within seconds, he'd plucked the correct change from my palm and produced a tiny cardboard stub to Braşov.

Thanking him, I set out to buy my Thanksgiving Day provisions for the journey ahead. The market stall next to the station sold only pumpkin seeds, paper cones of paprika, and spiky tangles of nettles. At nearby Non-Stop, I picked up water, a wrinkled apple, an ancient-looking bag of chips, stale bread, and the ubiquitous Vaca Care Râde cheese, adding Romanian to the list of languages in which I could now say "Laughing Cow."

It occurred to me how empty the couple of shops I'd visited had been. I thought of the dark, desperate gardens crammed onto Suceava's balconies and windowsills, the old-fashioned plows pulled by bony oxen in the countryside, and the almost total lack of restaurants throughout the city. The few customers at McDonald's were the best-dressed Romanians I'd seen.

The patches of ground where they tried to grow their own food were frozen solid, yet the people were some of the warmest and friendliest I'd ever met. In all my travels, Romania was the first place anyone had taken the time to walk with me to show me the way.

Andrea, the girl I'd spoken with on the train into Cluj, had been right. Here, I was one of the lucky ones. If for no other reason, than the fact that I could leave.

Carina Lofgren from Sweden, age 45.
February 3, 2010. Langkawi.

A 45-year-old Swedish female tourist died after being stung by a jellyfish while taking an evening swim off a beach in Langkawi. She suddenly shrieked with pain and became unconscious within seconds. Lesions, reportedly consistent with a chirodropid sting, were visible on her legs. She was immediately taken ashore, where cardiopulmonary resuscitation (CPR) was commenced. Her husband reported that an ambulance arrived 15 minutes later and the paramedics confirmed that she had been stung by a jellyfish.[6]

thirty-five

Haad Rin, Ko Pha Ngan, THAILAND

August 12, 2002

I T FELT AS if I would never be able leave Ko Pha Ngan. Sean had been dead for three days, and still the authorities refused to release his body.

Almost everything I heard, I heard through Anat and Talia. The hotel manager told them that the Thai prince was visiting, and the police couldn't spare an officer to finish the paperwork. Locals warned them that after seven days, the temple would cremate his body and there would be nothing we could do to stop it.

This bothered the girls. Judaism required a prompt burial, usually within twenty-four hours, and for the body to be buried whole.

Although Sean had told me he didn't want to be buried, his father had already begun arrangements for the family plot in Melbourne. Where and when he'd be buried seemed totally out of my control, but I did feel I needed to bring Sean's body back whole. I couldn't hand him in ashes to his parents, return their twenty-five-year-old son to them in a jar.

Only the August days were hot and sticky, and it was hard not to wonder what kind of state he would be in by the time I did finally manage to get him home.

"When is Sean's family coming?" Anat and Talia asked every day. "If fiancé means nothing to these police, they will at least have to listen to his parents."

But I didn't expect Sean's parents to come to Ko Pha Ngan. I knew Keith couldn't leave Audrey, who had completely collapsed. So when we spoke on the phone, his family had never offered and I never asked. Besides, it would take Sean's parents days to reach us—long enough that we would both be long gone before they arrived. The police could let us go at any time. Each day we spent on the island could be our last.

My own parents were increasingly anxious to join me. I told them over and over not to come. As official family, the Reillys could at least attempt to get Sean's body released sooner, or maybe prevent the autopsy ordered in Bangkok. "Honestly, Mum," I told her on the phone. "What can you possibly do here that will make this even a tiny bit better?"

I knew my parents wanted to try to take care of me, but I couldn't chance having to take care of them. Neither of them was totally comfortable traveling abroad, and neither of them had ever been to Thailand. The last time I'd traveled with my dad in New Zealand, he'd been uneasy, uptight, and unhappy. And although my mum hadn't batted an eyelid at insect-infested showers, hot dirty bus rides, or even aggressive monkeys during our trip the year before to Malaysia and Borneo, I'd been the one to handle all the planning, money, accommodation, and transport. At the moment, I was barely able to take care of myself and Sean's body. I just wasn't capable of anything more.

After another morning of phone calls and faxes in Haad Rin town, I stopped by the lobby of the Seaview Haadrin to see if there was any news from Bangkok, the Australian consulate, or the local police. I was avoiding the Internet, since I knew there was an unread email from Sean waiting in my inbox. Seeing it there in bold (*hey sexy*), reading his last message for the first time (*havent seen you for a while*), the lines he'd typed as I'd danced for him outside the shop window (*maybe if you are free*) would make it feel as if he were still alive (*we can have dinner sometime*), as if he were still trying to communicate with me (*i love you. sean*). Besides, his words were sure to be silly and flippant. So instead I stood, waiting and crying by the empty counter at reception.

"Hey, love, are you okay?" I recognized the languid drawl of an Australian accent and looked up. A young man with blue eyes and dark stubble was standing next to me at the counter.

I shook my head. "No."

The guy blinked a couple of times and took half a step backward, knocking his elbow against a stack of glossy brochures behind him. He stared at me for another second or so, before spinning on his heel and walking away.

He was the first Westerner to speak to me on the island since the Canadian couple had given me their flashlight the night Sean died. I turned back to the empty counter, but then changed my mind and decided to give up as well.

As I made my way through the adjoining restaurant, I caught the whispers that followed in my footsteps.

"Shhh! That's her."

"He was only twenty-five."

"I got stung a couple years ago in Hawaii and it fuckin' hurt like hell."

"Just overly sensitive."

"Why on earth would you be in the water if you were allergic?"

"I heard they'd only just met."

"Sooooooo sad."

For three days, I'd felt their eyes on my back. For three days, I'd heard their hushed voices. The whispers I understood, the ones in English, came in all the familiar accents: Aussies, Kiwis, Brits, Irish, South Africans, Canadians, and fellow Americans.

Inside my single cabana, I sank down onto the floor. Even on the other side of the locked door, I could still feel the crowd from that night around us on the beach. Pressing against my back, their feet shuffling closer on the damp sand, jostling and standing over him and watching. Again and again, I saw the tall thin girl walking along the water's edge, stopping twice to look down at his body, before turning and walking away.

I could still hear the sounds of the ocean, still hear their voices from that night. The British, North American, Israeli, and Thai inflections. The rough edges of their English words.

"It'll be okay."

"He drowned. Has water in his lungs. Turn him upside down."

"You're counting wrong. It's fifteen compressions to two breaths."

"He's choking. Turn him upside down. Empty his airways."

"His face was in the water. He has water in his lungs."

"Turn him upside down."

After Sean was loaded into the back of the truck, after Anat and Talia followed on foot to the clinic, they'd all stayed behind on the beach. Maybe talking about what they'd seen, before drifting apart in groups of two or four to drink, to eat, to dance, to smoke.

Would Sean and I have been any different? If it had been someone else who had been stung that night, what would we have done? As much as I hated to admit it, I knew we would not have behaved in the same way as Anat and Talia. I wanted to think that at least we would have tried, as the Canadian couple did with the flashlight. But when our offer of help was declined, we also probably would have walked away.

And as much as I appreciated the gesture, really what good was a flashlight? What could any of the other backpackers on Ko Pha Ngan have possibly done to help? I didn't want to sit and talk with them, go out for a meal or a beer. If someone had said they were sorry, asked if there was anything they could do, I would have said no and meant it.

Anat and Talia had never given me a choice. Even when I tried to politely refuse their help, they hadn't listened. They'd hardly left me alone since they'd pushed their way through that glass door and into the clinic, while everyone else had waited outside. Later that afternoon, when I left my cabana again, the girls were already walking up the sandy path between the palm trees toward me.

"Oh, Shannon. It is good to find you. You can go. Finally they said okay. Finally, they let you and Sean leave."

"Really?" My shoulders dropped. I felt something inside my chest unwind just a little.

"Yes. Already a driver is coming for Sean."

"When?"

"Maybe this afternoon. Probably this evening."

"Thank God."

"Yes," Talia agreed. "Now they cannot burn him. You can take Sean's body home. His parents can bury him whole."

"And it is good for you to leave this place. Because, Shannon . . ." Anat glanced at Talia. "There has been another person stung. Another girl. Now there are three."

Whatever had relaxed inside my chest recoiled. "Oh my God. She died?"

They both nodded. "This girl on the legs. Like Sean."

I felt a cold weight sink into my stomach. My skin became taut. "You guys need to leave too."

"We will. After you go."

"Yes, as soon as you leave," Talia said, blowing cigarette smoke over her shoulder. "And we don't swim in the water after Sean. These back-packers know and still swimming are crazy. Me, I never see the locals in the ocean."

The three of us then walked together into Haad Rin town. I spent my last afternoon on the island in the cramped AA Travel office making phone calls: to both our families, to his insurance, and to Warren Johnson, the Australian consul in Bangkok. The pretty, open-faced girl behind the travel agency desk was the first to try to explain to me that death was not such a big deal in Thailand.

"When you die, you die," she said, spinning a pencil between her fingers. The girl said that her husband had infected her with HIV after sleeping with prostitutes. When she'd told her mother and asked her to look after their children, her mother had shrugged and said this was just one of many lives. Across the desk, the girl's dark eyes were warm and clear, her forehead smooth, her mouth soft.

As I got up to leave, the girl stood with me. *"Sawasdee kha."* She pressed her palms together in front of her chest and bowed her head slightly. "I am sorry for you this one life is hard."

"You too." I brought my hands together and dropped my chin. *"Sawas-dee,"* I said, before walking out the door.

Back through the hot dusty streets of the town and on my way to the Seaview Haadrin, I wished I could also believe in reincarnation. It certainly explained a lot about the locals' reactions to Sean's death.

However, I couldn't contain my horror that I'd still seen no attempt by the locals to warn others of the dangers in the water. In the three days since Sean had been stung, I hadn't seen a single poster, sign, notice, or leaflet cautioning about jellyfish. Not in the town or on the beach. Three people had now died, and the tourists continued to swim, splashing and laughing. The sweeping sandy curve of Haad Rin Nok looked as idyllic and benign as it had the day we'd arrived.

Max Moudir from France, age 5.
August 23, 2014. Ko Pha Ngan.

Fatal case: a 5 year old French boy, stung by a multiple tentacle box jellyfish on August 23rd 2014 at Khuat beach on Pha-ngan island. He lost consciousness, fresh water was poured over the injuries, ice packs were applied, and resuscitation was attempted by his parents.[7]

thirty-six

Hell's Gate, Saba, NETHERLAND ANTILLES

August 1999

I WANT TO TRY Sean one last time. Standing at the rusting payphone in Hell's Gate on the island of Saba, I look out over the deep blue Caribbean Sea and pick up the receiver. Then I punch in the code from my calling card, hold my breath, and wait. Seconds pass as I hear various clicks and connections down the phone. I look from my tanned toes in worn-out flip-flops, and then up to towering Mount Scenery—covered in mist, green forest, ferns, and mango trees, its summit almost three thousand feet tall and 1,064 slippery moss-coated steps up.

"Is that you, Miss? Hang on a sec. I can't hear a thing." Ireland is five hours ahead of the Lesser Antilles, and I can make out clanging glasses, singing, and shouting. "Are you there, sexy?"

"Hi, weasel." I check my dive watch. "I've got forty minutes." In an hour, I'm supposed to be back on board *Margarita*, the forty-two-foot catamaran that one local skipper, Ian; ten teenage students; and I currently call home.

"I miss you." Sean slurs just a little.

"I miss you too."

We talk quickly, all too aware our time is running out. Sean tells me about his job cooking at Eddie Rocket's in Galway, his new flat, and pints of Guinness and peat fires in pubs on the Aran Islands during his days off. I tell him about diving the pinnacles off Saba. Columns of volcanic rock that rise up from hundreds of feet below the water, encrusted with soft corals and sponges, and circled by blue tang, blacktip sharks, and great barracuda.

I'm in the middle of telling him a story—I'd taken a group of teenagers diving in the early evening, working up to their first night dive, when a swarm of moon jellies surrounded us. Translucent and purple round blobs, six inches to a foot across, bumping against our elbows and floating in front of our faces. I'd seen my students' eyes grow wide behind their masks as some tried to jerk backward to get away. So I'd grabbed the back of Beth's tank, as she was most likely to bolt, and signaled to the students: *Watch me* and *okay*. Then I placed an open palm against the top of one jelly's curved bell, away from the delicate fringe of tentacles below, and gently pushed it to the side. I never let them touch anything underwater, and the kids had loved learning to—when I'm interrupted by a recorded voice announcing we only have one minute left on the phone card.

"Oh, and we're still on the waiting list for married student housing at UC Santa Cruz. And we can always look off campus," I say in a rush. We've been talking about getting married and Sean moving to California when I begin my PhD. But I hate when the phone card cuts out and the line goes dead before we have a chance to stay goodbye.

"We'll figure it out." Sean doesn't sound at all rushed. He pauses, and I imagine him taking a gulp of his drink or a drag from a cigarette, or both. "It's like you always say, Miss. The world isn't that big. And it's up to us, right?"

Chayanan Surin from Bangkok, age 31.
July 31, 2015. Ko Pha Ngan.

Thai woman aged 31 years was diagnosed as "Cardiac arrest with anaphylaxis following contact with a venomous animal" . . . The clinical manifestations of the female Thai victim were consistent with chirodropid envenomation. She collapsed and had no pulse within a few minutes.[8]

thirty-seven

Haad Rin, Ko Pha Ngan, THAILAND

August 12, 2002

I 'D THOUGHT OF trying to leave something behind on Haad Rin Nok, something more permanent than a message written in the wet sand. I wondered if I could make some kind of headstone or hand-painted sign, stick a driftwood cross in the rocks near where he died.

But when I got back to the Seaview Haadrin, after my last afternoon of phone calls at the AA Travel office in town, the driver who would take Sean's body to Bangkok was already there waiting. He opened the rear door of the banged-up silver hearse and motioned for me to look inside.

I braced myself and held my breath as a rush of cold air hit my face. An enormous closed coffin filled the space in the back of the car. The casket seemed big enough to hold both Sean and me. It had elaborately carved wooden sides and was lacquered a shade of red so dark that it seemed to absorb all the light around it.

"Okay?" the driver asked. But that was apparently the only English he knew. We took turns staring as the other spoke. He looked surprisingly young. Yet his cheeks were sunken, his eyes bruised, and his body skinny and twitchy. Eventually, he dragged over one of the hotel employees to translate.

They'd already moved Sean's body from the box at the temple and into this new coffin. I felt a stabbing pang of regret that I hadn't been there. They would go to Thong Sala for the night and take the ferry to the mainland in the morning.

"We leave him in the car tonight?" I asked.

"Yes. Okay. No problem. Is very cold inside," the guy from the hotel said. He spoke briefly to the driver and then continued, "He sleeps in front of car. Everything okay. No problem."

"Okay," the driver added, nodding.

I would have preferred to be the one to sleep in the car with Sean that night. I would have given just about anything to stay with his body.

"One thousand baht."

"Excuse me?"

"He say you take ferry off Ko Pha Ngan, then he send you to Bangkok in car with him for one thousand baht."

"Okay," I agreed immediately. Twenty-something dollars seemed a small price to pay. Being stuck next to the driver for the twelve-hour journey would be awkward at the least. But I would be with Sean.

The two men spoke again. "He say is okay for him, but against rules. You tell no one. No his family, no your family. No friends. You tell no one. No one know."

"Okay," I repeated.

"And two thousand baht."

Again, I agreed. Then everything seemed to happen in a hurry. The hotel manager came to collect the key to my cabana before I'd even had a chance to pack. "Okay. You go now. Okay. Okay. Goodbye." She waved me off. Her brother was already waiting by his car to take me. I'd spend the night in Thong Sala on my own, before taking the ferry off the island. I threw our things together, paid our bill in full, and went to find Anat and Talia to say goodbye and thank them one more time.

Throughout that warm summer evening, I kept running into the twitching driver. First around the Seaview Haadrin, and then later at the ferry kiosk and on the streets of Thong Sala. He'd see me and then rush to grab a local to translate. Again and again, he said that I could not tell a single person I'd be going. I couldn't tell anyone on Ko Pha Ngan or in Bangkok, the United States or Australia. No one could know

I would be in the car. But he wouldn't ever look me in the eye. And the fee for the ride kept going up. He insisted on cash, started asking for US dollars, and doubled the amount each time we spoke.

With each encounter I grew more and more uneasy. I hated to leave Sean's body, and I didn't care about the money. But I couldn't read the expression in the driver's dark shifting eyes. He was nervous and jumpy and I couldn't tell what was going on. At one point, his hand darted out to grab my wrist and he pulled me hard and close, his sour breath hot on my face. I finally decided to book a flight to Bangkok instead. Although I knew it was probably the right decision, it wasn't an easy one.

Then I returned to my hotel room in Thong Sala, took one look at our two large backpacks, and panicked. Sean had always insisted on carrying my Eagle Creek pack as well as his own, despite my protests. He'd carried them both as we'd backpacked through Europe and Morocco, traveled to Ireland, camped and fished on Wilsons Prom, vacationed in Perth, Santa Cruz and San Francisco, and finally on to China and Thailand.

When we'd landed in Bangkok, Sean had grabbed both of our packs from the *tuk-tuk* and handed me the map. It was hot, I was lost, and he was frustrated under the combined weight. But he refused to give up my pack.

For years, we'd had an ongoing competition to see who could travel lighter, comparing our packs on the scales at check-in and waiting for the winning numbers to flash in red. It was easier to keep the weight down traveling in a hot climate. Yet despite how little we'd each been carrying, I didn't see how I would ever manage both backpacks the way he had.

That night in Thong Sala, in my dreary hotel room, I emptied Sean's and my packs onto the creaking single bed. I couldn't throw anything away, not his spray deodorant or Fudge Hair Putty, his grimy jeans or grungy socks. So I tried various combinations, mixing everything we owned together on the bed, before dividing the heavier items between the two packs. Or using his pack for all the critical things (our passports and airline tickets, the clothes I still wanted to dress him in, his insurance paperwork and death certificate) and putting the less consequential pieces (our dressier outfits, the little makeup I'd brought, his board shorts, and my bikinis) in mine. Over and over again, I heaved our backpacks onto my shoulders and tried to walk across the hotel room. Even that short distance, I couldn't manage on my own.

I unpacked, reorganized, and repacked our things late into the night. I hated just the thought of handing his pack over to the driver. But I couldn't do it without Sean. I would never be able to carry his weight alone.

thirty-eight

Veliko Târnovo, BULGARIA

December 2002

I RECOGNIZED THE BACKPACKS before I recognized the boys. The towering blue overstuffed MacPac, with the worn patch of the Aussie flag, was especially conspicuous in Eastern Europe.

Both of the boys had been in the same coed dorm room as I had at the Elvis' Villa Hostel in Bucharest—Simon from Melbourne and Adam from Manhattan. Simon was tall and broad with a mop of tight brown curls, and Adam was darker and shorter with glasses. But I'd hardly spoken to either of them at Elvis, and hadn't realized they were also headed to Veliko Târnovo, in the mountains of northern Bulgaria.

A few hours earlier, I was debating visiting the Black Sea. I'd actually been relieved when the girls working at the hostel had told me everything on the coast would be closed in December. So instead, I'd found myself in line behind Simon and Adam at the train station in Bucharest.

Simon's blue backpack was practically as big as I was, and he was "double-packing it," carrying a second, slightly smaller pack on his front. When we reached the ticket counter, he dropped his bags onto the metal scale with a groan, all thirty-three kilos' worth.

My clothes were probably half his size, and I was wearing the same thermals, dingy jeans, and tan cable-knit sweater over and over again. Other than that, I only had a few books and toiletries. I pushed my own green pack onto the scale and waited for the winning numbers to flash in red. Thirteen kilos, though it still felt like more.

As we boarded the rickety train, I wasn't the least bit sure how I felt about traveling with Simon and Adam. The lack of a common language in Eastern Europe had provided me with a comfortable insulation so far. Immediately the boys started in with the usual questions. Backpackers always asked each other how long they'd been traveling—assigning numbers and credence to trip durations, countries visited, and sketchiest locations.

The handful of fellow English-speaking backpackers I'd told about Sean had responded by asking how long we'd been together, or how long I'd been pregnant. As if by assigning numbers to my loss, my grief could also be weighed on a scale.

The border crossing took five hours. We passed the time in the stationary train car playing cards with a mustached Bulgarian who passed around an old plastic soda bottle filled with fiery homemade *rakiya*, or fruit brandy. By the time we reached Veliko Târnovo, I'd decided not to tell Simon and Adam about Sean.

We pulled into the darkness of the station just as it began to snow, and I stretched to get my pack down from the overhead rack. But the luggage tag caught, and the train was already starting to pull away. I was about to climb up onto the seats to reach, when Simon leaned over to untangle the tag. Adam hopped off first and Simon got to the open doorway next, but then his pack buckle caught on the door. I released him, and we jumped from the moving train into the cold black night. I landed unsteadily, surprised when I didn't slip and fall.

There were no ATMs at the station, and there wasn't a single street-light on the way into town. We got lost wandering down an empty snowy highway, jumped a couple of yellow plastic road barriers, and kept trying to get our bearings or find someone to ask for directions. Disoriented in the freezing dark, I was now glad I wasn't alone.

When we finally reached the city center and the run-down Hotel Orbita, Simon noticed tiny dried spots of blood on the sheets.

"Dodgy little bastards." He stripped back the other two beds in the room and found more reddish-brown dots. "Bedbugs. I got 'em in Bratislava, and it was bloody awful for three days. Mad itching all over my body and my face swollen up like a freakin' balloon."

We switched rooms, only to find more spots. I hadn't even touched any of the sheets and my skin was starting to crawl.

"Is only rust." The receptionist picked at her nail polish and shrugged.

She was hardly convincing. But Adam said he couldn't afford the other hotels, and neither of the boys was willing to return to the guy in the yellow jacket we'd met on the street who'd been trying to push a private room. So we stayed, but decided we needed a few stiff drinks before we could actually sleep there.

The rest of the evening passed in a blur. Simon and I left Adam at the English Pub chatting up a couple of pretty local girls. Outside on the snow-covered street, we met a group of university students who talked us into the noise and the disco lights of the Spyder nightclub next door.

For the first time since Sean died, I felt like dancing. It was the same catchy playlist of pop I'd been hearing throughout Eastern Europe for months: t.A.T.u.'s "All the Things She Said," Nelly and Kelly Rowland's "Dilemma," Shakira's "Objection," and Madonna's "Die Another Day."

But every ten tracks or so, a Bulgarian folk song would come on and everyone in the nightclub would join in some kind of coordinated dance. I'd taken a variety of dance classes throughout my childhood in California, and had always been comfortable and confident. But as I tried to follow along that night—holding hands in a circle, kicking, turning, clapping, and skipping—I was always at least two or three steps behind.

For one cold December day, I was just a normal, single, twenty-eight-year-old girl backpacking through Eastern Europe.

Simon, Adam, and I had woken up late, hungover but happily bugbite-free. We spent the afternoon exploring the narrow frosted streets of the old town, walking along the slurry-colored Yantra River, and climbing the steep-sided gorge up to tiers of rustic houses, historic churches, an ancient citadel, and the slippery overhanging cliff-top at Execution Rock. The sky was a pale gray and everything was dusted in powdery white snow.

But that night, the three of us were sitting, drinking, and talking in Desperado, when I started sobbing and couldn't stop. I don't remember what they said, or if they said anything at all, when I told them about my dead fiancé. What I do remember were the surprised, scared looks on their faces. And that they never mentioned Sean again.

I shouldn't have been surprised by my own collapse, but I was scared. I felt shaky and unhinged. I wasn't even sure what triggered it. I just knew I'd never been so frighteningly out of control of my own emotions, and it took almost another twenty-four hours to regain any sense of composure. After I'd told Simon and Adam in the bar, I walked back to the hotel alone in the icy dark, passed out cold, and accidentally locked them both out of the room.

The next morning, I started bawling again first thing in the shower. Sean felt so far away, it almost seemed as if he never happened. It felt as if I'd been alone for ages. As if I could hardly remember a time when I'd been attached or belonged to someone. And it was hard to imagine ever truly connecting with another person again. I was stuck crying in the shower for almost an hour, shocked that the one time I really needed it, there seemed to be an endless supply of hot water.

When I did get out, I didn't want to be backpacking, I didn't want to be in Bulgaria, and I didn't want to be with the boys. I spent the entire day hiding from both of them and struggling to stop crying—first while typing out long messages home in a smoke-filled Internet café, then shivering as I walked along cliff edges and castle ruins buried in snow, and finally through the terrible Vin Diesel film *xXx* at the local cinema.

By the end of the day, I'd run out of hiding places. But when I returned to the hotel, Simon and Adam acted as if nothing had happened. I couldn't be sure they even remembered.

So the three of us went out again, this time to Mosquito, and there we ran into the same university students that we'd met our first night in Veliko Tàrnovo. The students were young, fun, and friendly, fashionably dressed, and with widely varying fluency in English.

We all sat together in a big group at the bar, holding different numbers of stotinki coins hidden in our fists and trying to guess how many total coins were being held between us. The loser had to buy the next round, which only came to about two leva, or one US dollar.

The students also introduced us to a shot they called "heroin." Bacardi and Triple Sec were poured together and lit on fire, with a spoon full of sugar held over the heat until the sugar caramelized. At the last minute, the spoon was dropped into the flames and the whole burning, bittersweet shot was drunk through a straw. I got singed early on, but managed to get through the rest of the night without burning myself again.

December 9th was Simon's twenty-seventh birthday, which he'd been talking about since the day we met and clearly wanted to celebrate. It was also the four-month anniversary of Sean's death. I'd started to find that the anxiety and trepidation leading up to an anniversary were worse than the actual date, although I usually suffered a crash a few days later.

Adam had left Veliko Tàrnovo earlier, but Simon and I had stayed on a little longer in the snowy, hilly university town. As we finally made our way by bus to the capital, Sofia, I not only had the distraction of the freezing winter temperatures, but also of Simon's disappointment in the turnout of his birthday email messages, and the added difficulties of traveling in Bulgaria.

The strange Cyrillic letters reminded me of trying to negotiate Chinese characters with Sean. Both Simon's and my *Lonely Planet*s listed all the street names in English, while the signs themselves were in Bulgarian Cyrillic. So we learned to find a major landmark and then try to count the blocks to our destination.

Adding to this confusion was the local custom of shaking heads for yes, and giving a quick nod for no. I found it almost impossible to adjust.

But it was easier traveling with Simon. It was a pleasant change to have someone else to help figure out which bus to catch, whom to pay, and where to get off. And I couldn't help but notice how much less I was stared at when I wasn't on my own. I realized I'd gotten used to feeling as if I were some kind of curious zoo animal.

As the bus approached Sofia, the white drifts of snow along the sides of the road began to turn to brown slush. The streets of the capital were crowded with huge, dilapidated apartment blocks. Beggars huddled around fires crackling in garbage cans, mangy hollow-ribbed dogs slunk in the shadows, and cars were parked haphazardly all over the sidewalks.

Maneuvering around the cars proved difficult on the icy sidewalks, and Simon and I slipped and fell and slid our way from the bus station to the Sofia Hostel. Cats whined and yowled in the alleyways of Chinese restaurants, and the city itself smelled as if it were hungover—the sickly sweet and sour fruity fragrance of fermented alcohol, combined with stale cigarette smoke and greasy takeaway food. It was a smell I recognized from the streets of Budapest, Bratislava, Warsaw, Sarajevo, Zagreb, and Bucharest.

We climbed the dimly lit stairs to the hostel and could hear peals of laughter. Two young girls sat curled together on a ratty couch—watching MTV, holding hands, and doubling over giggling.

"*Zdrasti,*" one of the girls said, wiping at the corners of her eyes. She straightened up on the couch and looked us up and down. "Where from? London?"

"Australia," Simon drawled, his accent even thicker than usual.

"US," I added.

"Oooh, international romance!" The girl's bright green eyes gleamed. "So, maybe you wanting your own dorm room for two—"

"No, no, no." Simon held up both his hands and flushed a deep red, starting from the base of his neck and creeping up to just below his curls. "Single dorm bed for me, thanks."

The girl with the green eyes got up from the couch and headed over to a small desk in the corner. "But maybe a dorm room for two later if you lucky, eh?" She winked, and nudged Simon in the ribs with her elbow as she passed him by.

In another life, I might have been attracted to Simon. He was tall and strong and friendly. He used a lot of the same Aussie phrases that Sean had, such as "happy as Larry" and "Bob's your uncle," and even used the same Fudge Hair Putty.

But I felt no rush of blood or physical pull toward him, and had absolutely no sense at all if he did toward me. I felt only insecure and out of touch, detached and disconnected. Simon and I had been traveling together for five days by the time we reached Sofia. I knew his extended trip around the world had been prompted by the marriage of his newly-ex-girlfriend to his newly-ex-best friend. Yet I still had no idea if he even remembered what I'd told him back at the Desperado bar in Veliko Târnovo. I didn't know how to talk about Sean, but I also didn't know how not to.

Almost everything about the way Simon and I traveled together was different. I'd spent nearly three months in Eastern Europe on my own, looking at churches, castles, and old cobblestone quarters, ticking a city's monuments off a list before moving on to the next town. I continued to spend a lot of time alone—visiting the enormous black-domed brick synagogue where Anat's mother's family might have worshiped yet now appeared practically deserted, or lighting a candle and making a farfetched wish under the fairytale-like snow-dusted green roofs and gold domes of the Church of St. Nicholas the Miracle-Maker.

But when I was with Simon, I slowed down. I sent out more emails, which my parents gratefully received, stayed out later at night, and even slept in. It was just a little bit more aligned with the way I used to travel with Sean.

And as it had been with Sean, traveling with Simon made it easier to meet and interact with the locals. I didn't have to wonder about the intentions of men, and young women were also more likely to approach. Maybe, like the girls continued to do at the hostel, they assumed Simon and I were a couple.

We spent a week exploring Sofia and its surroundings, and Paulina, the green-eyed girl, was almost always parked on the ratty couch in the lobby—giggling, talking, and teasing. I'd never met someone who laughed so much, and could see the infectious effect it had on the people around her.

As silly as Paulina could be, she had a fascinating story to tell. One afternoon during a blizzard, she and I sat together on the couch and she told me all about Bulgaria under Communist rule. Twenty-four now, she'd been eleven when the Eastern Bloc began to collapse. She remembered both the before and after well.

"Before, everyone in the whole country had only power for one hour on, then two hours off, one hour on, then two hours off. I was a student, and all the kids, we had to try to do our homework when we had the light. But in winter, we had no heat ever. So we had to wear thick gloves as we try to write as fast as we can before it goes dark again!"

Paulina mimicked scribbling frantically holding a pencil in a clumsy fist, before she fell back into the cushions in a fit of laughter.

"We had to travel to Romania to get pants or blankets. And there were three things we never, never had: bread, bananas, and toilet paper." Paulina ticked the items off on her fingers, and started laughing again. "We had to use newspaper! But if you ever saw a long, long line on the street, you just got in line at the end because you knew it had to be for one of these three things.

"But even without heat," Paulina continued. "Even without bread, bananas, or toilet paper, people in Bulgaria, they were happier then. Now, only a few people are better off and very, very rich. And these are all the Mafia and corrupt government officials. Most of the people are poorer and even worse off. Now, people they are starving to death because they don't have enough to eat."

The next morning, Paulina and her friend called me back into the lobby. They were jumping up and down, pointing at the TV screen.

"Oh, good good! Finally, you explain this song to us! Please you can tell us, what is she saying? What does she mean?"

I turned to see Jennifer Lopez in a hot-pink bikini, rolling around on a yacht with Ben Affleck on MTV. I stopped to listen for a few seconds.

"Um, okay. So what she's saying is: *'Don't be fooled by the rocks that I got. I'm still, I'm still Jenny from the block.'*"

"But what does this mean? What is 'the rocks'? What is 'the block'?" The two girls watched as J.Lo danced and pranced half-naked in red lipstick and furs.

"Uh, so 'the rocks' are diamonds. And she's trying to say that just because she has lots of money and jewels now, she's still the same girl who grew up in a poor neighborhood in New York, or came from 'the block.'"

"Hmm." Paulina nodded and was quiet for a moment. Then she burst out laughing.

My life from home was beginning to catch up to me in Bulgaria, and it wasn't just the MTV constantly playing in the lobby at the Sofia Hostel. During the last couple of weeks, I'd received my official acceptance as a visiting academic at Melbourne University for 2003, applied for my Australian student visa, and written a letter of reference for one of my volunteers from Kangaroo Island.

I didn't feel at all ready to return to my PhD, but I didn't know that I ever would. Money wasn't the issue. I was used to budget travel, and stretching my savings had been easier than I'd anticipated. But if I was going to finish the degree, I was running out of time. I'd already missed one field season, and the fifty-five sea lion pups I'd been studying since birth would continue to dive and develop with or without me. Soon, they'd be weaned and having to fend for themselves in the great big Southern Ocean.

Since my arrival in Budapest almost three months ago, I'd changed my departure out of Eastern Europe a number of times, and couldn't push it any later. I tried to comfort myself that after flying out of Sofia, I'd still have a couple of days in Frankfurt, a week in Malta, and more than two weeks in Spain.

I thought if I could manage to touch the ocean again off one of the small Maltese islands in the Mediterranean, then I might be able to sink back into marine biology. From there, I'd fly to Madrid to meet my mum on Christmas Eve so that we could *not* celebrate the holidays together, before we both finally flew out of Barcelona and back to California. Just a few weeks after that, I'd have to move to Melbourne on my own.

I had only five days left in Bulgaria. Simon and I exchanged email addresses and phone numbers, and he would leave a note on my dorm bunk my last night in Sofia, scrawled on a Kamenitza beer coaster: SHANNON, WAKE ME UP BE 4 YOU GO BUT NOT TOO EARLY ☺ IF NOT I WILL GIVE YOU A CALL IN AUS ➜ BON VOYAGE, SIMON. P.S. ENJOYED TRAVELLING WITH YOU ☺.

But before that, on one of our last days together, he and I went with a few other backpackers to Koprivshtitsa, a tiny village in the Sredna Gora Mountains with a name not a single one of us could pronounce.

The train headed east from Sofia at eight a.m., and as we made our way to the station in the dark that frigid fifteen-below morning, it felt like the blind leading the blind.

Simon and I had been stumbling our way through Cyrillic, and that morning our group included two guys from France—"Frenchie One" and "Frenchie Two," as the girls at the hostel called them—and another guy from Japan. None of us spoke the more common second languages in Bulgaria, Russian or German, and even I could hardly understand the other boys' attempts at negotiating train tickets or trying to buy a cup of coffee in English. My first meeting with Frenchie One had involved an awkward misunderstanding where he wanted to know if I was Norwegian, and I'd thought he was asking if I was not a virgin.

I spent the two-hour train journey writing in my journal, and when we arrived in Koprivshtitsa, it looked like a village caught in a snow globe. Steep cobblestone paths wound between old wooden houses, icicles hung from the low red-tiled roofs, and stone footbridges crossed over frozen streams. Snowflakes whirled through the air of the quiet streets and everything was covered in white.

It was difficult to walk on the icy, irregular cobblestones and the boys and I picked our way along the lanes and the frosted banks of the Topolnitsa River. Horses snorted clouds of breath as we passed and stomped their hooves in the snow. When our fingers and toes were numb from the cold, we stopped for lunch.

The menu at the run-down *mehana*, or tavern, provided English translations, but these were more entertaining than informative. There was *chicken mouthful*, *brains forest type specialty*, and *dead baby cow piece with legend*. I ordered the *stuffed fried with cheese*, the *egg on a roof*, and a Zagorka Special beer.

It turned out to be one of the best meals I had in Bulgaria. Nothing like Anat's mother's home-cooking, but the closest I'd come in weeks. The *stuffed fried with cheese*, or *kashkaval pane*, was breaded deep-fried cheese that was crispy, gooey, salty, and steaming hot. The dish had become a staple of mine throughout Eastern Europe, my body craving the warm comfort of calories and fat in the plummeting winter temperatures.

When my *egg on a roof* arrived, it was served in a red clay pot. Underneath the lid, the pot was filled with a bubbling mix of tomatoes, peppers, onions, and spicy sausage, topped with a couple of eggs, and sprinkled heavily with dark smoky paprika. The earthy richness of the food was offset by the cool, malty sweetness of the beer.

I scraped up every last bite. In addition to the warmth that calories provided, I'd also learned that up to a point, I could substitute eating for sleeping. When I lost my appetite, I was able to sleep longer to make up for it. Or, as was more often the case, I could compensate some for the relentless insomnia and restless nightmares by eating more.

The climb up the hill to the *mehana* for lunch proved easier than the walk back down. The cobbles were slick with ice, and while I was nearing the bottom, still gingerly stepping sideways, Frenchie One's feet slipped out from under him at the top. As if in a cartoon, his body was frozen in midair for a split second, before he crashed into a heap, and slid past me down the hill.

He skidded to a stop and was just trying to scramble up to standing when Frenchie Two stumbled and came flying down after him. Spread out on his back like a snow angel, Frenchie Two spun down the hill and hurtled into Frenchie One, knocking him back off his feet, where they ended up in a soggy, tangled pile of waterproof jackets and hiking boots.

The sounds from my own mouth startled me. The physicality also took me by surprise—the vibrations in my throat, the movement of my chest, the muscles tightening in my stomach.

It was the first time I'd laughed since Thailand, and even as I couldn't stop myself, I was aware of how foreign it felt. It seemed as if I were watching from a distance, as if the snow globe had been shaken and I was looking in from the outside. Simon standing next to me, hooting and pointing. His cheeks flushed and his dark curls speckled with white. My feet braced on the icy street, doubled over with one hand against my thigh and the other hand wiping at the tears falling from my eyes.

thirty-nine

San Diego, California, UNITED STATES

July 1982

I'M WAITING for the tide to drop and my grandma Joy to finish swimming her laps so we can go explore the tide pools. It's the summer after second grade, and I've only just begun to fall in love with the ocean. Sitting in a wet swimsuit under a yellow-striped beach umbrella at La Jolla Shores, a sandy tuna and pickle sandwich on my lap, wondering if Grandpa Bob might buy me an ice cream cone later. Mint chocolate chip, or butter pecan.

But I'm more excited about the tide pools. There'll be the sharp edges of mussels and gooseneck barnacles to watch out for, the crumbly tubes of sandcastle worms, fuzzy purple sand dollars, and squishy green sea anemones. Yesterday there was even a tiny brown baby two-spot octopus hiding among the rocks and I'm hoping it's still there.

The waves in front of me slowly build and curl before crashing to shore, the color of the water turning from blue to green to white. I smell sunscreen, seaweed, and the fishy brine of my tuna sandwich. My toes are still numb from the cold Pacific, and I dig them into the hot sand in the sun and take another bite. Wiping the salt water from my eyes, I can just make out my grandma on the other side of the whitecaps—her arms arcing out of the sea, her feet kicking up spray. She swims the length of the beach, back and forth, again and again. Until finally, she turns and catches a wave at its crest. She bodysurfs the foam all the way in, her white swim cap tucked down and her arms straight out in front of her like a superhero.

The moment she hits the sand and stands up out of the surf, her body sags slightly to one side and her limp starts again, over the crumpled left foot polio had twisted when she was a child. It reminds me of Hans Christian Andersen's Little Mermaid, whose every step on land was an ordeal. My grandma disentangles herself from the kelp before hobbling across the beach toward me, and I think how everything is different in the water. My grandma is always comfortable and competent, but in the ocean, buoyed by the salt, she becomes strong and graceful, lissome and unencumbered. The vastness of the Pacific opens up behind her, and the possibilities seem infinite.

Saskia Thies from Germany, age 20.
October 6, 2015. Ko Samui.

Other cases in this study also had similar clinical manifestations which were indicative of chirodropid envenomations. One such case was the fatal sting of a German woman on October 6th, 2015. The injured individuals all suffered from tremendous pain after being stung and also had systemic reactions. They had difficulty breathing and had a very high heart rate. Thaikruea et al. (2015) conducted the investigations and found that seven out of the eight cases collapsed and all of them had tentacle marks on their bodies.[9]

forty

Ko Pha Ngan to Barcelona

2002

A S I STOOD THERE on that slippery cobblestone street that freezing cold afternoon in Koprivshtitsa, it finally felt as if the beach on Ko Pha Ngan really was almost seven thousand miles away. Even if it was only for a moment or two.

I had gotten used to feeling as if Thailand were around every corner. I'd been hoping that after four months and ten countries, I might have come further. But distance can be deceptive. My own path through grief never followed the neat upward trajectories plotted in Hollywood films. Maybe by not traveling in a straight line, I'd ended up covering more ground. Maybe Paulina's infectious laughter just took a while to catch up with me.

The circuitous journey I'd taken after leaving Ko Pha Ngan had certainly been longer and harder than I ever could have imagined. Everything *was* different, and there were times when every step did feel like an ordeal. But there'd also been the moments of kindness and beauty I'd never anticipated. There were moments when nothing seemed to make sense, and moments I wouldn't truly understand for many years.

After handing Sean's backpack over to the driver on Ko Pha Ngan, I'd flown alone to Bangkok. Sean's father, Keith, had booked a room for me at a four-star hotel near the airport and the Australian embassy. The consul was straightforward and sympathetic. Since I wasn't family, there was nothing I could do to prevent an autopsy.

That night I lost Sean's baby, in the white air-conditioned hotel bathroom. It was painful and awful and long. I'd never even taken a pregnancy test, but had always assumed it would be a boy. Thirteen years later, I still see children who would be the same age and think of him.

Sean's brother and uncle arrived in Bangkok the next day. We went to see his body, naked and cold. A Y-shaped incision that cut across his chest and down his stomach had been stitched back together and staples were punched tight along his skull. The blue of his eyes had already faded, and his pupils clouded over. We left Thailand the day after that and, together, flew his coffin home.

In four months, I'd flown from Melbourne to California to Budapest. Then on to Slovakia, Poland, Israel, Bosnia, Croatia, Romania, and Bulgaria.

And from Bulgaria, I flew to Frankfurt. Everything in Germany was so big, clean, and modern, and everyone was so cheerful, clean, and rich. Everyone spoke English; I stopped even asking. The shops took credit cards, and there were fitted sheets and elevators. After all that time, the sights, smells, and sounds of Eastern Europe had become strangely familiar. I'd been tired of the cold, the stares, and the difficulties, but it had felt raw and real there. Germany's perfectly ordered immaculate world triggered the most startling culture shock I've ever experienced.

At the Frankfurt Hostel, I asked an Austrian girl how I might find out about trains back to the airport. She wrinkled her brow and looked at me sideways. "You go to the train station and you look at the schedule."

"But they don't have schedules in English?"

"Of course in English. It's very easy."

"And the schedules are up-to-date? Not from ten years ago, and only in summer?"

"Yes, yes. They are all up-to-date and in season and on time. It is very easy."

"And they're in English?" I couldn't believe it. *It can't be that easy*, I thought. *It must be a trick.*

But there was no trick, and soon after that I flew to Malta for a week. When I'd first booked my tickets, I'd foolishly thought I'd be ready to fall in love with the ocean once more. Every direction I looked I could see the water, and couples crowded the beachfront promenades at sunset. The harbors around Sliema and St. Julian's were filled with *luzzu*, traditional long narrow wooden fishing boats painted in bright reds, yellows, greens, and blues—a pair of stylized eyes on each bow to protect the fishermen at sea.

I spent a rainy afternoon on the island of Gozo, biking past Dwejra Bay to the Inland Sea and Tieqa Żerqa, or Azure Window, a natural limestone arch almost a hundred feet above the ocean. The location was stunning—the water a dark slate blue, yellow cliffs rising from the sea, the limestone forming a perfect arc in the gray sky high above the waves. In the depths below was a site Jacques Cousteau had ranked as one of his top ten dives, and I wasn't even tempted. Just the thought of touching the water made me panicky, queasy, and frightened. Instead, I explored the islands' prehistoric Megalithic Temples and decided there wasn't any rush.

On Christmas Eve, I flew to Spain to meet my mum. Together, we avoided Christmas in Madrid—seeing a matinee of *The Two Towers*, looking at the outsides of palaces and museums that were closed, and never once mentioning the holiday.

We moved on to Cuenca, Toledo, and then to New Year's Eve in Seville. We spent the night packed into the crowd at Plaza Nueva, drinking from shared bottles of cava before they were smashed onto the pavement. We'd hardly eaten all day because we hadn't known the restaurants would be closed. Blue and white Christmas lights flickered on the trees, and there was the smoke and noise of fireworks, broken glass everywhere, and rumors in Spanish that someone had been knifed. As the clock struck twelve, everyone else around us crammed grapes into their mouths—one grape for each bell—hoping to bring good luck in the coming year.

From Seville, we went to Ronda, and finally Barcelona. There, my mum and I ate tapas: boozy *chorizo al diablo*, pungent *queso de Cabrales*, and small *pincho* sandwiches, before the waiters counted the discarded toothpicks for the bill. We drank strong bitter *sidra*, the bartenders pouring theatrically from high above their heads to increase the bubbles and intensify the flavor. And we watched Futbol Club Barcelona beat last-place Huelva Recreativo 3–0, the men in the stadium throwing their hands into the air each time Barcelona missed another goal.

I took my mum to Sagrada Família, Gaudí's towering, crazy, and chaotic church, which Sean and I had been to together. Work had continued long since Gaudí's death in 1926, and the estimated date of completion had been brought forward since we'd visited, from 2085 to 2020. Though it was hard for me to see significant progress.

I knew I had a long way still to go myself. Visiting the places I'd been to with Sean, traveling in a country where I spoke the language, and being with someone who loved me sometimes made the trip easier and sometimes made it harder. Sean's presence was constant and palpable—drinking a Jack and Coke at Flaherty's Irish Bar near the wharf, eating a cheap *bocadillo de tortilla de patata* on a cold bench in Plaça de Catalunya, caught in a crowd of young backpackers laughing and jostling along La Rambla—spoken and unspoken during every single conversation with my mum.

Spain was where Sean and I had fallen in love, and where we were planning to honeymoon. It was in Barcelona, exactly four years earlier, where Sean and I had first met and had our first kiss. Before going home to start a life without him, I ended my journey there—at the beginning.

forty-one

Shànghǎi, Guìzhōu, CHINA

August 2002

S EAN'S ARRANGED FOR a Communist Party car to take us to the Shànghǎi Pudong International Airport. I've noticed the high speeds and lack of apparent road rules in China, so I reach for my seat belt. The driver takes it personally.

"There is no need. I will never crash."

I put the seat belt on, despite the driver's protests and the dirty looks he gives me through the rearview mirror. Riding shotgun, Sean shrugs and complies, preferring as usual to avoid confrontation.

Sean and the driver joke as we swerve through the chaotic traffic and choking-thick purple smog. Men driving motorbikes wear cardboard ice cream containers as helmets. Women sit behind, sidesaddle, with their legs crossed in tight skirts and nothing on their heads. One woman clutches a bundled blanket to her chest. As we pass, I see the tiny baby in her arms.

Traveling through China has been hard work. It will be such a relief to have menus in English and drink beer without formaldehyde. In only a few hours, there'll be green curry and green papaya salad. We'll be able to eat satay, sriracha sauce, and fresh seafood. Sean and I can hardly wait. Soon, we'll be able to just relax together on a beach in Thailand.

We arrive at the airport and jump out onto the curb. Sean grins and points at my chest. My white T-shirt is stained with grease and dust from the long-neglected seat belt.

The driver smiles. "See, no crash."

Inside, I decide I want to change my shirt before we check in and get our boarding passes. But Sean circles his arm around my waist and pulls me closer to him. He laughs as he leans down, and he kisses me.

"Seriously, Miss. Who cares?"

Shannon and Sean. Shànghǎi. August 2, 2002.
Courtesy of the author

epilogue

I N THAILAND, I'd been told over and over again that Sean was the first to die in decades, that the locals had never heard of jellyfish deaths there. I'd thought he was allergic, and just incredibly unlucky. Until two days later when Anat and Talia told me Mounya had died. After that, I didn't know what to think.

When I finally left Ko Pha Ngan, my mum warned me not to look online. She'd found some article where an official was quoted as saying Sean's death had been excruciating. I hadn't thought of searching the Internet until she said this. Then I couldn't get online quickly enough.

I found another official claiming that after Sean's death, police on the island handed out leaflets advising against swimming, but that travelers had disregarded the warnings. And a thread that said news of a deadly jellyfish was very bad for the tourist industry. Someone named Jane posted:

I live on the island of Koh Phangan and watched the locals hide the fact that jellyfish were in the sea. The police had posted signs (very small 8x11" sheets that were posted only at the clinic) and the bungalow owners removed them and refused to warn people.

I certainly never saw any leaflets or signs. Anat and Talia stayed longer on the island than I did, and they never saw any. When a cousin of one of their friends visited Haad Rin Nok three months later, in November 2002, there still wasn't any indication anything had ever happened.

Yet there had been other deaths. In December 1995, two people were killed by jellyfish off Langkawi Island, near the border between Malaysia and Thailand. Then on May 6, 1996, two teenagers died in the same location. On October 20, 1999, a twenty-six-year-old British tourist was visiting Ko Samui with his brother when he was stung and killed.

All of these deaths were likely caused by *Chironex fleckeri*, the largest species of box jellyfish and arguably the most venomous creature on the planet. Almost totally transparent, a single jelly has sixty tentacles, each up to ten feet long and with every inch containing 2.5 million stinging cells, or nematocysts. A victim only needs to come into contact with a few feet of tentacles to be injected by billions of stingers. As early as 2003, Australian box jellyfish expert Jamie Seymour was quoted in *New Scientist*: *People are getting stung and killed all over the tropics without anybody realizing it.*

Then on April 3, 2008, Moa Bergman from Sweden was playing in the water off Ko Lanta when she was stung and killed by a box jellyfish. She was eleven years old.

Less than two years later, on February 3, 2010, Carina Lofgren, also from Sweden, was stung and killed, again off Langkawi. On November 14th of that same year, Ann Nordh, yet another Swede, died off Cha-Am. While there are questions about Ann's death (which of these deaths didn't leave questions?), Carina's husband and brother were with her when she was stung in shallow water and died, despite their efforts at resuscitation, minutes later on the beach. Yet both of these deaths were officially ruled as drownings.

These are only the deaths in, or immediately near, Thailand (other deaths in Malaysia include a twenty-six-year-old tourist from Brunei in June 2000, an eight-year-old South Korean girl in November 2006, and a four-year-old Japanese boy, Reo Ohta, in January 2013). It also doesn't include a number of near-fatal stings documented throughout the area.

Previously thought to be confined to waters off northern Australia, box jellyfish populations appear to be expanding. Global warming, pollution, ocean acidification, introduced species, decreasing numbers of sea turtles who eat jellyfish, and overfishing may all be contributing factors. There have now been fatalities in Indonesia, India, China, Japan, Papua New Guinea, Borneo, the Solomon Islands, and the Philippines.

And then again, on August 23, 2014, a five-year-old boy from France, Max Moudir, was stung by a box jellyfish at Haad Khuad beach back on Ko Pha Ngan. Twelve years and less than eight miles from where this book began. Like Sean, Max was stung in the early evening, fell unconscious almost immediately, and was dead within minutes. His father, Karim, tried CPR and they rushed Max to a hospital, but it was too late. Like Sean, and there were still no warnings, no vinegar, and no antivenom.

In the months that followed, Karim and I corresponded over email. *I don't know what I can to do to make a sense of the life and the death of my son. Did you think I could save him or it will be impossible? I put fresh water and ice when I took him out the sea. Maybe, if I do not . . . Maybe I don't try enough to revive him. Now, death is with me, on me.*

Less than a year later, I got a different email from Karim. On July 31, 2015, there'd been another death at Haad Rin. A thirty-one-year-old woman, Chayanan Surin, had traveled from Bangkok to Ko Pha Ngan to celebrate the Full Moon Party. She was swimming with three friends when she was stung severely. She died before she got to the hospital.

And again on October 6, 2015. A twenty-year-old German tourist, Saskia Thies, was stung and killed during an evening swim at Lamai beach back on neighboring Ko Samui. Her friend Jiovana Rassi was stung on the hand trying to save Saskia, but she managed to survive. Although there'd been sightings of large numbers of box jellyfish earlier in the area, no one seems to have warned the girls.

These are also only the deaths that have been published. Thailand's Disease Control Department reported twelve box jellyfish fatalities from 1998 to 2013. Yet after three additional deaths in 2014 and '15, the department again reported a total of twelve fatal stings. Even when officially recognized, the victims seem all too quickly forgotten. None of the articles from 2002 ever discussed the twenty-six-year-old Brit who'd been killed on Ko Samui less than three years earlier. In the most recent media reports regarding Chayanan and Saskia, Max's death is sometimes cited, but there's not a single line mentioning Sean, Mounya, or Moa.

So what I've never been sure about is how many people died with Sean that weekend in 2002 on Ko Pha Ngan. While I was there, I was certain two girls had been killed. But maybe one of their deaths was ruled a drunk drowning; maybe whoever was with her couldn't produce four male witnesses. Because the accounts immediately after Sean's death mention only one girl. Except sometimes she's from Morocco and sometimes she's from Switzerland. Sometimes she dives face first into three jellies and dies within minutes. Sometimes she's stung on the legs and dies in the hospital one day later, sometimes two days. Sometimes she is a twenty-three-year-old female; sometimes her name is Mounya. But one thing doesn't change. No matter how many articles I search, she never survives.

And the deaths continue. This story—Sean's story, my story, our story—turns out to be one of many.

afterword

Kangaroo Island to London

2003–2016

FTER THE JOURNEY, after having to leave all those countries and 2002 behind, I went back to my PhD. But it was different. I was different. My heart could never be in it in the same way. My last field season with the Australian sea lions on Kangaroo Island, I caught the mothers and pups with my team on the sandy beaches at Seal Bay, but still couldn't bring myself to touch the ocean.

I finally stepped back into the water on the first year anniversary of Sean's death. I'd traveled alone to Noosa on the Sunshine Coast of Australia and rented a surfboard, disappointed to have to take one in pink. But there weren't any waves that day. The winter sky was big and blue, and the ocean was flat. I waded into the sea until it was chest-deep and then I went under. I tasted the salt, felt the chill of the water on my shoulders, and nothing changed. It wasn't the big cinematic moment I'd expected it to be. I went under one more time, and waded straight back out of the ocean again.

Two months later, on a solo vacation in Vanuatu, I let my feet leave the sand and actually looked around underwater. I fed baby hawksbill sea turtles in a rock pool, went snorkeling, and spent days scuba diving the SS *President Coolidge*, a World War II wreck a hundred feet below. But it was back on land—walking down a dirt road on Efate—when there was one instant, one long, deep, physical inhale. It was like coming up for air, and for the first time in fourteen months, it felt as if I could breathe.

The following summer, in 2004, I taught diving and tropical marine ecology to teenagers at the Island School on Eleuthera in the Bahamas. I passed off the lecture on cnidarians (sea anemones, corals, sea pens, and jellyfish) to another teacher. If a bay was filled with *Cassiopea*, or upside-down jellies, during our morning jog-swims, I'd take the students on a different route. The second anniversary of Sean's death, I was back at the ocean, at Pink Sands Beach on nearby Harbour Island, raising my glass and writing messages in the wet sand.

I finished my PhD in September 2005, and my first job after graduating was as the marine mammal biologist on board an expedition ship in Antarctica. The MS *Explorer*, or Little Red Ship, left Ushuaia in Argentina and set out to cross the Drake Passage. I spent two days on deck in the freezing cold, staring out to sea and occasionally tossed about by twenty-five-foot waves. When we finally arrived at the Antarctic Peninsula, there were humpback whales bubble-net feeding in the midnight sun, leopard seals skinning and eating chinstrap penguins in the surf, killer whales breaching and spy-hopping next to the ship, crabeater seals sleeping on ice floes.

Late one afternoon, after hiking through hundreds of clamoring Adélie penguins and up to the top of Devil Island, we were loading the inflatable Zodiac boats to return to the *Explorer* when a group of passengers excitedly called me over. They were pulling out cameras and pointing to the ice-strewn water. I was expecting a floating half-eaten penguin chick, or a leopard seal cruising through the rocky shallows. I leaned out over the Zodiac's rubber side but didn't see anything until it drifted up inches from my face. It was the size of a basketball, translucent pinkish-purple, with a mass of trailing dark orange frills and tentacles at least fifteen feet long. My stomach flip-flopped. I couldn't say a word. And I realized that even in Antarctica, there would be jellyfish.

But there were also Weddell seals and southern elephant seals, minke whales and fin whales, Commerson's dolphins and hourglass dolphins. I watched glaciers calve ice as big as houses, saw wandering albatrosses court their lifelong mates, sat next to gentoo penguin chicks as they hatched from their eggs, had Antarctic fur seal pups climb into my lap, and drank whiskey at the great explorer Ernest Shackleton's grave.

My second season in Antarctica, in January 2007, I met my future husband. He was from the UK, an assistant expedition leader on board the *Explorer*, and among many duties, he assigned the shared staff cabins. With few female staff, he offered to arrange my own cabin if I dressed up one night, unannounced, as a pirate. He then assigned us to write the ship's log together, and taught me to drive the Zodiacs that were lowered by crane off the side and into the water. The first night we kissed, late and alone in the forward lounge bar, I spilled almost an entire bottle of red wine across the pink carpet.

Before we could join the ship for another Antarctic season together, the *Explorer* hit ice. We watched online from a tiny, dark rented flat in London as everyone on board escaped into the Zodiacs and lifeboats and she slowly went under. Our portside cabin 201, my pirate costume, his boots and waders, and the red wine stain in the forward lounge all sank four thousand feet to the bottom of the Bransfield Strait.

Over two and a half years later, in June 2010, and at the opposite end of the world, we got married on Fuglesangen, a tiny uninhabited island in the Arctic Ocean. Almost eighty degrees north, the rocky snow-covered beach faced out over the Nordvestøyane, or Northwestern Islands, of Arctic Norway. Only three of us stood on the beach in the sunshine—the guy who performed the ceremony was someone we'd worked with in Antarctica. But we'd seen ten polar bears that morning and a colony of little auks twittered behind us (*fuglesang* means "birdsong") as reindeer crossed the snowy slopes above. We all wore lifejackets and waterproofs and each carried a rifle, a necessary precaution because of the bears. His ring was a part from a marine radio. I was six months pregnant.

* * *

This is a story about finding love and learning to live with loss. But mostly, it's a story about all the places in between.

In the books that I read and the movies I watched after Sean died, I was always taken aback by how quickly the plot fast-forwarded through grief and on to recovery and the lessons learned. My own journey has not been a tidy story of triumph over grief. It took a lot longer, and was a hell of a lot harder, than I ever thought it would be.

So this story is about the months following Sean's death, the time missing in all those books and movies, when all I could do was try to figure out how to put one foot in front of the other. There would still be years of insomnia, flashbacks and nightmares, anniversaries and avoiding holidays. I had to figure out how to behave like a widow, and then I had to figure out how to stop behaving like one.

Even the end doesn't look like I thought it would—my husband and I were together almost nine years, married for over five and a half, and we have the three most charming and noisy children together. I've surprised everyone, including myself, by staying in the UK after we separated. So here I am, living in a big city like London, far from the sea and instead surrounded in my own home by little boys with British accents and a babbling baby girl.

But this book is not about my family now. As much as they fill my days so completely, loving them does not mean I don't miss Sean. Losing Sean is not something I will ever get over, or move past, or recover from. I'll always be haunted by his death. I'll always be enchanted by his life.

Over the years, I've slowly settled on my own ways to remember. At first I kept Sean's heavy silver ring on a chain around my neck, continued to wear the Claddagh ring engraved with his name on my left hand. I still sometimes light candles for Sean, raise a toast on birthdays and anniversaries. The cardboard box with most of his things (his glasses and Chinese passport, the photos of us together in the Czech Republic, Morocco, Slovenia, and Spain, his favorite blue-checked shirt, the Futbol Club Barcelona scarf, dried roses from his casket, that stupid purple sundress I was wearing when he died) has been moved to the attic. The two silver rings are now in my grandma Joy's old butterfly jewelry box, along with his funeral card, his Cadbury Schweppes business card, and the fortune I got from a Chinese cookie on what should have been Sean's twenty-seventh birthday: *There are times when sorrow seems to be the only truth.*

Because the truth is, the world isn't full of Hollywood happy endings. Sometimes the princess doesn't rescue the prince. Sometimes children never find their way home. In the original version, unlike the Disney film, at sunrise the Little Mermaid despairs and throws herself into the sea.

I've now loved Sean longer dead than I knew him alive. I still can't help but sometimes wonder, *Would we have had a smaller house and a bigger garden together in Melbourne? What would our children have looked like? Would we have been happy?* Sean will always be gone. He'll never get married, buy a house, or hold his first child. When I first started writing this story down, an early reader said, "I didn't find the silver lining." But this is what Poland taught me—that real tragedies don't need to be redeemed, they need to be remembered.

Believe it or not but I never forget the 9th of August, Talia emailed me shortly after the thirteen-year anniversary of Sean's death. She and her boyfriend had just moved in together in Tel Aviv. He works for one of the biggest tourism companies in Israel; she's an information security manager. They've been together a year, and he makes her happy. Anat is still in the military. She married the boyfriend I met in 2002 and together they have three children.

There are still moments when I think about what might have happened if Anat and Talia hadn't followed the truck on foot from the beach, if they hadn't chosen to walk through the door of that clinic. I would have signed documents I didn't understand. His death would have been ruled a drunk drowning. His insurance could have refused coverage. His parents and the police might have blamed me. And for all these years, I wouldn't have had the support of two friends who realized exactly what I had been through on Ko Pha Ngan.

This is what Israel and its rules for sitting shiva taught me—that as much as grief needs solitude, memories need to be shared and mourning needs to be recognized. Grief needs time and space, but it also needs company.

Because after Sean's death, there were times when I felt let down by everything I knew—the country and culture I grew up in, the ocean I thought I understood, some of my closest and oldest friends. But then there was the kindness of these two young strangers, and I don't think it's any coincidence that they were from Israel. It was their compassion, their courage, their companionship, and their chutzpah that saved me.

In the study of our terrace house in London, overlooking our tiny garden of potted plants, I've held on to my old journals, one in shamrock green, and my thumb-worn *Lonely Planet* guide to Eastern Europe. They sit on the bookshelf by the desk, surrounded by photos (my ex-husband and me in Venice and on the Ross Ice Shelf, the boys' baby pictures and sonograms of my daughter). On top of the bookshelf, there's a folder filled with Cyrillic ticket stubs and foreign beer labels from 2002; there are receipts for bus journeys to Oświęcim and Brzezinka, postcards from Jerusalem and Jaffa, the carefully folded cartoon *Survival Map*.

For three years after Sean's death, the *Survival Map* hung on my bedroom wall. First, in a house I shared with four other girls in Melbourne, and then back in the condo my parents own in Capitola. When I'd first bought the map, it was a sort of guidebook, a local's perspective on the city. But it came to mean much more. I was still trying to plot my own survival, and wanted to remember Sarajevans' resilience and how they'd taken control of their story. In the map publishers' own words, Sarajevans had fought terror *with tolerance, death with humor, and fascism with culture!* And this is what Bosnia taught me—that grief can be met with creativity, power, and beauty.

There's a part of me that longs to return to Sarajevo someday. It's a place I would love to show my three children when they are older. But it can never be the Sarajevo I experienced in 2002, the one depicted on my *Survival Map*.

These days, it's my grandpa's waterproof maps that hang on the walls of our house in London—the red arrows of currents sweeping through the South China Sea in our guestroom, the swirling blue lines of the great North Pacific in our living room.

Some things might have been different if I hadn't had the miscarriage in Bangkok. Maybe there would have been many more Christmases with the Reillys in Melbourne. "That Jack Reilly, he's got a bit of dash," Sean used to say, picturing our future son. But he's gone too.

It took a long time for me to let go of that life, of the family I thought I would join. It wasn't until I finally had my own children that I could truly understand.

I know how incredibly lucky I've been. I had to travel to the ends of the earth to find my husband, and although our marriage didn't last, our children are healthy, happy, and a handful. They hold two passports to countries that most of the world can only dream about. And I can't imagine life without their boisterous, demanding, curious, and delighted energy bouncing around the room.

So I look at my kids now and I imagine what it must have been like to get that phone call at three a.m. *Some girl* on the other end telling me that my twenty-five-year-old son is dead. *Some girl*, when I carried him for nine months, nursed him for eighteen. When I changed him and rocked him and sang to him and was there to catch him when he fell. When I loved him so much, it made everything else pale in comparison. When I watched him grow up, only to have *her* tell me he was gone.

Any parent will say that having a child changes everything. No matter how many times someone says this, you're still never prepared. When I heard Max had been stung on Ko Pha Ngan, I kept picturing the scene—

his tiny body collapsing on the beach, the terror, chaos, confusion, and helplessness, the hopeless ride to the hospital. But mostly, I couldn't stop thinking about his parents.

Because after Sean's death, my life split in two: *before* and *after*. I see a photo of myself and instantly know which girl is looking back at me from the picture. The girl who danced for Sean on a dusky street through a shop window, a little bit dirty and making him laugh. Or the girl who couldn't tell her little brother what he needed to hear.

But my life split again when I became a mum. Someone mentions an event or occasion, and I immediately know if it was before or after I had my first son. So it's Audrey, Sean's mother, I find my thoughts now turning to each Mother's Day, the anniversary, his birthday, and Christmas. Because more than anything else, having my own children has changed the way I felt about Sean's death and his family. It's changed the way I felt about love.

My parents have now retired in Santa Cruz. They live a couple of blocks from the beach, where the wind is heavy with salt and the sounds of pounding surf and barking California sea lions drift into their bedroom windows. Each walk down West Cliff Drive, I'm reminded—as I first was on that ferry in Croatia——how beautiful, and how powerful, the ocean can be.

On one of my family's visits from London, I took my eldest for a tour of my old lab at Long Marine at UC Santa Cruz. We saw the motley crew of unreleasable animals: Sprouts, a bubble-blowing twenty-five-year-old harbor seal; Tunu, a spotted seal found still alive inside his mother after she was killed by Eskimo hunters; and Puka and Primo, two Atlantic bottlenose dolphins who'd washed out of the US Navy. My son patted Sprouts on the back and watched the dolphins have their teeth cleaned as he asked question after question after question in his British accent. He wanted to know if he would be a scuba diver when he was bigger, if the dolphins ate ice cream, and if I was scared of the waves.

Sometimes I'm still finding my way forward. The steps I take for my kids are the easy ones. I haven't figured out yet what I'll tell them about jellyfish (which come up surprisingly often with a pirate-obsessed toddler). But as we stood together in the sun by the dolphin pool I said that yes, I'd love to teach him to scuba dive when he was older. That bottlenose dolphins ate fish and squid. And that no, I wasn't afraid of the waves.

notes

1   P. J. Fenner, J. M. Lippmann, L.-A. Gershwin, "Fatal and Nonfatal Severe Jellyfish Stings in Thai Waters," *Journal of Travel Medicine* 17, no. 2 (2010): 133–138.

2   Ibid.

3   Ibid.

4   Ibid.

5   Ibid.

6   P. J. Fenner, J. M. Lippmann, L.-A. Gershwin, K. Winkel, "Fatal and Severe Box Jellyfish Stings, Including Irukandji Stings, in Malaysia," *Journal of Travel Medicine* 18, no. 4 (2011): 275–281.

7   L. Thaikruea, P. Siriariyaporn, "The Magnitude of Severe Box Jellyfish Cases on Koh Samui and Koh Pha-ngan in the Gulf of Thailand," *BMC Research Notes* 9, no. 108 (2016): 108.

8   Ibid.

9   Ibid.

acknowledgments

H UGH AND Karen Fowler for their unending love and support, and for being an enormous help watching G, B, and D. And to Chris, Irene and Tony Dolder, Katy Hill, Paula Parreño Martínez, Julian and Veronique Musson, Monika Vida-Girbicz, and the small army of people who went above and beyond to help watch the kids so I could write. The Anderson Center for Interdisciplinary Arts, Ledig House International Writers Residency, Ragdale Foundation, Soapstone Writing Retreat, and Ucross Foundation for providing the generous and much appreciated gifts of time and space. Judith Barrington, Maria Black, Mollie Jeffrey, Justine Labelestier, Kenneth Lin, Kelly Link, Jon Magidsohn, Elizabeth McKenzie, Clare Olson, Micah Perks, Melissa Sanderself, Manil Suri, and Jill Wolfson for reading and commenting on early drafts. My agent, Renée Zuckerbrot, who always totally and completely believed in this book, and my editor, Marysue Rucci, for her incredibly thoughtful and thorough comments and suggestions. Zachary Knoll and Marie Florio for the attention, care, help, and hard work, after hours and on holiday.

Anat and Talia, who chose to walk through the door of the clinic on Ko Pha Ngan instead of walking away. Mayhill Courtney Fowler, Mary Reed, and again both Justine Labelestier and my mum—because *acknowledgments*

every single time I checked email in Eastern Europe, yours were the messages that were always there waiting.

Andrew Jones, whose four year-old son, Lewis, was stung by a box jellyfish and nearly died in December 2007 on Ko Mak. Since then, Andrew has done everything in his power to try to make Thailand's beaches safer, through awareness, education, and prevention (thaibox jellyfish.blogspot.com).

Of course, for Sean. And also for Audrey.

*A Conversation with Shannon Leone Fowler
and her mother, Karen Joy Fowler*

KAREN JOY FOWLER – When you were in the fourth grade, you wrote a book called *The Zookeeper Capers*. I think the narrator was a chimp?

SHANNON LEONE FOWLER – Yes, it was from the point of a view of a chimpanzee, and was all about the misadventures of the chimp's zookeeper. I named the zookeeper Rolf after Rolf Benirschke, the kicker for the San Diego Chargers because he donated money with each kick to research of endangered animals at the San Diego Zoo.

KJF – That's right – you were so taken with him when you were nine years old. You had quite a considerable success with that book.

SLF – I did. I won Best Originality at the Davis Book Fair.

KJF – And *Zookeeper Capers* was so clearly the prototype for my novel all these years later, *We Are All Completely Beside Ourselves*. But in spite of this early success, I remember both you and your brother telling me you didn't want to be writers. You thought it looked lonely to go off in a room all by yourself and not talk to anybody for hours.

SLF – Nothing changes how you value being alone like having your own kids. Now that I'm a single mum of three very young children, having a job where I get to be alone is a dream come true. I can't think of anything better than to have hours on end when no one is making demands of me, pulling on my clothes, or insisting on coming with me when I go to the bathroom.

KJF – So you wrote *Travelling with Ghosts* while raising your kids. And you're still interested in animals – the book has a lot of marine biology, and of course Sean's death from a box jellyfish. This is a grief memoir, and you've gotten a lot of response to the grief part, but it's also a travel memoir, and my impression is that there's been less response to the travel part.

SLF – Yes, the vast majority of personal messages from readers as well as the media have been about Sean's death, and I wasn't entirely anticipating that. Because although the book is very much centered around Sean's death, the bulk of the story is the journey after and the travel that I did following. I think the lessons I learned that were the most surprising and profound were the lessons I learned travelling. So I wasn't entirely prepared for the focus on Sean's death, although I guess I should have been because it's so shocking. But it was difficult at the beginning because I was thinking I was going to have conversations about these amazing Israeli girls or the resilience of Bosnia, and instead I kept finding myself back on the beach in Thailand.

KJF – The travels of course weren't a fun trip at all. But, like animals, it's been a constant thread in your life that you love to travel. From the time you were a very little girl, you always liked to go to new places and see new things. Do you have any sense of when that bug bit?

SLF – I think, as you know, the first trip that we took was when we went to England and Scotland when I was fourteen.

KJF – Yeah, it's a kind of strange fact about the family that you went to another country before you went out of state.

SLF – I know, my eldest has already been to thirteen countries.

KJF – And he's six years old.

SLF – The baby is two and she's been to nine countries. But I was fourteen before I left the US, and then I loved it. While I was in high school, we also went to Canada and Mexico, and I loved every place we visited.

I think there's something about the unknown, something about waking up and not having any idea where the day is going to take you. Not knowing where I'm going to sleep, how I'm going to get money, what I'm going to eat. Although that often ends in disappointment, with terrible places to stay and awful food, when it ends well, it's such a gift, and there are so few truly wonderful surprises in life.

I think it's the same reason I love the ocean. You sink below the surface and suddenly there's no internet, no telephones, no traffic – it's cold and dark and quiet. You're practically weightless, and surrounded by different forms of life, big and microscopic. It's the unknown, this other world; it's exploration, and leaving everything that you understand behind. Plunging yourself in somewhere foreign, where you have to figure it out and find new ways of doing things. So I think my love of the ocean and my love of travel are related.

KJF – Well, that's interesting. I never put the two of them together quite like that. Because you took your first international trip when you were fourteen, but you had spent summer after summer by then at the ocean. Do you think your initial attraction to ocean was as you described?

SLF – Where I grew up, where we lived, in Davis – this inland, idyllic, tiny university town – we could bike everywhere, but it was far from the ocean. So the ocean represented everything that wasn't. Wasn't day-to-day, wasn't understood. Travel and the ocean to me are this expanse into the unknown. I think spending the summers in San Diego with Grandpa Bob had a huge impact, because he was like a guidebook to the ocean. He was like having a *Lonely Planet* guide to this new world, and he could teach me how to try to navigate it safely and tell me all these little secrets about the sea.

KJF – Well, speaking of safety and the risk of the unknown, as your mother, when I read this book, I cannot help but notice you doing a lot of things that could have turned out so badly. And now you're a mother yourself, can you look at some of the choices you made and think maybe that wasn't such a good idea even though it worked out?

SLF – Certainly when I was writing, particularly the Sarajevo chapter, I could see how bad some of my decisions were after Sean's death. The fact that I went with this crazy woman from the bus station and stayed in a cellar . . .

KJF – This windowless basement!

SLF – Below a shop, and I couldn't even lock my door, and no one else was staying there, and I had no phone. That was absurd. It turned out fine, but it really could not have. Would I want my children doing that? Absolutely not. But because Sean died and we weren't taking any risks – in Thailand we were playing it safe, we thought we were being boring – a part of me then thought, *What the hell was the point in trying to be careful?* I'm very lucky Sarajevo turned out the way it did; the people in Bosnia were amazing. But years later, we watched that movie together . . .

KJF – *The Whistleblower*, with Rachel Weisz. I know, that was terrifying.

SLF – And that sex trafficking was going on while I was there, with the US security forces, and the UN troops turning a blind eye, all after the siege had ended. So we watched that movie, and both thought, *Oh my God.*

KJF – Yes. And I didn't even know you were in Sarajevo, so you could have just disappeared off the face of the earth.

SLF – No one knew I was in Sarajevo. I mentioned to the Israeli girls that I was thinking about Bosnia, but I hadn't told anyone I was going because I didn't want anyone to worry.

And of course things like arriving into Cluj-Napoca at midnight – I've got no Romanian money and no idea where I'm staying or where anything is. But it was totally fine, people were really helpful! Yet would I want my kid landing somewhere at midnight with no local currency and no reservations and no idea? No. No.

KJF – Good, that's all I ask. Moving on – I've done very little personal essay writing myself, but people have lots of ideas about what's fair and what's not in memoir. There's a sense everything you include should be true, which is already tricky because our memories can be unreliable. But I've heard some say it's even unfair to cut things . . .

SLF – Wow.

KJF – That any shaping of it makes it artificial. As a memoirist, how do you feel about that?

SLF – Because I had my journals, and I wrote in my journals obsessively, filled pages daily . . .

KJF – You do have an astonishing level of detail: the waiter had this kind of moustache and this song was playing in the background.

SLF – And that's because I wrote it all down. The level of detail I had, even though I started writing the book five years later, was almost overwhelming. When I write how much I paid for a meal at a milk bar in Poland, I know because I wrote it all down: how I paid, the menu translation, what the server looked like, who I sat next to. So if I'd had to write this book without cutting anything, it would have been a book no one wanted to read. If you can't shape the story, it's not a story, it's just someone's journal and stream of consciousness.

I guess that's where the line between fiction and non-fiction gets blurred. I remember taking a short class in memoir and the teacher said, 'Writing memoir is easy, you just write down what happened.' But I think this couldn't be further from the truth. For me, with memoir, you already have the characters and the plot and you can't change that, but everything else is up for grabs. The order you tell the story in, which little details you use, which little details you don't, the secrets you let the reader in on and at which points. I think that's all very much like writing fiction. You can't change the characters and you can't change what happened, and in some ways I found that a relief. Sometimes my editor or my agent might say, 'I'd really like it if you came off a bit better in this scene.' And I could only say, 'Sorry, but I didn't! It's not the way it happened'. I liked that concrete aspect. But I could still play with *how* I decided to tell all the things I couldn't change.

KJF – One of the major impetuses for writing *Travelling with Ghosts* was that you found the American way of dealing with death and grief so unhelpful. You responded well to the rules the Israeli girls had when they dealt with you. And there was a time when there were a lot of rules in America about grief. There were specific time frames: heavy mourning, half mourning and light mourning, and the clothing would reflect this so everybody would know. Do you think that would be a good idea? Or I know you also liked being anonymous sometimes.

SLF – I think the problem with rules, always, is that they are going to work for some people and not for everyone. For me, as you know, I've never been very good at pretending. So although I thought I might like that idea of being anonymous, it never worked out very well for me because I usually ended up breaking down and telling someone after I'd had a drink or something. I've never been someone who can really pull that off, but I'm sure many people are much better at it. I did find the rules of shiva incredibly helpful, that it was dictated how a mourner behaves, and how people around the mourner behave.

KJF – It seemed more how the people around the mourner behave.

SLF – But that's because only the girls knew what they were doing. There are rules for the mourner too – rules about ripping your clothing, lighting candles, not cutting your hair – but I wasn't following these because I didn't know. So the shiva rules I wrote about in the book were what the two girls were doing for me.

Maybe some people would find these rules confining. But I think having a set of traditions, if anything, helps people to be around someone in mourning. Our culture is at such a loss as to how to deal with grief that people in mourning are avoided, and that's probably the worst thing that can happen. As I say at the end of the book, 'Grief needs time and space, but it also needs company.'

KJF – This is an intensely personal story. I think one of the reasons that I shy away from memoir is a sense of protective privacy. You are so openly out there in *Travelling with Ghosts*, and in interviews and responses you're getting such personal, sometimes intrusive questions. Are you comfortable with that?

SLF – I am, mostly. As an American living in London, I think Americans tend to be quite open. Because I wrote the book based on my journals, there was already a deeply personal voice I was using to write. And I've told you many times that the only way I could write the book was to not worry about what people would think – my family, my kids when they were older, my friends and neighbors. So that was the only way I could write this story: to not think about anyone actually reading it. Then I finished the book and started revising, and then I sold the book and was editing, and then copy-editing. I really didn't think about having my personal story out there in the world until the excerpt appeared in the *Guardian* newspaper right before publication.

I was with my kids and we were making pancakes – flour everywhere and the counters sticky with boysenberry syrup – and it was this really typical weekend morning except all of a sudden, the darkest, deepest, saddest parts of my life were on the internet and strangers were responding online. And the only people I could immediately share this with were my very young children who couldn't possibly understand.

I remember calling you up and telling you that maybe I'd made a mistake, that I didn't know if it was the right thing to have done, and by then of course, it was too late. So it was harder than I thought it would be.

But the book came out in February and it's now August, and every week I continue to get incredibly personal messages from readers. It's almost always people who've lost someone – they've lost a lover or a parent or a child – and their stories are harrowing and so sad. But they've connected with my words, and found some kind of comfort. I think that makes up for whatever uncomfortableness I have at having my own story out there. So when I called you up and said that I think I might have made a mistake, you told me that if it helps anyone, then it's a more important book than a bestseller. That if it reaches people and makes a difference in someone's life, what more can you ask for?

KJF – What more can you ask for? Absolutely.